The Rhetoric of Alexander Hamilton

STATUE OF ALEXANDER HAMILTON
BY ORDWAY PARTRIDGE

The RHETORIC *of*

Alexander Hamilton

By BOWER ALY

New York

RUSSELL & RUSSELL

1965

FOREWORD

Hᴵˢᵀᴼᴿʸ has a way with men, and justice is often not the end that history serves. Their names become symbols, sometimes even grossly false symbols, standing in the public mind for qualities they never had in life. Thus Machiavelli, thought of by some close students as a disappointed moralist, becomes the symbol for triumphant cunning in politics. And it is generally supposed to be appropriate that the grave of Alexander Hamilton should be at the top of Wall Street, although Wall Street is the symbol of a strong appetite for money and Hamilton never showed even a normal interest in money. This can all be explained, of course. Symbols make slow and gradual shifts until they reach their fixed meanings on partial truths. Hamilton was the leader of the conservatives in early American politics, and for that reason all the liberal writers since his death have ascribed to him almost any quality they happened to dislike. This makes him one of the most-heard-of and least-known men in American history. The important element in his character, however, is still his extraordinary power.

Dr. Aly does not try to settle the thorny question, what kind of man was Hamilton? He is doing a more useful work in examining specifically and technically the instrument by which Hamilton exercised most of his power, his great skill in persuasion. Aristotle, to whom Dr. Aly goes back for guidance and the basis of analysis, said long ago that spoken discourse should be judged by its effect when spoken. The invention and wide diffusion of printing, which has brought plenty of evil mixed with its great blessings, have made us forget that speeches are designed to be heard. Hamilton is not often spoken of in histories of American eloquence, but he evidently had the ability to persuade the people of his day. Dr. Aly's study of the contemporary circumstances of one very important series of speeches is an admirable example of the method by which the power of such eloquence may be understood and assigned to its proper role as an influence in the making of history.

Lyman Bryson

New York
July 1, 1941

PREFACE

D URING the thirty years of his active life in New York and in the United States of America, from his early youth until his death, Alexander Hamilton was almost constantly engaged in controversy. In legislatures, conventions, and courts, as well as in conferences and discussions, he sought to explain, to convince, and to persuade. Yet the forensic and polemic aspects of his career have received comparatively little specific attention. To the student of rhetoric, the speeches and writings of Alexander Hamilton are interesting because they are notable examples of discourse; to the student of history they are interesting because they are the work of a man who influenced the whole course of events in the American states. A complete study of Hamilton's public life, therefore, should have meaning both for the rhetorician and for the historian and should cast light on that shadow ground which lies between the ancient arts of rhetoric and politics.

The ensuing account makes no pretensions to being the complete study which I envision. It is a preliminary treatment, in which I have endeavored to contribute a point of view rather than a final reckoning.

Although I have naturally depended upon some of the means and methods of historical research, I have been primarily interested in rhetorical criticism rather than in a historical record; and although I have manifested a collateral interest in Hamilton as a writer, I have been chiefly interested in Hamilton as an orator.

At the conclusion of my labor, I have the pleasure of acknowledging my debt to helpful scholars and friends who share the credit for any merits the book may have, without being in any sense responsible for its demerits. To Charles A. Beard, Merle Curti, and Milton Smith I am indebted for encouragement given to the idea and structure of the study. As the work developed, I received the generous advice of Herbert A. Wichelns, Magdalene Kramer, John L. Childs, Arthur E. Bestor, Jr., Erling Hunt, Roy F. Nichols, Allan Abbott, Samuel McKee, Jr., Edward F. Reisner, and Edward L. Hodnett.

Among others who read the manuscript and made helpful suggestions, I am privileged to thank W. H. Blake, A. Craig Baird, Loren D. Reid, W. Norwood Brigance, Russell H. Wagner, Louise I. Stephens, James H. McBurney, H. L. Ewbank, Karl R. Wallace, Donald C. Bryant, and E. Wilder Spaulding.

To my colleagues at the University of Missouri, whose candid criticisms have delivered me from many errors, I owe a special debt which it is a pleasure to acknowledge by mentioning their names: Minnie M. Brashear, A. H. R. Fairchild, Wilbur E. Gilman, Lee S. Hultzén, Theophil W. H. Irion, and the late Edward G. Ainsworth, Jr.

To Lyman Bryson, whose patient counsel has guided this essay from first to last, I am happy to express my gratitude.

To the librarians of Hamilton College, the University of Missouri, the University of Wisconsin, Columbia University, the Library of Congress, the New York Public Library, the New York State Library, the New York Historical Society, and the Huntington Library, I offer my appreciation for attitudes which have been uniformly considerate and helpful. My obligation to Mrs. Helen Thompson Newman and Mrs. Verna B. Andrews for assistance with the manuscript is genuine and is gratefully acknowledged. To the Advanced School of Education, Teachers College, Columbia University, I am deeply obligated for the scholarship and liberal grant in aid which made it possible for me to complete this study.

BOWER ALY

Columbia, Missouri
May 1, 1941

CONTENTS

The Rhetoric of Alexander Hamilton

I. THE HAMILTON BIOGRAPHY AND CRITICISM

HAMILTON *is really a colossus to the anti-republican party. Without numbers, he is a host in himself.*—THOMAS JEFFERSON

MORE THAN 150 years ago Alexander Hamilton, having already given the final number of *The Federalist* to Mc-Lean to be printed in the shop in Hanover Square, began to deliver his famous speeches in the debates at Poughkeepsie. Yet apparently no volume devoted solely or even chiefly to a criticism of his writings or his speeches has ever been published.[1] There have been learned studies of Hamilton's ideas of the protective tariff, of Hamilton's finance, of Hamilton's theories of government, but Hamilton as writer and speaker has received only incidental treatment in sketches or biographies.

To Hamilton, language was, it is true, an instrument to be used in daily practice, always subordinate to an end beyond itself. But it is precisely Hamilton's use of language as an instrument which should bring him attention today; for historians recognize that few American writers have been more genuinely influential than Alexander Hamilton; and few men in any age have so well advanced their fortunes by tongue and pen as he.

---

[1] Partial studies have been made. De Vilbiss's essay, "A Rhetorical Criticism of the Early Pamphlets of Alexander Hamilton," offers a criticism of Hamilton's pamphlets written in the controversy with Seabury. Dyer's study, "Hamilton's Rhetoric in *The Federalist*," is an analysis of the proof found in *The Federalist*, essays LXVIII to LXXXIII. Fulton's thesis, "The Speeches of Alexander Hamilton in the New York Convention: A Critical Study in Argumentation," is limited to a consideration of the types of argument employed by Hamilton in certain speeches delivered in the New York convention for the ratification of the constitution.

Hamilton as pamphleteer, Hamilton as letter-writer, Hamilton as Washington's corresponding secretary—all deserve close attention; the present study, however, is a criticism of Hamilton's oratory, particularly of his speeches in the convention at Poughkeepsie, where his career as a parliamentary speaker reached a dramatic climax.

BIOGRAPHY AND CRITICISM

Although the critic of oratory must understand the speeches, the audience, and the times, he must also know the speaker. Here the critic must wait upon the biographer; and this circumstance leads immediately to the following questions: (1) What is the status of the Hamilton biography? (2) What criticism of Hamilton's rhetoric appears in biographies and elsewhere to date?

THE STATUS OF THE HAMILTON BIOGRAPHY

Manifestly, no one, least of all the critic, should expect perfection in biography. All biographies are subject to the human limitations of error, prejudice, or mischance, as well as to changing fashion, no matter what the circumstance of their origin. Alexander Hamilton has perhaps suffered more than most public men from the lack of a clear and comprehensive account of his life; and it is an open question whether he has had to endure more from attack by his enemies or praise by his friends. Be that as it may, in the years that have passed since Alexander Hamilton was killed by Aaron Burr at Weehawken no adequate account of the man has appeared. Biographies there have been, in plenty; but the only one which attempted to be definitive was not critical; and the many that have been essayed in the critical method have not been definitive. Moreover, in no case, apparently, has the biographer adequately considered Hamilton's writing and speaking; and, considering the extent of Hamilton's uses of language, a definitive biography, whenever written, must include a thoroughgoing rhetorical analysis.

The reasons for the failure of Hamilton's biographers are easy to conjecture. In the first place, the task of writing Hamilton's life, even though he died a comparatively young man, is one of some magnitude. Hamilton was a person of tremendous energy, as well as brilliance of mind, and his output of letters, speeches, briefs, and reports was extensive. Even so, despite the existence of a mass of evidence, many materials necessary for a proper understanding of his personality, if not of his public life, must surely have gone up in flames when Schuyler's papers were burned in the holocaust described by Tuckerman;[2] and there is no knowing what similar events have deprived us of other means of understanding him. Hamilton, moreover, was not merely a person of energy and brilliance; he was also one of influence. Indeed, it is difficult to find fault with Morison's considered judgment that "at no period in the history of the United States has one man possessed so potent an influence over the federal government as Alexander Hamilton exerted during Washington's second administration, and the first half of his successor's."[3] The ramifications of Hamilton's great influence have obviously contributed to the problem of his biographers, for it could never be traced out entirely in documents. His personal power must have been extended, in more than ordinary measure, through conversations, discussions, and conferences which are now and forever unavailable.

Some of the difficulty encountered by the biographers has come from the obscurity of Hamilton's early days. Born in relative humility and breaking home-ties early, Hamilton did not provide his biographers with neat packages of biographical materials ready for the documentation of his infancy and

[2] Tuckerman, *Life of General Philip Schuyler*, p. 253.
[3] Morison, *The Life and Letters of Harrison Gray Otis, Federalist, 1765-1848*, I, 157.

childhood. Consequently, some of the most elementary facts concerning his origins are still in dispute.

Despite the manifest difficulties arising out of both the abundance and the dearth of evidence, another obstruction has been even more perilous to the biographers. Alexander Hamilton is still an object of controversy. As the villain of demagogues, on the one hand, and as the hero of reactionaries, on the other, Hamilton is, even at the present moment, a participant by proxy in political battles. As recently as 1922, Arthur H. Vandenberg, with singular misunderstanding both of Hamilton's genius and of his relation to the Constitution, was able "to speak for Hamilton in relation to the menaced spirit of the Constitution" and to have Hamilton say "he would consider that he lived and died in vain and that his poor memory was shorn of its last, sympathetic friend, if any Constitutional crisis, great or small, ever shall arise in the story of the United States, in which it should be undenied that he could ever countenance, by the timidity of silence, so much as a single gesture against the Constitutional Rock whence we are hewn." [4]

Hamilton's contemporary position in controversy is not a new one. Not only in the present age but in every generation since his death, Hamilton has been either a partisan hero or a partisan villain. In his study of Hamilton, Samuel Schmucker expressed the opinion, more pious than correct, that the

fierce passions and jealousies of that memorable era in which Hamilton figured and flourished, have now been laid to rest in the slumber of the tomb; and he who attempts at the present day to write the history of this great man, may claim at least one advantage over his predecessors—that he has no temptation from party prejudice and bias, either to color, exaggerate, or suppress the truth. [5]

Precisely how far Schmucker was justified in his opinion may be judged by his own words, for he goes on to say, with the

[4] Vandenberg, *If Hamilton Were Here Today*, p. ix.
[5] Schmucker, *The Life and Times of Alexander Hamilton*, p. vi.

appearance of something less than dispassionate judgment, that the

remarkable incidents of Hamilton's career will never lose their singular power to attract and instruct mankind; for they furnish impressive illustrations both of the brightest and the basest elements of human character. The brightest all appertained to himself; the basest belonged to those by whom he was surrounded and assailed.[6]

Schmucker's reference to Hamilton's being assailed is warranted. Hamilton was hardly more than buried when there appeared, partly in answer to the many eulogies delivered on him, an account which was destined later to be known as the *Life of Hamilton*.[7] The author of this early biography was John Williams. This same John Williams is referred to by Macaulay in his "Review of the *Memoirs of the Life of Warren Hastings*" in the statement that "Hastings stooped so low as to court the aid of that malignant and filthy baboon John Williams, who called himself Anthony Pasquin. It was necessary to subsidise such allies largely." [8]

Although Macaulay may not have escaped some prejudices of his own concerning Hastings's assistant, "Anthony Pasquin," who achieved an unsavoury reputation both in England and America, was doubtless an unpleasant fellow, hardly the first choice of any one for a biographer. His account of Hamilton is detractive, derogatory, and prejudiced. It exhibits Hamil-

[6] *Ibid.*

[7] The note concerning the Hamilton Club edition of Williams's *Life of Alexander Hamilton* in *Bibliotheca Americana* (XXVIII, 427) quotes from Paul L. Ford's *Bibliotheca Hamiltoniana* (1886, p. 81), evidently accepting Ford's judgment that the title is fraudulent and that Hoffman, of the Hamilton Club, probably reprinted the work from some newspaper of the period. I have not been able to find the source of Hoffman's title; but the source of the subject matter of his Hamilton Club edition of the *Life of Alexander Hamilton* could easily have been an extended footnote appended by John Williams to the *Hamiltoniad*. It is thus hardly necessary to suppose, as Ford does, a reprinting from a contemporary newspaper as yet undiscovered.

[8] Macaulay, *Works* (London, 1879), VI, 639.

ton's faults, minimizes his virtues, and sets forth his British factionalism by a method so devious as to leave little room for argument.[9]

THE CONTINUING PREJUDICES

If the approach to Hamilton's biography exemplified by Vandenberg, Schmucker, and Williams were confined to them, it might be ignored; but unfortunately works which entertain more serious pretensions to representing Hamilton's life are open to the same objections of prejudice. Something of the spirit of Schmucker, for example, in combination with the mood of filial piety, animates the most complete treatment of Hamilton—the two works by his son, John Church Hamilton.[10] In the earlier of these, the biographer stated quite frankly that when he was first requested to undertake the work, a "deep conviction of my incapacity, the want of the necessary preparatory studies, and a distrust of the natural bias of my feelings, prompted me to decline it." [11] The distrust of "the bias of feelings" is clearly justified, both in the *Life* and in the *History*. As the title suggests, the second work is more history than biography; but what there is of biography is based on the premise that Hamilton could do no wrong. If the premise be understood, the volumes may be useful, and, as a matter of fact, they have provided the basis for the generally accepted accounts of Hamilton's life.

THE TYPES OF BIOGRAPHY

Of the titles here considered in the category of Hamilton biography, five, including the two separate works by his son, have already been mentioned. The others seem to fall into

[9] Williams (*pseud.*, Anthony Pasquin), *The Hamiltoniad*, p. 25.
[10] John Church Hamilton, *The Life of Alexander Hamilton* (New York, 1840); John Church Hamilton, *Life of Alexander Hamilton: A History of the Republic of the United States . . .* (Boston, 1879).
[11] John Church Hamilton, *Life* (1840), I, iii.

three classes: the general studies, the accounts devoted primarily to his statesmanship, and the volumes with a thesis.   The first class includes *Alexander Hamilton*,[12] by Conant, hardly more than a sketch; *Lives of John Jay and Alexander Hamilton*,[13] by Renwick; *The Life and Epoch of Alexander Hamilton*,[14] by Shea; *The Intimate Life of Alexander Hamilton*,[15] by Allan McLane Hamilton; the novelized biography entitled *The Conqueror*,[16] by Mrs. Atherton; *Alexander Hamilton*,[17] by Howard Hicks; *An American Colossus: The Singular Career of Alexander Hamilton*,[18] by Ralph Edward Bailey; and the recent biography by David Loth, entitled *Alexander Hamilton: Portrait of a Prodigy*.[19]

The biographies which deal with Hamilton primarily as a statesman are frequently not without theses; but they have in common a certain preoccupation with politics, albeit not always with the same concepts. John T. Morse's *Life of Alexander Hamilton* [20] and Lodge's *Alexander Hamilton* [21] proceed from what is essentially the same point of view of Hamilton as statesman-patriot, both works being indebted to the earlier volumes by John Church Hamilton. Cheetham's "Biography of Mr. Hamilton," appended to his *Narrative of the Suppression by Col. Burr of the History of the Administration of John Adams*, deserves no more than mention.[22] Granrud's dissertation reveals the writer's strong personal faith in Hamilton's honesty and devotion to the Union.[23] Oliver's *Alexander Hamilton: An Essay on American Union*,[24] a pretentious study, reveals the author's strong bias against Jefferson. Claude G.

---

[12] Boston, 1901. The full title of each of the works mentioned in this chapter is given in the bibliography.

[13] New York, 1841.   [15] New York, 1910.

[14] Boston, 1881.   [16] New York, 1916.

[17] New York, 1928. The book represents a type, of which other titles could be listed, designed for the schoolboy.

[18] Boston, 1933.   [22] Baltimore, *ca.* 1802.

[19] New York, 1939.   [23] Ithaca, 1894.

[20] Boston, 1876.   [24] New York, 1920.

[21] Boston, 1882.

Bowers's *Jefferson and Hamilton*,[25] on the other hand, although maintaining the semblance of impartiality, is Jeffersonian in its prejudices. Henry J. Ford's *Alexander Hamilton* [26] appears, in some respects, to be the most carefully conceived of the works dealing with Hamilton as a statesman.

The third class of biographies includes those with a case to prove. Culbertson's *Alexander Hamilton: An Essay* [27] is designed to show that Hamilton was a nationalist rather than a capitalist. Baldwin's *Party Leaders* [28] exhibits Hamilton as leader of the Federalists, while Riethmuller attempts to prove, in his *Alexander Hamilton and His Contemporaries*,[29] that Hamilton would have favored the South in the Civil War. F. T. Fox, in his *Study in Alexander Hamilton*,[30] desires to prove that Hamilton was no gentleman; and Boutell, in *Alexander Hamilton: The Constructive Statesman*,[31] wishes to show that he was a great builder. In *Alexander Hamilton: First American Business Man*,[32] Warshow develops Hamilton as a great commercial leader. Sumner undertakes to show, in his *Alexander Hamilton*,[33] how Hamilton developed the American state. Smertenko's *Alexander Hamilton* [34] is a study in the newer psychology, a representation of Hamilton's character in terms of neurosis and libido.

Hamilton's life and works are discussed not only in formal biographical studies, but also in the general American histories and in essays and standard works of reference. These do not require comment here, but will be considered later in a discussion of the treatment accorded Hamilton by the historians of literature and oratory. Hamilton is often appraised with a brief statement in the schoolbooks or in the popular biographies of his contemporaries; but since these appraisals apparently derive rather easily from each other, they need not be examined systematically.

[25] Boston, 1925.
[26] New York, 1925.
[27] New Haven, 1916.
[28] New York, 1855.
[29] London, 1864.

[30] New York, 1911.
[31] Chicago, 1890.
[32] New York, 1931.
[33] New York, 1890.
[34] New York, 1932.

HAMILTONIAN CRITICISM

How have Hamilton's biographers gone about the criticism of his works? Any answer undertaken in the proper spirit should consider not only what the writers have set down about Hamilton's speeches and pamphlets but also what principles, or lack of them, have motivated the biographers in their selection, reporting, and criticism. In attempting to understand the point of view of the biographers, one should not draw too narrow a line between the criticism of the pamphlet and that of the speech. The problems of the speaker and the pamphleteer have often so many elements in common that some light can be shed on the biographer's principles of the criticism of oratory by considering them together with his revealed principles for the criticism of persuasive writing.

THE CLASSES OF CRITICISM

As critics, Hamilton's biographers do not discover, for the most part, the speaker's means of persuasion; they do not think rhetorically. If for the sake of convenience we group their criticism into three main classes—the narrative, the literary, and the comprehensive—their neglect of systematic rhetorical judgment is only too apparent. The narrative treatment, without actually ignoring Hamilton's use of language, attempts to avoid more than a story of it. The literary method goes beyond the story to an evaluation and criticism, the criticism being based on literary principles applied to the text. The comprehensive criticisms involve, for better or for worse, a realization of some of the factors peculiar to persuasive writing and speaking.

The works of Atherton, Hicks, Riethmuller, Fox, Boutell, Culbertson, Cheetham, Warshow, and Vandenberg either do not deal with Hamilton's works at all or do so in such a way as to discourage attention to them. The six biographies primarily narrative in method, however, will require some comment.

NARRATIVE TREATMENT

Sumner is interested in Hamilton's ideas, particularly as they show him to be a maker of the American state. Consequently, he says concerning the Poughkeepsie convention that Hamilton "employed his utmost eloquence to carry the ratification";[35] but nothing is said about the eloquence itself. It is taken for granted.

Claude G. Bowers offers the assurance that it will be

impossible to comprehend the genius of Hamilton, his domination of his party, and his power, despite his unpopularity with the masses, without a foreknowledge of his force with the pen. It was his scepter and his sword.[36]

Bowers, furthermore, attempts a paragraph of synthesis concerning Hamilton's oratory; but he does not find room for analysis.

David Loth, in his recent treatment, is primarily interested in writing a well-rounded narrative, and, although he includes a short chapter on *The Federalist* and the adoption of the Constitution, he does not undertake problems of criticism. Insofar as Loth considers Hamilton's discourse, however, he shows an understanding of it; for Loth's point of view never allows him to suppose that Hamilton was writing or speaking primarily for posterity or to assume that Hamilton's primary aim was a purely literary one.

Allan McLane Hamilton's book provides a discursive chapter on Hamilton as a writer and orator; but criticism is not seriously attempted. Shea's work is useful, but it is anecdotal rather than critical. The two works by John Church Hamilton are likewise uncritical The *Life* is circumstantial and does not, in general, undertake analytical discussion of topics or their relation to a possible audience. Concerning Hamilton's exchange of pamphlets with Seabury, for example, the reader must con-

[35] Sumner, *Alexander Hamilton*, p. 137.
[36] Bowers, *Jefferson and Hamilton*, p. 26.

tent himself with the knowledge that "these pamphlets will be admitted to possess merits of which the most practised statesman might be proud." [37] The *History* is more useful, even though it does not seriously attempt judgments. Abstracts of the speeches and pamphlets are allowed, as a general rule, to speak for themselves; and the general rule is proved excellent by such breaches as the following description of Hamilton's position in the Constitutional convention. The author explains that the

policy of Clinton had placed him [Alexander Hamilton] there to become a cipher and a sacrifice. He felt it all, but he felt, with the cold palsy of the State upon his vote, that the warm life of a nation was in his heart—a heart ever alive to the sense of duty and of honor. In these he found the path of courageous wisdom.[38]

THE LITERARY STANDARD

Of those biographers who, in addition to relating a sequence of events, proceed to establish a judgment, some recognize chiefly a "literary" standard, and others are at least aware of canons of rhetoric. The former group will be considered first.

Baldwin, who discusses Hamilton as a party leader, can be appraised by his judgment of Hamilton's contributions to *The Federalist*, which must, he says, "be regarded as curiosities of political literature." [39] Granrud, also, reveals his canons by his criticism. He observes of *The Federalist* that the "diction, though copious and varied, is largely made up of words of Latin origin, and there is no nice discrimination of synonyms." [40] Granrud's chapters are interesting for their understanding of the Poughkeepsie occasion; but they are even more striking in their failure to relate the speaking to it.

Samuel Schmucker has little to say about oratory; but his

---

[37] *Life*, 1840, I, 38.   [38] *History*, 1879, III, 275.
[39] J. G. Baldwin, *Party Leaders*, p. 33.
[40] Granrud, *Five Years of Alexander Hamilton's Public Life*, p. 30.

chapter devoted to *The Federalist* exhibits his system. He finds two lines for the relation of *The Federalist* to its immediate objective, i.e., the securing of the adoption of the Federal Constitution; he gives over three pages to an account of *The Federalist* and posterity; and he allows the rest of his discussion to deal with "the literary peculiarities, and . . . some of the doctrines discussed in this remarkable production." [41] Consequently, the chapter hardly suggests that the papers were part of a controversy; instead, it offers the information that the "style of Hamilton bore the impress of the peculiar qualities of his mind. It was clear, nervous, ornate." And examples are provided of "great beauty of diction," of "imagery," and of "symmetry." [42] Schmucker values the artist above the rhetorician; and he wishes Hamilton to have the higher sanction.

Henry Cabot Lodge's *Alexander Hamilton* presents an interesting contrast to Schmucker's volume, for, like Schmucker, Lodge is concerned with establishing the fame of Hamilton and the merits of *The Federalist*; and he goes to some trouble to present a case for the papers as political documents, as "intellectual possessions," even as literature. But unlike Schmucker, he feels compelled finally to offer something in the nature of an apology. Fine though *The Federalist* is, it lacks, Lodge believes, some of the literary proprieties, and hence must fall before the judgment that "literature with an object and as a means to an end instead of one cultivated purely for its own sake, can never be of the highest order." [43] Such a pronouncement in favor of the self-conscious artist in literature may meet objections from many quarters; but the present concern is that Lodge should evidently have overlooked the possibility of any other canons of criticism than the purely literary.[44]

Something of Lodge's deficiency may be present in the work

---

[41] Schmucker, *op. cit.*, p. 274.   [42] *Ibid.*, p. 263.
[43] Lodge, *Alexander Hamilton*, p. 69.
[44] Lodge is interested in Hamilton's oratory (*op. cit.*, p. 276), but the interest seems to be incidental, not primary.

of Henry Jones Ford. In his summary judgment, Ford con-
cludes that Hamilton's

talents were great but not unequalled. In philosophy and eloquence
he is so inferior to Burke that there is no basis for comparison; but
in Burke's writings we have the polished result of skilful artistry,
while Hamilton's writings were hastily produced as mere incidents
of his political activity.[45]

As to the philosophies of Burke and Hamilton, Ford may perhaps be advised; but concerning the eloquence of the two men,
the reader wishes in vain for a statement of relevant grounds
of criticism.

COMPREHENSIVE JUDGMENTS

The word "comprehensive," used to classify a number of
biographies, is designed to imply merely that they comprehend more than a literary or textual consideration of Hamilton's speeches and papers. It cannot be too clearly stated that
there has been no thoroughgoing criticism of Hamilton's works.
Nevertheless, there is a clearly recognizable difference between
the treatment by Lodge, just cited, and, for example, that by
Morse. Morse does not attempt to deal with *The Federalist* on
the scale that Lodge does; but Morse does what Lodge does
not: he offers not only an account but a criticism of Hamilton's
oratory. Indeed, Morse gives significantly more careful treatment to Hamilton's speaking than to his writing. More important than the extent of Morse's treatment is the realism of
it. Even though one may regret the exclusion of *inventio* from
rhetoric in the observation that Hamilton "was an orator as
well as a thinker," one notes with rising interest the subsequent
comment:

What he had thought out with the Scottish logic which he was
entitled to through his father, he uttered with the French fire which
came from his maternal ancestry. He spoke with that fervid vigor

---

[45] Ford, *op. cit.*, p. 371.

which not only evinced his own conviction, but forced conviction upon his hearers. He compelled attention; his large and brilliant eyes held his audience by a fascination more agreeable but not less potent than belonged to the glance of the Ancient Mariner. Listeners never yawned or allowed their eyes to wander or their lids to droop when he was speaking even on the dryest points of constitutional law.[46]

Discounting the doctrine of hereditary transmission of logic and fire, one observes almost for the first time that Hamilton had listeners, i.e., that his problem was immediate and real. This fine thread of understanding the speaker's problem ties loosely together with that of Morse the otherwise widely diverging biographies by Conant, Oliver, Renwick, Bailey, Smertenko, and Williams.

In his sketch, Conant asserts without explication that *The Federalist*, although a purely political argument, has survived the occasion which called it forth as one of the master arguments of political writing. As to the position of *The Federalist* in literature, Conant is less sure of himself and abdicates as a judge in favor of Barrett Wendell. His observations concerning Hamilton's oratory, however, display a somewhat different temper. Notably, he says that Hamilton's "dark, deep-set eyes were lighted in debate with a fire which controlled great audiences and cowed his enemies. But it was chiefly the power of pure intellect which gave him control over the minds of other men." [47] How pure intellect functions as proof, Conant does not explain; but he reveals a sense of the problem in the words "audiences" and "control."

Although Oliver is concerned not with spoken but with written language, he likewise reveals the sense of the problem. Of *The Federalist*, he writes that the

crowning merit of these papers, which were produced under great pressure—often while the printer's boy was waiting in the office—is

---

[46] J. T. Morse, *The Life of Alexander Hamilton*, I, 147.
[47] Conant, *Alexander Hamilton*, p. 6.

that they succeeded in accomplishing what they set out to accomplish. They were the greatest force that worked on men's minds to make them consent to the adoption of the constitution.[48]

At the present moment, it is of no concern that Oliver's judgment about the effectiveness of *The Federalist* is unsubstantiated and very probably false. It is of immediate interest that Oliver should discover *the crowning merit* of the papers in their supposed effectiveness. Oliver further reveals his concept of controversial literature in his criticism of the Declaration of Independence which, since it is Jefferson's, he does not wish to praise too highly. Yet he admits that it "has the essential quality of great oratory, for it blew upon the smouldering embers in the hearts of the men to whom it was addressed until they burst into flame." [49] And, in making a comparison between the Declaration of Independence and the *Farewell Address,* which he attributes to Hamilton, Oliver observes, "The *Farewell Address* being less dramatic in its occasion afforded fewer opportunities to the spirit of oratory." [50] The inference from Oliver is that the "spirit of oratory" is emotional, that it does not involve a clear dependence upon the enthymeme; but again, even while entertaining doubts as to the fullness of his concepts and the correctness of his conclusions, one is interested to observe the occasion and the *audience* in Oliver's assumptions.

One distrusts Renwick's observations, for they are made, for the most part, through rose-colored glasses. His little book, furthermore, does not provide sufficient room for analysis. Nevertheless, implicit in his discussion of *The Federalist* and of Hamilton's speeches is the immediately practical situation. With him, the purpose, the occasion, and the means taken are by assumption those of the politico-rhetorician, rather than those of the literary artist. His book, moreover, is unique in Hamiltonian biography in some of its surmises about the edu-

---

[48] Oliver, *Alexander Hamilton,* p. 168.
[49] *Ibid.,* p. 364.   [50] *Ibid.,* p. 365.

cation of the orator. With reference to Hamilton's clerkship with Cruger, Renwick observes:

> The habits of order and regularity in a well-conducted commercial establishment are never forgotten, and are applicable to every possible pursuit. Nor is the exercise of a mercantile correspondence without its value in a literary point of view. To those with little previous education, or who have not an opportunity of improving themselves afterward, this exercise may communicate no elegance of style; but where the use of language has once been attained, the compression of thought and conciseness of expression on which merchants pride themselves, give a terseness and precision of diction which those educated in any other profession can rarely equal.[51]

Ralph Edward Bailey is fully as conscious as Renwick of a rhetorical situation; he reveals his understanding of the Westchester pamphlets by the evidence he notes of Hamilton's versatility: "When he [Hamilton] presented the argument to the farmers . . . he completely changed style." [52] Bailey also reports Hamilton's training in a debating society and his use of strategy in timing. Altogether, although no complete analysis is attempted and insufficient concern is shown for the lines of Hamilton's argument, Bailey's treatment of the campaign in New York furnishes abundant evidence of the author's clear conception of the nature of the speaking situation.

Smertenko, in his interpretation, demonstrates clearly his perception of Hamilton's argumentative problems and methods. Smertenko's is essentially a Freudian interpretation of Hamilton; but he observes with respect to Hamilton's *dictamen* that beginning "with this description [of the hurricane] the letter, public or private, was Hamilton's favorite weapon of advance and defense. It was the axe with which he hacked out the steps up the mountain peak of fame." [53]

---

[51] Renwick, *Lives of John Jay and Alexander Hamilton*, p. 153.
[52] Bailey, *An American Colossus*, p. 42.
[53] Smertenko, *Alexander Hamilton*, p. 22.

Smertenko's account of Hamilton's exchange with Seabury is a short but satisfying criticism of a brilliant debate. Hamilton's task is well understood, and his writing is related to the readers, to the opponent, and to the young debater's own problems. The account represents one of the few instances in Hamiltonian biography in which Hamilton's capacity for polemic is adequately presented. Smertenko correctly sees, also, in the refutation of Seabury, the initial evidence of Hamilton's method: "He adopted what became his invariable method of defense, a militant attack on the facts and arguments of his opponent." [54] Smertenko's criticism is thus not confined to "literary peculiarities." It carries the smell of battle. Distinctive though Smertenko's paragraphs may be, however, they are subordinated to his central Freudian idea.

In fact, in order to find a story of Hamilton's life which gives a relatively large share of the whole to a discussion of the orator and writer, it is necessary to return to one of the earliest topical treatments. John Williams (Anthony Pasquin) was sincerely anxious to disparage Hamilton, the "King of the Feds"; and, not bothering himself about nice questions of taste, he published *The Hamiltoniad* before Hamilton had been dead a month. In the short biography of Hamilton which he appended, Williams clearly thought it necessary to deal directly and extensively with Hamilton as writer and orator. Williams's critical opinions should obviously be viewed with caution; but reading between his lines, one observes that his attempts at detraction often serve to represent Hamilton in better light as an orator than does the indiscriminate praise of later biographers.

To the attack on Hamilton as a writer, Williams brings the charge, sanctified by ancient usage in many another critique, that "he was a sophist, rather than a reasoner." He goes on specifically to say that Hamilton "was too circuitous and declamatory, and had less of that estimable gift in composition,

[54] *Ibid.*, p. 28.

which the ancients called *ad unguem*, than any other writer we have known, who had obtained any celebrity in society." [55]

Continuing the attack on Hamilton's prestige, Williams deals with the orator somewhat more fully than with the writer:

As an ORATOR he was more plausible than commanding. He rather won his award by an insinuation of manner, than by a bold and impetuous stream of eloquence. He was deficient in those lofty energies of soul, which characterized PATRICK HENRY, when he had determined to relieve his country from bondage.—He had none of the florid copiousness of Mirabeau; the rapid conception of Charles Fox; or the poignancy of Sheridan. His manner was his own, and better suited to forensic disputation, than legislative discussion. He was habituated to be pleasing, by his address, but he was not fitted to astonish, by his power: nor could he have shaken and controuled a senate, for the emancipation of his fellow-citizens, provided the prejudices of his mind would have allowed him to have been a vindicator of the natural privileges of society. He had a propensity to sophistication, which was indicative of the crookedness of his ambition; for the furtherance of which he was necessitated to take a *Protean* diversity of shapes,—but these circumfluent movements, would not have been expedient, had he uniformly meant what he uttered.—True generosity and true merit delight in sunshine, and feeling themselves amiable, they are most happy in being explicit.[56]

Whatever the deficiency of Williams's spirit, one observes with interest his point of view. Since it seemed not to occur to Williams that Hamilton was speaking or writing for posterity, his criticism, while obviously prejudiced, is related to genuine problems of controversy.

CRITICISM IN INFORMAL STUDIES

One finds scant recognition of the problems of controversy in most of the critical essays and shorter commentaries remaining for consideration. Save for Shaw's *History of American*

[55] Williams, *op. cit.*, p. 9.   [56] *Ibid.*, p. 16.

Oratory,[57] which is not comprehensive, there is no history of American oratory, nor even a compendium comparable to Goodrich's *Select British Eloquence*.[58] Hardwicke's *History of Oratory and Orators*,[59] Sears's *History of Oratory*,[60] and Platz's *History of Public Speaking* [61] are small in compass and large in scope, thus sparing little space for any single figure.

It is perhaps not to be expected that the general histories would find space for extended development of the history of oratory; at any rate, with the possible exception of George Ticknor Curtis's *Constitutional History of the United States*,[62] they seem to provide nothing worthy of remark about Hamilton's theory or practice of public speaking. When the historian considers oratory and controversial writing, he evidently considers them to be literature, or at least, except as source material, something other than history. But the historians of American literature seem generally to have regarded controversial writing as very doubtful literature; and oratory is now evidently quite without the pale. To be specific, Moses Coit Tyler's *Literary History of the American Revolution*,[63] which is confined to the period prior to 1783, is restricted so far as Hamilton is concerned to the Westchester pamphlets and deals with them in terms which are clearly unrealistic. Barrett Wendell, in his *Literary History of America*, does not consider the speeches at all; and he seems to approach *The Federalist* with condescension. What is said about *The Federalist* resolves itself into the conclusion that "it is phrased with a rhythmical balance and urbane polish which give it a claim to literary distinction." [64] The reader notes the specific prerequisites to literary distinction, to wit, balance of rhythm and urbanity of polish; but he remains in a state of indecision concerning the functions of a literature of controversy.

[57] Indianapolis, 1928.
[58] New York, 1852.
[59] New York, 1896.
[60] Chicago, 1897.
[61] New York, 1935.
[62] New York, 1889.
[63] New York, 1897.
[64] New York, 1900, p. 118.

One looks in vain to Trent's *History of American Literature* [65] for any greater light than that offered by Wendell; and, indeed, the literary historians seem generally to have preferred the historiography of the fine to that of the useful arts. A reservation should obviously be made concerning Parrington, who, in his *Main Currents in American Thought*,[66] has given generous attention to Alexander Hamilton and to *The Federalist*. But Parrington's work, while it is notable for the freshness and heartiness with which the author approached his task, nevertheless reveals the author's preoccupation with Hamilton's politics, to the neglect of Hamilton's persuasion.

Of the literary histories there remains the account in the *Cambridge History of American Literature*,[67] which does suggest for *The Federalist*, though not for any of Hamilton's speeches, a relation to a genuine audience as well as to a "permanent influence."

The most thoughtful consideration of Hamilton as a writer of prose is found in Prescott's introductory essay to his selection from the writings of Hamilton and Jefferson.[68] "The inclusion of Hamilton and Jefferson in a series devoted to American literature," Prescott writes, "may at first seem questionable." [69] But the writer shows why Hamilton and Jefferson deserve to be studied and notes, concerning Hamilton, that he wrote well "with an orderly clearness and masterful confidence, perhaps sometimes betrayed by rapidity." [70] Tracing the origin of Hamilton's thought, Prescott describes the conflict between the principles of Locke and Hobbes and, with reference to Hamilton's *inventio*, raises the question, "What were the theories of government, inherited by Hamilton and his contemporaries, between which they might choose to find 'arguments' fitted to support their 'claims'?" [71] Prescott is thus concerned with aspects of Hamilton's rhetoric; but he is not interested primar-

---

[65] New York, 1903.   [66] New York, 1927.   [67] New York, 1917.
[68] *Alexander Hamilton and Thomas Jefferson. . .* , New York, 1934.
[69] *Ibid.*, p. xi.   [70] *Ibid.*   [71] *Ibid.*, pp. xii-xiii.

ily in its immediately controversial aspects, nor does he deal with Hamilton directly as a speaker.

The essayists in biography present still another problem. Ames's sketch, written "immediately after the death of the ever to be lamented Hamilton," suggests how rare it is

that a man, who owes so much to nature, descends to seek more from industry; but he seemed to depend on industry, as if nature had done nothing for him. His habits of investigation were very remarkable; his mind seemed to cling to his subject till he had exhausted it. Hence the uncommon superiority of his reasoning powers.[72]

As a note on Hamilton's method, Ames's account will do service; but it, like the remainder of the essay, is an observation rather than a criticism.

The sketch provided in Lord's *Beacon Lights of History* represents neither observation nor criticism. So far is *The Federalist* removed from the hurly-burly, in this version, that all feeling of conflict is eliminated. *The Federalist*, the essayist is certain, "was not written for money or fame, but from patriotism, to enlighten the minds of the people." [73] And with reference to Hamilton's speeches, one finds only the assurance that "the ablest debater of the [Constitutional] convention was Hamilton, and his speeches were impressive and convincing." [74]

The life of Hamilton provided in *The Dictionary of American Biography* is of an entirely different order. Nevins presents a summary of the received account of Hamilton, and gives discerning estimates of the papers and speeches. Although the limitations of space obviously prohibit extended justification of his conclusion, Nevins states that in "political management and general political contests Hamilton was one among several able leaders of his day, and was likely to err through passion or prejudice; but in parliamentary battle he was to have no

[72] Ames, *Works*, II, 260.
[73] Lord, *Beacon Lights of History*, IV, 392.
[74] *Ibid.*, IV, 388.

real equal until the senatorial giants of the generation of Webster and Clay appeared." [75]

Philbrick's article in the *Encyclopaedia Britannica* [76] is of the same type as that of Nevins. There is careful estimate, but little analysis.

A variation is provided by the description in Fiske's essay entitled "Alexander Hamilton and the Federalist Party." Although he does not refrain from judgments concerning *The Federalist* and the speeches, Fiske reverses the critical process, to judge the hearers by what is addressed to them, and, in the process, implies his own general estimate:

As the speeches in Xenophon's "Anabasis" give one a very brief opinion of the intelligence of the Greek soldiers to whom such arguments might even be supposed to be addressed, so the essays in the "Federalist" give one a very high opinion of the intelligence of our great-grandfathers. The American people have never received a higher compliment than in having had such a book addressed to them. That they deserved it was shown by the effect produced, and it is in this democratic appeal to the general intelligence that we get the pleasantest impression of Hamilton's power. [77]

SUMMARY

From the foregoing analysis it appears that no biographer has written a definitive account of Hamilton's life and, furthermore, that no critic has considered Hamilton primarily from the point of view of rhetoric. The ensuing chapter will describe briefly the applicable theories of rhetoric and define the available principles of criticism.

[75] *The Dictionary of American Biography*, VIII, 174.
[76] Fourteenth ed., XI, 121.
[77] Fiske, *Essays: Historical and Literary*, I, 123.

II. THE CRITICISM OF ORATORY

FOR US *who live today under the government of speech, of whom it may be said that our daily interests are at the mercy of an oration, or the impossibility of replying to it, it is necessary to learn to speak, and, like the Greeks and Romans, we have more need of rhetoric than our fathers had.*—FERDINAND BRUNETIÈRE

A MERICAN oratory has not often been the subject of criticism. In his influential and thought-provoking study, Wichelns suggests the reasons: the association of oratory with statecraft; the momentary nature of the spoken word; the historical nature of the occasion; and the difficulty of reconciling the text with the utterance.[1] That these are weighty reasons cannot be doubted. Yet over and above these reasons appears the circumstance that oratory, regarded as a branch of literature, has not had a province of its own. The responsibilities of criticism have thus generally fallen to literary men.

CRITICISM IN AMERICA

The past generation in America considered the aims, methods, values, and standards of criticism. The experimental attitude and the skeptical spirit pervaded all the arts; but in none was controversy more vigorous than in the discussions of literature. The essential elements of the debates among the critics were as old as letters and were based on differences in temperament as old as human nature itself; but in many of their

[1] Herbert A. Wichelns, "The Literary Criticism of Oratory," in *Studies in Rhetoric and Public Speaking in Honor of James Albert Winans*, p. 181.

courses the lines of argument revealed an interesting repetition, with American variations, of the criticism of criticism which had engaged France and England a generation earlier. Among the critics one principle seems generally to have been held in common. Literature was defined by the nature of the controversy as a fine art. Oratory, not being considered a fine art, was therefore neglected by the literary critics; or, if criticism was attempted, it was based upon a system which confused the canons of rhetoric with those of poetic. The lack of proper discrimination between rhetoric and poetic was not peculiar to the period; for their distinction has often been beyond the occasion of criticism.[2]

RHETORIC AND POETIC

The distinction between rhetoric and poetic must be made, however, if any adequate criticism of oratory is to be undertaken. The distinction is at once clearer and more subtle than has generally been realized.[3] The difference between rhetoric and poetic is not simply that between prose and poetry. The familiar essay, for example, is likely to be poetic, while a satire in blank verse may very well be rhetoric. Neither does the relation of rhetoric to poetic have anything to do with the form of presentation. Originally, both rhetoric and poetic were oral, and their adaptation to the written word is not a matter

[2] Charles Sears Baldwin, *Ancient Rhetoric and Poetic*, p. 224.

[3] Interpretations of the theory of rhetoric have busied readers and writers for centuries. The present writer is not so ambitious as to wish to add to the number; yet it is necessary for the sake of clarity to set down the concepts governing this study, and, in this note, to indicate their sources. Among the works consulted, the following have been most helpful: Aristotle's *Rhetoric* in the translation by Roberts; C. S. Baldwin's *Ancient Rhetoric and Poetic*, and his *Medieval Rhetoric and Poetic*; Butcher's *The Poetics of Aristotle*; Clark's *Rhetoric and Poetry in the Renaissance*; Cooper's *The Rhetoric of Aristotle*; Cope's *Introduction to Aristotle's Rhetoric*; Jowett's *The Dialogues of Plato*; and Saint-Hilaire's *Rhetorique d'Aristote*.

of present concern. The rhetorical problem is the same, in essence, whether the vehicle be a pamphlet or a speech, the differences being primarily those of adaptation to the audience.

Nor is the distinction to be found, as is sometimes supposed, in the audience factor alone. Since poetic has its own audience relation, the discerning critic will not assume the audience as peculiar to rhetoric. It is true that the romantic movement has emphasized self-expression for poetry, at the expense of communication; but the characteristic difference between rhetoric and poetic must be sought elsewhere.

The distinction will be found not in the form of construction nor in the manner of presentation nor yet in the audience factor. It exists in the mental structure of the creator of discourse at the moment of composition and delivery and it is reflected in differing types of audience response. The creator of poetic discourse is concerned, in the first instance, with portraying life; the creator of rhetorical discourse is concerned, in the first instance, with influencing it. The former is primarily interested in his subject, the latter in his audience. The immediate end which the creator of poetic discourse seeks to achieve in terms of his hearers is the stimulation of mind and spirit. The creator of rhetorical discourse looks forward, in terms of his hearers, to the securing of their understanding, belief, or action.

The characteristic difference in the mental structure of the creator of discourse thus reflected in the attitude toward the audience problem has profound significance for the orator. His problem of impelling to action or of securing acquiescence or acceptance of a state of being suggests neither the mood of contemplation nor the attitude of the spectator. The specific requirement of action or acquiescence by an immediate audience thus determines the nature of oratory and forms the mold of its criticism. This requirement of action or acquiescence underlies the simple assumption of the present study: The criticism of oratory should be based on principles of rhetoric.

ATTITUDES TOWARD RHETORIC

The question, "What principles of rhetoric?" arises immediately. The meaning involved in the term "mere rhetoric" can be dismissed at once. The concept of rhetoric as an ornamental addition to language, a kind of extra baggage carried without good purpose, is held, it is true, by persons who should know better; but even if such a concept were warranted by the tradition of the subject, it would not suffice as the basis for a philosophy from which fundamental principles are to be drawn. The long history of rhetoric reveals three attitudes which have at one time or another been so prevalent as to warrant some exposition. The attitudes can easily be named the sophistic, the Platonic, and the Aristotelian, provided their continuing and contemporary influence be kept in mind.[4]

It was the misfortune of the sophists to incur the ill will of Plato and so to be damned for all time as the practitioners of the devious art of making the worse appear the better reason. The sophists who incurred the displeasure of Plato, and of Aristotle for that matter, were actually charged with malpractice in dialectic rather than with the misuse of rhetoric; but by long tradition the term "sophist" has been applied to orators as well as to dialecticians. The school of sophists has had many teachers, and some discrimination should be exercised in judging them. The art of some sophists has been, and is today, a bag of tricks, designed to provide the student of public speaking with an easy guide to eloquence. The objective is no more than the securing of a superficial gloss in the speaker's manner. Although other teachers and practitioners of the sophistic school have had more fundamental interests

---

[4] Reference could be made to Isocrates, to Quintilian, to Cicero, and to others; but the attitudes here characterized as sophistic, Platonic, and Aristotelian are believed to represent those fundamental approaches to rhetorical situations which have been most influential in governing human conduct.

in the education of the whole person, the primary characteristic of sophistic has been its absorption in one aspect of rhetoric, that is, the style and method of the public speaker.

The second attitude toward rhetoric, the Platonic, arose out of Plato's protest against the sophists. The dislike with which Plato regarded the sophists of his day has been represented in a continuing suspicion of rhetoric; but since rhetoric seems to be necessarily a universal art and practice in society, it has been, even though often suspect, a part of every education. The educator as creator of utopia has frequently distrusted the rhetorician and questioned his value in an ideal social order; but in progressing toward his utopia, the educator has been under the ironic necessity of practicing the art or craft which he has assumed to despise. The intellectual idealist, likewise, has distrusted the rhetorician as the popularizer and energizer of knowledge. Often convinced of the correctness of doctrines for which he has been unable to secure general acceptance, the intellectual idealist has had difficulty in accepting Aristotle's dictum that men have a natural tendency toward whatever is true and that, as a corollary, the advocate of any right principle which fails of popular acceptance deserves to be reprehended.

The common man, also, has often been suspicious of rhetoric whenever he has been conscious of its use. The public speaker has thus sometimes found it expedient to conceal his art behind disarming qualities; and an awkwardness of person and homeliness of phrase, or their appearance, have served him, paradoxically enough, as a means of persuasion. "I am no orator as Brutus is," Shakespeare had Mark Antony assure the Roman mob, "but, as you know me all, a plain blunt man!"

Aristotle saw more in rhetoric than the sophists or Plato had perceived. Aristotle disapproved of the shallow conception of rhetoric common in his day quite as heartily as Plato did; in the introduction to the first book of his *Rhetoric* he stated his objections clearly: The makers of previous systems had considered only a small part of rhetoric; busying themselves with details, they had neglected to complete a system comprehensive enough to include the rhetorical syllogism.[5] Unlike Plato, however, Aristotle proceeded at once from a realistic rather than from an idealistic point of view. Although Aristotle was matter-of-fact about the art of rhetoric and fell short of admiring it, he nevertheless maintained a positive rather than a negative attitude toward it. Ruling out the relationship of rhetoric to *truth*, which had engrossed the attention of Plato, Aristotle observed that the art of rhetoric is actually based on the concept of *probability*. Instead of retreating from the art, or attacking it, Aristotle set out to place all its aspects into a coherent and orderly form. The result of his endeavor is the *Rhetoric*, the first really systematic treatise on the subject.

The first systematic treatise, it is also the most significant; for its influence has been pervasive. Cicero and Quintilian were indebted to it; Bacon was influenced by it; and writers nearer our own time, such as Blair and Campbell and Whately, were dependent on it. Modern scholars, like those of other eras, have pronounced it valid. Baldwin found Aristotle's *Rhetoric* to be not merely a manual but a philosophical survey in which the "scope of rhetoric is measured not by any scheme of education, but by the relations of knowledge to conduct and affairs." [6] Roberts observed, concerning the *Rhetoric* and the *Poetics*, that these two great treatises on language "bring the long and amazing procession of Aristotle's thought to a fitting close." [7] And Lane Cooper has stated unequivocally that the *Rhetoric* of Aristotle is today "the most helpful book extant for writers of prose and for speakers of every sort." [8]

The teaching of public speaking in schools and colleges in many generations has been influenced by the cogency of the *Rhetoric*; and the present emphasis on thought and communi-

---

[5] Aristotle, *Rhetoric*, 1354a.
[6] C. S. Baldwin, *Ancient Rhetoric and Poetic*, p. 8.
[7] See Roberts's preface to his translation of Aristotle's *Rhetoric*.
[8] Cooper, *The Rhetoric of Aristotle*, p. xvii.

cation in courses in public speaking represents a departure from the sophistic of elocution common a generation ago and a return to the Aristotelian tradition. The work of Aristotle represents a philosophy of rhetoric, yet a philosophy which deals with audience phenomena rather than with individual ideation. Its universal quality can be accounted for only by the complete insight which the author had into the nature of the occasion, the purposes of oratory, and the relation of orator to audience. In contrast with the sophists, who looked upon rhetoric as a private concern, and in contrast with Plato, who regarded rhetoric with suspicion, Aristotle saw rhetoric as a social force which, like wealth, or strength, or any other form of power, might be used either for good or for evil.[9] It is thus the positive social attitude of Aristotle, rather than the narrow concept of the sophists or the negation of Plato, which should be chosen to determine the principles of criticism of American oratory.

ARISTOTLE'S PHILOSOPHY OF RHETORIC

If Aristotle's philosophy of rhetoric is to serve as the source for a theory of criticism, his work should be examined more closely. Rhetoric, in Aristotle's view, is not a mere adjunct of politics, ethics, or education. It has a function of its own in any given instance, and, like logic, is of universal applicability. It is a pervasive working-principle with characteristics differentiating it from other disciplines. The special province of rhetoric is the line of argument. In short, rhetoric is the faculty of observing in any given case the available means of persuasion. Speeches may be made about politics, or medicine, or economics; but no matter what the subject, there is a constant, a principle underlying them all. This constant, this working-principle of discerning the available means of persuasion, is rhetoric.[10]

[9] Aristotle, *Rhetoric*, 1355b.   [10] *Ibid.*, 1355b.

If audiences were perfect, the only means necessary to persuasion could be found in the enthymeme, a kind of rhetorical
syllogism constituting reasonable proof. But since audiences are
not perfect, the public speaker must employ other means of
persuasion as well, of which there are two: emotional proof,
the creating of a favorable disposition in the hearers; and ethical
proof, the securing of a favorable attitude toward the speaker.[11]

The audience, in the Aristotelian theory, determines also
the three classes or divisions of oratory. Deliberative or political
speaking, looking toward the future, urges expedient courses
of action. Forensic or legal oratory, looking back into the past,
attacks or defends some person in order to promote justice
or injustice. Ceremonial or occasional oratory, chiefly concerned
with the present, attempts to secure honor or dishonor by means
of praise or blame.[12] The *Rhetoric* of Aristotle thus derives
from the audience, the hearer; and the point of view throughout is toward the audience-speaker relation. Of the three books
which make it up, the first is devoted primarily to the speaker,
the second to the audience, and the third to the speech. Implicit in the whole is the occasion, the background of the speaking situation.

Aristotle's plan and point of view will be utilized in this essay
in criticism, not only because they are generally applicable and
sound, but also for convenience. At the same time, the oratory
of Alexander Hamilton must be considered in the light of
Hamilton's own ideas and means of persuasion, as they can be
developed throughout this study. Accordingly, a chapter will be
devoted to Hamilton as a speaker, another to the occasion,
another to the audience, and still another to the speeches.

[11] Aristotle, *Rhetoric*, 1356a.   [12] *Ibid.*, 1358b.

III. THE SPEAKER

WE ARE *to form, then, the perfect orator, who cannot exist unless as a good man; and we require in him, therefore, not only consummate ability in speaking, but every excellence of mind.*—QUINTILIAN

ALEXANDER HAMILTON was born a British subject on the island of Nevis, in the West Indies. The generally accepted date of his birth is January 11, 1757;[1] but an early biographer recorded the year of his birth as "about . . . 1753";[2] and a recent account of his life suggests 1752 or 1753.[3] There appear to be no official records of Hamilton's birth, and unusual caution must be exercised in arriving at any judgments in which his exact age and his paternity are factors of importance.

Hamilton's mother was Rachel Fawcett, the daughter of a French physician of Nevis. Prior to Hamilton's birth, his mother had been married to and separated from a Danish citizen of the island of St. Croix named Michael Levine; after her separation from Levine, she entered into a legally irregular but socially accepted relation with James Hamilton, a Scotchman of the island of St. Christopher, and it is he whom Alexander Hamilton recognized as father.[4]

---

[1] Lodge, *Alexander Hamilton*, p. 1; Bailey, *An American Colossus*, p. 18; J. T. Morse, *The Life of Alexander Hamilton*, I, 2; H. J. Ford, *Alexander Hamilton*, p. 2.

[2] Cheetham, *A Narrative of the Suppression by Col. Burr of the History of the Administration of John Adams*, p. 52.

[3] Smertenko, *Alexander Hamilton*, p. 4.

[4] Alexander Hamilton to James Hamilton, Jr., June 23, 1783. Allan McLane Hamilton, *The Intimate Life of Alexander Hamilton*, p. 6.

Rachel Levine died in 1768.[5] James Hamilton was a failure
in business and, although he lived until 1799, offered little or
no assistance to Alexander Hamilton, boy or man. Following
his mother's death, the boy went to work for Nicholas Cruger,
a merchant of Christianstadt on the island of St. Croix, and
continued working for him until 1772.

THE SPEAKER'S SCHOOLING

Hamilton's early training was received from his mother,
who was a woman of some education, and from Hugh Knox,
a Presbyterian clergyman who had studied with the Rev. Aaron
Burr, president of the College of New Jersey.

The general store of Nicholas Cruger furthered the youth's
education by providing genuine learning situations, and his
business letters of the period demonstrate that he took advantage of his opportunities.[6] But the work was dull. There was no
opportunity to shine, to rise in the world. Young Hamilton
wished for an opportunity to distinguish himself in a war.[7]
But there was no war, and so, in 1772, he entered Francis
Barber's school at Elizabethtown, New Jersey, to prepare for
college. In 1773 he matriculated at King's College, now Columbia University, in New York.[8]

Little enough is certainly known about Hamilton's formal
studies in college. It appears that he was ambitious enough to
enroll for all subjects, including the courses in the medical college, and that he had private lessons in mathematics.[9] His be-

[5] Photograph, Burial Register of St. John's Episcopal Church, Christianstadt, in the island of St. Croix. Atherton, *A Few of Hamilton's Letters*, p. 260.
[6] Hamilton to Cruger, Nov. 16, 1771. Alexander Hamilton, *Works*,
John Church Hamilton, ed., I, 2.
[7] Hamilton to Stevens, Nov. 11, 1769. Alexander Hamilton, *Works*,
John Church Hamilton, ed., I, 1.
[8] John Church Hamilton, *History*, I, 45.
[9] Bailey, *op. cit.*, p. 29.

havior was evidently good, for his name was not listed in
President Cooper's "Black Book," a record of student offenses;
and he was inspired, during his early student days, with a religious fervor which led him to reflection and prayer.[10]

At the time of Hamilton's attendance, King's College, like
other educational institutions of the day, supported a curriculum
heavy in the classics, including those of rhetoric and oratory.
The original rules and regulations of the college, set up in
1755, established as one of the entrance requirements the ability
to read the first three of Tully's select orations. At the same
time, a rule for college exercises provided that the "Pupils
in each of their Turns shall be obliged, at Such times as the
President shall appoint, to make Exercises in the Severall
Branches of Learning Suitable to their Standing both in Latin
and English, Such as Declamations, and Disputations on Various Questions Pro and Con, and frequently Thesis and Syllogis-
tical Reasonings." [11]

In 1762 there developed an idea that the growing college
needed a new plan, and accordingly a committee was appointed
by the Board of Governors to inquire into the state and circumstances of the college. The committee reported in writing at
a meeting of the Governors held on March 1, 1763, and the
report was enacted. The new plan was the result of a thoroughgoing review of the administration and curriculum of the college and it recommended "Additions, Amendments, & Altera-
tions." In order to give the new plan greater weight and sanction, it was published "with a becoming solemnity in the-Col-
lege Hall," in the presence of governors, professors, masters,
and students. The several professors, masters, and tutors were
solemnly notified to carry the new plan into effect.[12]

The plan involved such matters as the fixing of fees and the

[10] *Ibid.*, p. 31.
[11] Minutes, The Board of Governors of King's College, June 3, 1755.
Columbiana, Library, Columbia University.
[12] *Ibid.*, March 1, 1763.

assignment of rooms, but it also presented a revised curriculum. For the first year, the studies included Sallust, Ovid, Caesar, and Virgil, in addition to translations and grammar; and in the second year rhetoric and "Restrictions to learn the Art of Speaking" were added. The third-year course required the study of Cicero's orations, Cicero's *De oratore*, and Aristotle's *Ethics* and *Poetics;* and, in the fourth year, the list of studies was enlarged to include metaphysics and moral philosophy, as well as Longinus, Demosthenes, Dionysius of Halicarnassus, and Isocrates. "Disputations in the Hall" were continued also. The minutes of the Board of Governors reveal no major changes during the ten-year period between the instituting of the revised curriculum and Hamilton's entrance. If, as seems probable, the revised curriculum of 1763 was in effect during his student days, Hamilton must have received thorough instruction in rhetoric and public speaking, even though he did not finish the complete course in residence.[13]

The commencement exercises of the period indicate the continued importance assigned to speech-making. The commencement of 1771 was celebrated with a forensic disputation on the question "Whether a lively *Imagination* is conducive to Happiness?" with orations "On Cheerfulness," "On the Passions," and "On Pneumatics," among others, and a valedictory address on "The Effects of Ambition." [14]

It may be, however, that Hamilton's most significant collegiate experiences in public speaking were extra-curricular. A "Literary Society" was functioning at King's College as early as 1768, when Gouverneur Morris and Benjamin Moore were awarded silver medals by the "Literary Society for superior excellence in oratory and composition." Hamilton, during his

[13] Minutes, The Board of Governors of King's College, March 1, 1763.
[14] *Order of Commencement in King's College, New-York, May 21, 1771.* Columbiana, Library, Columbia University. For newspaper accounts of early commencements, see the article by Milton Halsey Thomas, "King's College Commencement in the Newspapers," *Columbia University Quarterly*, XXII (June, 1930), 226-47.

student days, belonged to the society and delivered before it
some youthful speeches which were long remembered by his
fellows.[15]

THE SOLDIER

But the war which the boy had wished for was brewing;
and from the debating exercises of a college society, the young
man turned to more realistic controversy in speech and pamphlet and eventually to the more forceful argument of the
sword. The war spirit disrupted King's College. In the spring
of 1776 the college buildings were taken over by the military
as a hospital.[16] Hamilton had already participated in the organization of The Hearts of Oak, a defense unit; and his soldier's career began as his formal schooling ended, when he was
appointed to command an artillery company.[17] He participated
in the campaigns of 1776 and 1777, notably in the defense
of Harlem Heights and in the attack on Trenton and Princeton.[18] But Washington needed skillful writers even more than
he needed captains. On March 1, 1777, Hamilton became aide-
de-camp to Washington and was entrusted with much of the
military correspondence during the fateful years from 1777 to
1781.[19] In 1781 Hamilton, chagrined at a rebuke administered
by his commander, resigned as aide-de-camp and asked for an

[15] Cardozo, *A History of the Philolexian Society of Columbia University from 1802-1902.*
[16] Minutes of the Board of Governors of King's College, May 14,
1776.
[17] Letter, Hamilton to the Provincial Congress of New York, May 26,
1776. Alexander Hamilton, *Works*, John Church Hamilton, ed., I, 7.
[18] Francis Vinton Greene, *The Revolutionary War and the Military
Policy of the United States*, pp. 52, 68.
[19] Significant portions of Washington's military correspondence are in
Hamilton's handwriting. See *The Writings of George Washington from
the Original Manuscript Sources, 1745-1799*, John C. Fitzpatrick, ed.,
Vols. VII to XXI. In his introduction (I, xliv) the editor observes ". . .
when young Alexander Hamilton served as aide, it is noticeable that
the letters to Congress, to governors, and State legislatures were usually
drafted by him." In a letter to John Sullivan, Feb. 4, 1781 (XXI, 181)

appointment in the field. He received an assignment in time
to demonstrate his personal courage in an attack on a redoubt
at Yorktown.[20]

AFTER THE WAR

Even though he was busily engaged in war, Hamilton had
found time, in December, 1780, to be married to Elizabeth
Schuyler, daughter of Gen. Philip Schuyler, the rich and respected patriot of New York.[21] When Cornwallis surrendered
at Yorktown, Hamilton returned to his wife in Albany and
settled down to the intensive study of the law. A few months
sufficed to prepare him for admission to the bar, and, after
a term in the Continental Congress, he began his practice
in the city of New York. At this time Hamilton intended to
remain a private citizen and to care for his own business; but
he was greatly irritated by the lack of energy in the central
government and found himself constantly drawn into public
affairs.[22] Even his law practice tended toward this end, for
in one celebrated case, that of *Rutgers vs. Waddington,* his
plea was the supervening authority of Federal treaties over
state law.[23] In the end, his strong opinions led him to be one
of the foremost of the advocates of a stronger union. He was a
participant in the Annapolis convention of 1786; he stead-
fastly supported the granting of the impost rights to the Continental Congress; and, finally, he was one of three delegates

---

written shortly before Hamilton's precipitate resignation (Feb. 16, 1781),
Washington expressed the following judgment of his aide: ". . . I can
venture to advance from a thorough knowledge of him, that there are
few men to be found, of his age, who has a more general knowledge
than he possesses, and none whose Soul is more firmly engaged in the
cause, or who exceeds him in probity and Sterling virtue."

[20] F. V. Greene, *op. cit.,* p. 274.

[21] John Church Hamilton, *History,* II, 145.

[22] Hamilton to Lafayette, Nov. 3, 1782. Alexander Hamilton, *Works,*
John Church Hamilton, ed., I, 320.

[23] Alexander Hamilton's "Notes for Argument in the Trespass Case."
Allan McLane Hamilton, *op. cit.,* p. 457.

from New York to the constitutional convention at Philadelphia in 1787.[24]

Alexander Hamilton, destined to be the leader of the Poughkeepsie convention, was thus, although still in his early thirties, a man of wide experience. He was young, but he was mature; for it had been twenty years since his mother's death had thrown him on his own resources, and in those twenty years he had earned his living in a general store, moved alone from his childhood home to another colony, prepared for and attended college, achieved a lieutenant-colonelcy as aide-de-camp to one of the great men of the epoch, married a daughter of one of the foremost families of New York, entered and achieved distinction in the practice of law, and served in congress and legislature. In the twenty years, also, he had undergone the full development of person, disposition, and mind which left him in 1788 much as he was to be for the remaining years of his life; he had acquired a reputation among men; and by reading, writing, and speaking had gained competence in the use of language.

THE SPEAKER'S PERSON

Although many portraits and statues of Hamilton are available, as a group they are more confusing than helpful in furnishing a picture of the orator not merely because they cannot capture voice and spirit, but also because there is marked dissimilarity in likeness among them. The striking statue of Hamilton by Ordway Partridge which stands at the entrance of Hamilton Hall, Columbia University, seems to offer the representation which best accords with credible descriptions. Fortunately, there is satisfying evidence concerning Hamilton's personal appearance.[25] In his maturity, he was not a large man,

[24] John Church Hamilton, *History*, III, 163 *et seq.*
[25] Shea, *The Life and Epoch of Alexander Hamilton*, p. 45; Allan McLane Hamilton, *op. cit.*, p. 29; James A. Hamilton, *Reminiscences of James A. Hamilton*, p. 3.

being about five feet seven inches in height; he was lithe, grace-
ful, and energetic. He had a Roman nose and a strong chin;
his complexion was fair, his hair reddish-brown, and his features
of the type commonly thought of as Scottish. The most notable
aspects of his countenance were his deep-set, deep-blue eyes,
and, on occasion, a captivating smile. His countenance was
severe, even stern, in repose, but in moments of relaxation it
was animated and merry. One man, at least, seeing him at such
a time, thought him boyish and giddy.[26] But the dignity of
his bearing and the air of command which he exercised in serious matters was notable and proceeded in part from his deliber-
ate speech. Hamilton's voice was engagingly pleasant, and the
charm of his manner was such as to make him attractive both
to friends and to strangers, to men and to women.[27] He was
careful in his dress, and observed the fashions of his day, without appearing to be foppish; he regarded himself as an aristo-
crat and he dressed, lived, and acted the part.

THE SPEAKER'S DISPOSITION

Like his countenance, Hamilton's disposition reflected varying aspects. James A. Hamilton, his third child, who was born
April 14, 1788, has recorded a son's early memories of the
tender and affectionate relations between Hamilton and his
children.[28] Hamilton's care for the orphan daughter of his old
comrade, Colonel Autle; his consideration for Earle, the unfortunate artist imprisoned for debt; his generous concern for
Duer, victim of speculation; with a host of other instances,
reveal his idea of friendship.[29]

Certainly one of the sources of Hamilton's power was pre-

[26] *The Journal of William Maclay, United States Senator from Pennsylvania, 1789-1791*, p. 302.

[27] Letter XLIX, Oct. 10, 1833. William Sullivan, *Familiar Letters on
Public Characters and Public Events* (Boston, 1834), p. 235.

[28] James A. Hamilton, *op. cit.*, p. 3.

[29] *Ibid.*, pp. 3-5.

cisely his capacity for friendship, which, rising above the level of winning friends to use them, embraced a genuine quality of fidelity. Throughout his life Hamilton made friends and enemies, but he rarely lost either. Even Hamilton's enemies knew his personal charm and the power of his language.[30] To his opponents he was as severe as to his friends he was generous. He was capable of unyielding prejudices, not only concerning ideas but also concerning persons. His constant thwarting of Aaron Burr, his inept attacks on John Adams, his consistent dislike for Thomas Jefferson, all testify to his capacity for vigorous antagonism.

While his generous friendships and his forthright enmities present Alexander Hamilton as a passionate, interesting, and human individual, they reveal, at the same time, his greatest weakness as a controversialist and as a public speaker. He was not consistently tactful. It is impossible to believe that Hamilton's blunders grew out of stupidity. He knew men, and on more than one occasion, including his mastery of the situation at Poughkeepsie, he demonstrated his ability to be pleasing. One who reads Hamilton's letters carefully and follows consecutively the events of his career will ascribe the marks of seeming ineptitude in many instances not to the lack of ability but to the lack of a sufficient willingness to be tactful. Obviously there were instances of devious practice in Hamilton's public and private life, notably the clandestine amour with Mrs. Reynolds,[31] the suggestion to Jay of a doubtful procedure in

[30] Jefferson to The President of the United States, Sept. 9, 1792. Thomas Jefferson, *Writings*, Albert Ellery Bergh, ed., VIII, 399. See also Jefferson to Madison, April 3, 1794, *ibid.*, IX, 281; Jefferson to Madison, Sept. 21, 1795, *ibid.*, IX, 309; Adams to Jefferson, July, 1813, *ibid.*, XIII, 301.

[31] "Observations on Certain Documents Contained in Nos. V. and VI. of *The History of the United States for the Year 1796*, in which the Charge of Speculation against Alexander Hamilton, late Secretary of the Treasury, is fully refuted. Written by himself. Philadelphia: Printed for John Fenno, by John Bioren, 1797." Alexander Hamilton, *Works*, Henry Cabot Lodge, ed., VII, 369.

the choosing of presidential electors in 1800,[32] and the attempt
at instigating the Christian Constitutional Societies against
Jefferson.[33] Nevertheless, despite his lapses, one is impressed in
Hamilton's correspondence and speeches with the use of the
word "candid" as a key to his ideal, if not to his consistent
practice, in conduct. Doubtless Hamilton's pride was also involved in his attitudes; for he knew his powers and often
exhibited impatience with the slowness or stupidity of others.
In the choice which every controversialist has to make between
expressing himself and seeking to persuade the other person,
Hamilton seemed, on occasion, to choose the release of his own
feelings to that inhibition of them sometimes necessary to win
adherents to a cause. This element of Hamilton's disposition
affected not only his ability as a controversialist, but also offered
no little aid and comfort to the forces engaged in building up
Antifederalism in the United States.

THE SPEAKER'S REPUTATION

In considering Hamilton's reputation in 1788, it is necessary first of all to cast out of account some of the evidence which
bears on his disposition, especially that which concerns the fric-
tions and animosities of the later years of his public life, from
1789 to 1800. When he went to Poughkeepsie in 1788, Hamilton had not yet quarreled with the Livingstons over the senatorship from New York; he had not made the bitter fight
against Clinton's retaining the governorship; he had not incurred the enmity of Aaron Burr. Neither Thomas Jefferson
nor James Monroe bore him any ill will; and James Madison,
far from being his political opponent, was his chief collaborator
in urging the adoption of the new constitution.[34] It is true that

[32] Hamilton to Jay, May 7, 1800. Alexander Hamilton, *Works*, John
Church Hamilton, ed., VI, 438.
[33] Hamilton to Bayard, April, 1802. Alexander Hamilton, *Works*, John
Church Hamilton, ed., VI, 540.
[34] Hamilton to Madison, April 3, 1788. Alexander Hamilton, *Works*,
John Church Hamilton, ed., I, 450.

Yates and Lansing, his fellow delegates at the Philadelphia convention, differed with him sharply, as did Governor Clinton; but the bitterest enmities were still to be incited. The issues of the assumption of state debts, of the national bank, and of the payment of soldier's claims had not arisen to establish a great body of men against Hamilton, and his personal popularity, even with the masses of the people, appears to have been noteworthy.[35] As for the rich and well-born, Hamilton was commonly regarded by them with unqualified admiration. The high opinion which George Washington had of the young man was no secret, and his friends included not only such citizens of New York as John Jay and Chancellor Livingston but also such national figures as Baron Steuben and Robert Morris.

At the same time, at least three elements in Hamilton's reputation were calculated to disturb the populace. In the first place, he was a lawyer, and plain people quite generally regarded lawyers with suspicion. In the second place, he was an active member of the Order of the Cincinnati, and the Order was commonly believed to be dangerous to the welfare of the people.[36] In the third place, Hamilton counseled moderation and restraint in dealing with those who had remained loyal to Britain in the Revolution, and such counsels were not cordially received by ardent patriots.[37]

[35] *Daily Advertiser*, New York, Aug. 2, 1788.

[36] John Church Hamilton, *History*, III, 122. The Order of the Cincinnati was believed to represent the beginnings of hereditary aristocracy. Hamilton was elected vice president while the convention was in session at Poughkeepsie. (*Country Journal and Poughkeepsie Advertiser*, July 8, 1788.) Maclay, a few years later, noted Hamilton's use of the organization. (Maclay, *op. cit.*, pp. 181, 204.)

[37] The charge of Toryism against Hamilton was one of long continuance. Cheetham (*op. cit.*, p. 55) observed, about 1802, that the "American Tory against whom he had fought, he now began to defend, and in every suit where a loyalist was concerned, Mr. Hamilton was the royal pleader." Beard (Maclay, *op. cit.*, p. viii) has commented on the irritation felt by the agrarians at the alignment of the propertied Tories with the proponents of Federalism. See also Nevins, *The American States during and after the Revolution*, *1775-1789*, pp. 268 *et seq.*

Beyond the general recognition of his brilliance, and in addition to his personal friendships, including his relation with Washington, which Hamilton himself recognized as one of great significance to himself,[38] there were at least three elements of strength in his popular reputation. In the first place, he indubitably had a brilliant war record, and the soldiers of the Revolution had already begun to expect and to receive popular esteem for their services.[39] In the second place, he had a wide acquaintance among merchants and business men in New York, dating in some instances from pre-Revolutionary days, and the respect of the mercantile interest was distinctly an asset.[40] In the third place, he had married the daughter of Philip Schuyler, had established his own home, and was the father of three children; and his position both as the head of a family and as the son-in-law of Philip Schuyler placed his social status beyond cavil.[41]

One further question has intimate relation not only to Hamilton's reputation but also to his character and career. John Adams stated that Hamilton was ignorant not only of Pennsylvania and the nation but of "his own city and State of New York." [42] Parton, the biographer of Aaron Burr, too easily assumed that Hamilton was alien.[43] And Woodrow Wilson, in a later generation, lent the historian's support to the idea that Hamilton was not truly an American.[44]

---

[38] Hamilton to Mrs. Washington, Jan. 12, 1800. Alexander Hamilton, *Works*, John Church Hamilton, ed., VI, 418.

[39] Daggett, *An Oration, Pronounced in the Brick Meeting-House, in the City of New-Haven, on the Fourth of July, A. D. 1787; It Being the Eleventh Anniversary of the Independence of the United States of America*, p. 11.

[40] Narrative of Hercules Mulligan. O'Brien, *Hercules Mulligan: Confidential Correspondent of General Washington*, p. 182.

[41] Tuckerman, *Life of General Philip Schuyler*, p. 9 et seq.

[42] Adams to Lloyd. John Adams, *Works*, Charles Francis Adams, ed., X, 125.

[43] Parton, *The Life and Times of Aaron Burr*, I, 212.

[44] Wilson, *A History of the American People*, V, 64, 74.

The effort to interpret Hamilton as a foreigner in America
is not well-considered. Concerning the New England town
meeting, for example, Alexander Hamilton was no more under-
privileged than John Jay, George Clinton, or, for that matter,
than James Madison and Thomas Jefferson. The town meeting
was a phenomenon peculiar to New England. The West Indies
in Hamilton's boyhood were, like the several separate provinces
on the continent, British possessions; and the relations between
the islands and New York were no more constrained by limitations of foreign prejudice than were those between New York
and the Carolinas. The West Indies were not so much a foreign
country as a sister province. It is significant that Adams, in
deploring Hamilton's lack of understanding of America, identified him quite definitely with New York; so did people generally in Hamilton's own day. In the heated controversies which
accompanied or followed his career in the Treasury, Hamilton
was not infrequently called a bastard, a self-confessed adulterer,
and worst of all, a monarchist.[45] But at that time, apparently, it
was not usually considered expedient to attack him as an alien.
Wilson's dictum would be much more accurate if it were merely
that Hamilton was not a Jeffersonian; for Hamilton was an
American, not an ordinary one, but nevertheless a conservative
American identified with a tradition which has been curiously
neglected by American historians. But the conservative philosophy represented by Hamilton is, in many respects, as charac-

[45] James Thomsen Callender, *The American Annual Register, or His-
torical Memoirs . . . for the Year 1796*, p. 173.
"The man who *dares* even to hint that the President of the United
States is proud or avaricious, is locked up in solitary confinement—Oh
Liberty!!! Whilst honors and emoluments are heaped upon the head of
the adulterer by the same President, who often approaches the throne of
his maker. Oh! decency." *Aurora and General Advertiser*, Philadelphia,
Nov. 10, 1798.
"What can ail the six per cent people at Irishmen? Their own Grand
Lama, the truly illustrious Alexander Hamilton, as far as his maternal
descent can be traced was the son of an IRISH CAMP GIRL." *Aurora and
General Advertiser*, March 17, 1798.

teristically American as the rival theories of liberalism. It would be a mistake, in attempting to understand Hamilton's reputation in 1788, to describe him as a foreigner. He was regarded as a New Yorker, as a member of the aristocracy, as a lawyer, as a soldier and aide-de-camp to Washington; but he was not considered to be an alien.

THE SPEAKER'S MIND

No study of Alexander Hamilton would be complete without special consideration of his mentality. His biographers write of his brilliance.[46] The word "brilliance" will suffice only if it be interpreted to include more than a surface quality; for, although Hamilton indubitably possessed a mentality of high order, he did not, like Charles James Fox, rely greatly on insight and inspiration. A significant part of Hamilton's brilliance was nothing more nor less than highly organized nervous energy systematically directed toward tasks of great difficulty. The man possessed tremendous psychic drive, a force which cannot be accounted for by reason of physical well-being, for, following hardships which he endured during the Revolution, he seems never to have been robust and often lashed himself into activity which prudence would have forbidden. The outstanding intellectual power which accompanied Hamilton's tremendous drive may be described as the ability to see and understand essential issues and relationships. Or, if we may accept Talleyrand's testimony, the secret of his power may be found in his possession of a kind of divination. Talleyrand, who knew and had probably conversed with every major figure of his epoch, considered Napoleon, Fox, and Hamilton to be the greatest of them; and of the three, he gave first place unhesitatingly to Hamilton.

[46] H. J. Ford, *op. cit.*, p. 370; Bowers, *Jefferson and Hamilton*, p. 27; Chancellor Kent, concerning Hamilton, speaks of "the matchless resources of his mighty mind." James Kent, *An Anniversary Discourse Delivered before the New-York Historical Society*, December 6, 1828, p. 34.

Hamilton, according to Talleyrand, "avait *deviné* l'Europe." [47]

Hamilton's insight, divination, or grasp of issues, with his urge to apply himself completely to problems, was accompanied by another attribute so consistent within him during his maturity as to appear as a part of his mentality and a color of his thought. Alexander Hamilton did not think well of the human race. Loyal to his friends, affectionate with his family, nevertheless he viewed the race as a whole without approbation. [48] Successful governments can be contrived, he was certain, only by making the human creature's self-interest identical, insofar as possible, with that of the group. It is significant that neither Jefferson nor Hamilton believed in mankind, *per se;* but the essential difference in the quality of their thought—and the difference characterizes both—is that while Jefferson believed education to be necessary in order to keep men in a natural state of virtue, Hamilton thought discipline necessary to prevent men from succumbing to their natural propensities for evil. In an age when forces were moving toward the democratic ideals espoused under the Jeffersonian concept of mankind, Hamilton's position appeared to be conservative, as indeed it was. Yet the precise nature of Hamilton's conservatism has too often escaped the attention of commentators. Like many American conservatives since his time, Hamilton was not a complete adherent to an unalterable *status quo.* His support of the colonies against Great Britain—a matter of choice with him—does not mark the complete conservative; neither does his strong support of a central government against the ruling sovereignties in the several states. The strict conservative in support of the order existing in this period would be found among the Tories and among the proponents of states rights.

[47] Marquis de Talleyrand-Perigord, *Étude sur la république,* p. 192. Shea, *op. cit.,* p. 35.

[48] Hamilton to Gouverneur Morris, March 4, 1802. Alexander Hamilton, *Works,* John Church Hamilton, ed., VI, 532. Hamilton to Gouverneur Morris, Feb. 27, 1802. *Ibid.,* VI, 530.

Neither is there sufficient evidence to support the thesis, popularly accepted, that Hamilton's mentality was in all respects antagonistic to democratic forms of government. A source of error to modern readers is that the word "democracy" does not mean today what it meant in 1788. The democracy which Hamilton feared was demagoguery, and he feared it as the inevitable preparation for tyranny. For reasons quite different from those of Jefferson, Hamilton approved and supported some of the ideas commonly attributed to the founder of democracy. Hamilton thus urged manhood suffrage, not as a natural right, but as an expedient means of securing a proper identification of the body of citizens with their government. He was an active supporter of public education; [49] he opposed slavery in a period when some Virginia democrats still found the peculiar institution necessary; [50] and he supported the civil rights, perhaps as much out of respect to his ruling passion for law and order as out of belief in the sanctity of human liberties. [51]

One finds the key to Hamilton's thinking in the idea of the ordered state. He was neither an optimist nor a defeatist concerning humanity. He held to the simple concept of a society naturally chaotic, becoming meaningful only by a process of order through man's internal self-discipline and the external discipline of the state. The stated end of his actions was to institute a government stable enough "to promote the encreasing respectability of the American name; to answer the calls of justice; to restore landed property to its due value; to furnish new resources both to agriculture and commerce; to cement more closely the union of the states; to add to their security against foreign attack; to establish public order on the basis of an upright and liberal policy." [52]

---

[49] Nevins, *op. cit.*, p. 468.

[50] *New York Journal and Weekly Register*, May 24, 1787.

[51] Hamilton to Gouverneur Morris, April 6, 1802. Alexander Hamilton, *Works*, John Church Hamilton, ed., VI, 537.

[52] *Report of the Secretary of the Treasury to the House of Representatives*, United States Treasury Department, Jan. 9, 1790, p. 4.

THE SPEAKER'S READING

Alexander Hamilton knew his own propensity for "literary pursuits" [53] and appears always to have been an avid reader. When he left King's College to become a captain in the service of New York, he continued his education under his own auspices. Hamilton kept the Pay-Book for his company of artillery; and in it he listed books and notes of his reading and reflection. Among the books were Rousseau's *Emilius*, Bacon's *Essays*, Montaigne's *Essays*, Ralt's *Dictionary of Trade and Commerce*, Plutarch's *Morals*, and Demosthenes's *Orations*.[54] The influence which Hamilton's reading had on his thinking and speaking must have been considerable, but it was evidently diffuse rather than specific. That he, like other American leaders of his day, was indebted to Montesquieu is clear to any reader of *The Federalist*.[55] That he was influenced by Hume [56] and by Grotius [57] is also apparent. His references to the histories or legends of Greece indicate a reading of ancient history,[58] and the list of readings in his Pay-Book furnishes evidence of an early interest in the history of Europe and America as well.[59] He also gave thought to some of the orations of Demosthenes. Written in his captain's Pay-Book, along with observations on coinage and on the ratio of increase among diverse populations, is an extract which serves admirably to characterize Hamilton's continuing and prevailing principle of action in controversy: "As a general marches at the head of his troops, so ought wise politicians, if I dare use the expression, to march at the head

[53] Hamilton to Hamilton, May 2, 1797, Alexander Hamilton, *Works*, John Church Hamilton, ed., VI, 243.

[54] "Pay-Book of the State Company of Artillery, Commanded by Alex'r Hamilton." Alexander Hamilton, *Works*, John Church Hamilton, ed., I, 4.

[55] See *The Federalist*, Nos. 9 and 78.   [57] *Ibid.*, No. 84.

[56] *Ibid.*, No. 85.   [58] *Ibid.*, Nos. 18 and 70.

[59] Among the volumes listed were *Grecian History*, *History of Prussia*, Millot's *History of France*, Smith's *History of New-York*, and Winn's *History of America*.

of affairs; insomuch that they ought not to await *the event*,
to know what measures to take; but the measures which they
have taken ought to produce the *event*." [60]

Hamilton's reading did not cease with his youth. After his
marriage, his sister-in-law, Mrs. Church, searched London for
books for him [61] and sent him, among other works, a copy of
Adam Smith's *Wealth of Nations*. Hamilton was proficient in
French, and, for a time at least, read three French journals:
La Chronique mensuelle, Le Trône mensuel, and the *Journal
etoile*. At his death, his library contained many French books,
bequeathed to him by his former client, William Constable.[62]

However much Hamilton may have been indebted to books,
he was not in any sense subject to them; his reading was related
to the world of his experience—to Cruger's Counting House,
to Hercules Mulligan and the merchants of New York, to the
army, and to his fellow lawyers. Among the titles in the youthful captain's Pay-Book, works of serious purpose predominate.
One need not suppose that Hamilton was ignorant of poetry or
fantasy to observe the parallel between the character of his
book list and the steady seriousness which marked both his
writing and his public speaking.

THE SPEAKER'S LETTERS

To understand Hamilton as a speaker in 1788, one must
remember that he had for many years practiced the art of persuasive correspondence. The letter was for him often either a
means of securing the attention of responsible persons or of
persuading them to his own way of thinking. Indeed the first
writing of Hamilton's ever published, so far as known, is a

---

[60] "Extracts from Demosthenes' Orations. Philippic I." Alexander
Hamilton, *Works,* John Church Hamilton, ed., I, 6.

[61] Mrs. Church to Mrs. Hamilton, Feb. 4, 1790. Quoted in Allan
McLane Hamilton, *op. cit.,* p. 75.

[62] Allan McLane Hamilton, *op. cit.,* p. 75 *n.*

letter written in 1772.[63] The letter, not at all remarkable except
in relation to its author, describes in somewhat sophomoric language a hurricane which devastated the island of St. Croix.

Where now, Oh! vile worm [wrote the young Hamilton], is all
thy boasted fortitude and resolution? what is become of thy arrogance
and self-sufficiency?—why dost thou tremble and stand aghast? how
humble—how helpless—how contemptible you now appear. . . .
Learn to know thy best support. Despise thyself and adore thy
God. . . .

The letter continues at some length in the same vein, but closes
with the matter-of-fact statement that "Our general has several
very salutary and human regulations, and both in his public and
private measures has shown himself *the man*." Hamilton's
later correspondence took its characteristic tone from the closing
paragraph rather than from the pietistic elevation of those
preceding.

Although Hamilton was not so prolific a letter-writer as
Thomas Jefferson, he wrote to good purpose. An examination
of his formal correspondence prior to 1788 reveals that he had
not only a grasp of his subject in a given instance but a full
appreciation of the effective line of argument. A letter written
to Gates, protesting the manner in which Gates had carried out
an order for the disposition of troops, illustrates Hamilton's
firmness of character; but it also reveals his understanding of
the tactics of persuasion.[64] In a long letter written to James
Duane, in 1780, Hamilton exhibits a comprehensive view of
political questions; but at the same time he demonstrates an
application of the principles of persuasion to a situation.[65]

[63] Hamilton to Hamilton, Sept. 6, 1772. "The Royal Danish-American
Gazette," Vol. III, No. 234, Saturday, Oct. 3d, 1772. Ed. by Thibou,
Christianstadt, St. Croix. Quoted from Atherton, *A Few of Hamilton's
Letters*, p. 261 *et seq.*
[64] Hamilton to Gates, Nov. 5, 1777. Atherton, *op. cit.*, p. 25.
[65] Hamilton to Duane, Sept. 3, 1780. Alexander Hamilton, *Works*,
John Church Hamilton, ed., I, 150.

Hamilton's letters to Robert Morris and his formal correspondence generally are examples of his rhetorical practice.[66]

THE SPEAKER AS PAMPHLETEER

Since Hamilton did not draw a fine distinction in his practice
of persuasion between the letter and the pamphlet, some of his
private letters are really pamphlets addressed to an audience
of one, and many of his pamphlets are simply letters addressed
to a larger audience. Hamilton's first pamphlets were written
in an exchange with President Myles Cooper, while Hamilton
was still a student in King's College; [67] but it was in answer to
Seabury that Hamilton first showed his ability as a controversialist.[68] After the adjournment of the First Continental
Congress, Samuel Seabury, writing under the pseudonym of
A. W. Farmer, published two articles attacking the Congress.
Seabury was a man of considerable attainments, and he set
forth effective arguments for the Tories. To these arguments,
Hamilton replied in two pamphlets entitled *A Full Vindication*
and *The Farmer Refuted*. There are pamphlets in the English
language which are superior to these in sublimity of diction;
there are pamphlets more remarkable for dignity of style and
for elevation of language. But one will need to search carefully
through the English and American literature of controversy to
find their superior in conception, arrangement, disposition, and
adaptation to a popular audience. In *A Full Vindication*, the
argument throughout is organized with full reference to the
available evidence. Two matters are to be considered—justice
and policy. Having reconciled his cause with justice, the young
pamphleteer proceeds in a manner somewhat like that of the
college debater to consider the requisites of good policy: "First,
that the necessity of the times requires it; secondly, that it be

[66] Hamilton to Morris, n.d. Alexander Hamilton, *Works*, John Church
Hamilton, ed., I, 116.
[67] *A History of Columbia University: 1754-1904*, p. 47.
[68] Alexander Hamilton, *Works*, Henry Cabot Lodge, ed., I, 3-177.

not the probable source of greater evils than those it pretends
to remedy; and lastly, that it have a probability of success." [69]
In the latter part of *A Full Vindication,* in particular, in which
he addressed himself directly to the farmers of New York,
Hamilton demonstrated a mastery of the techniques of persuasive writing. Direct, forceful, and clear, the address to the
farmers of New York will not attract those who search for
literary grandeur; but its very simplicity and lack of pretense,
its complete avoidance of straining after literary effects, reveal
the writer's understanding of the function of controversial writing. In these early pamphlets Hamilton proved his ability to
refute without giving ground. Presumably on the defensive, he
carried the battle into the enemy's territory immediately. His
rhetorical syllogisms, furthermore, are not chosen from some
remote Achaean League or Amphictyonic Council; they come
directly from the farmers. He establishes his own personal
authority in the very beginning of his argument and subtly
attacks his opponent, by frankly explaining his own position:

The reason I address myself to you, in particular, is not because I
am one of your number, or connected with you in interest, more than
with any other branch of the community. I love to speak the truth,
and would scorn to prejudice you in favor of what I have to say, by
taking upon me a fictitious character, as other people have done. I
can venture to assure you that the true writer of the piece signed
A. W. Farmer, is not in reality a Farmer.[70]

In the second of the pamphlets, *The Farmer Refuted,* Hamilton prefaces the argument with an advertisement which makes
use of apparent reversal of opinion as a rhetorical plan.

The writer of the ensuing sheets can, with truth [he declares], say
more than the generality of those who either espouse or oppose the
claim of the BRITISH PARLIAMENT; which is, that *his* political opinions
have been the result of mature deliberation and rational inquiry. . . .
To those who are possessed of greater candor, and who yet may be

---

[69] *Ibid.,* I, 14.   [70] *Ibid.,* I, 33.

disposed to ask how *he* can be sure that his opinions have not been influenced by prejudice, *he* answers, Because he remembers the time when he had strong prejudices on the side *he* now opposes.[71]

The pamphlet debate with Seabury proved Hamilton's capacity for persuasive writing and his ability to address himself to a populace. Although his later writings, coming from more complete experience, are sometimes more profound in subject matter, in none does Hamilton reveal greater distinction in the arts of persuasion than in the pamphlet series of 1774-75.

He did not lack opportunity to continue his experience in pamphleteering. Before entering the army, Hamilton wrote his "Remarks on the Quebec Bill," an attack on British policy in Quebec, with particular reference to its effect on the colonies.[72] While he was still serving as Washington's aide-de-camp, he wrote for Holt's *Journal* the scathing letters which he signed "Publius," attacking speculation in army supplies.[73] And as the war was nearing a close, in 1781, he set forth in ordered sequence a plea for a Federal union in a series called *The Continentalist.*

There is something noble and magnificent [he wrote] in the perspective of a great Federal Republic, closely linked in the pursuit of a common interest, tranquil and prosperous at home, respectable abroad; but there is something proportionably diminutive and contemptible in the prospect of a number of petty States, with the appearance only of union, jarring, jealous, and perverse, without any determined direction, fluctuating and unhappy at home, weak and insignificant by their dissensions in the eyes of other nations.[74]

After the war was over, in 1784, Hamilton wrote two pamphlets, over the pseudonym of Phocion, which were an earnest plea for the civil rights and for toleration for the Loyalists.[75] The basis of Hamilton's reasoning here, as always, is the

[71] Alexander Hamilton, *Works*, Henry Cabot Lodge, ed., I, 54.
[72] *Ibid.*, I, 181-96.   [74] *Ibid.*, I, 286.
[73] *Ibid.*, I, 199-209.   [75] *Ibid.*, IV, 230-90.

ordered state. He shows again a comprehension not only of affairs but of lines of argument.

But it is upon *The Federalist* that his claim to distinction as a writer is usually based.[76] As a state paper, *The Federalist* has been acclaimed by statesmen, beginning with George Washington and continuing to the present day.[77] As a contribution to the philosophy of politics, it has received the approbation of scholars at home and abroad; and Hamilton's major contribution to it has been adequately recognized. In relation to Hamilton's oratory, however, there are questions more pertinent than the quality of *The Federalist* as a state paper or as a work of scholarship. What does *The Federalist* reveal about Hamilton's abilities in persuasion? And what evidence does it offer concerning his grasp of the subject matter of his subsequent speeches? With reference to the first question, John Fiske has expressed the belief that *The Federalist* did more to insure "the adoption of the Constitution than anything else that was said or done in that eventful year." [78]

Since many forces were at work for and against the proposed constitution, it is difficult to accept Fiske's statement without evidence, and he offers none. As a matter of fact, *The Federalist* must have been of doubtful efficacy as a campaign document. As for its influence outside New York, a majority of the necessary ratifications had been secured for the proposed constitution before *The Federalist* was halfway through the press. If due allowance be made for the time necessary for electing delegates —a decisive step—and for transporting the mails carrying the

[76] *The Federalist* first appeared in newspapers in the city of New York, beginning Oct. 27, 1787. The first edition in book form was that of McLean, published in 1788. Since that time many editions have appeared, including the Sesquicentennial Edition, published with an introduction by Professor Edward Mead Earle, in 1937. National Home Library Foundation, Washington, D. C.

[77] Washington to Hamilton, Aug. 28, 1788. George Washington, *Writings*, W. C. Ford, ed., XI, 314.

[78] Fiske, *The Critical Period of American History: 1783-1789*, p. 366. Lodge shares Fiske's opinion. See Lodge, *Alexander Hamilton*, p. 67.

papers, it is clear that the effect of the essays as a whole on the majority of the necessary ratifications was at least doubtful. In New York, although their possible function in consolidating the Federalist group should not be minimized,[79] the essays were chiefly acclaimed by those who would have welcomed them in any case. There is no indication that George Clinton and his followers were convinced of the error of their ways by reading *The Federalist;* and, what is more important, it does not appear that the masses of the people, enfranchised for the purpose of voting on the proposed constitution, were persuaded in its favor by any arguments set forth by Hamilton, Madison, and Jay. The essays constituting *The Federalist* were addressed, as a campaign document, to the people of the state of New York; but neither Hamilton nor any one of his collaborators was successful in adapting them to the new audience, i.e., the whole body of the citizens. They are logically impressive, they are exhaustive in treatment; but as campaign documents addressed to a populace they are notably inferior to Hamilton's pamphlet to the farmers of New York, written before the Revolution.[80] That the essays had some influence on Hamilton's natural audience, the discerning few, is possible; that they had some immediate effect on the issue is likely; but that they were, as Fiske states, the primary agent effecting the enactment of the proposed constitution appears, on consideration, to be doubtful. One suspects a quality of *post hoc ergo propter hoc* in Fiske's unsubstantiated statement.

But though the essays do not offer proof of Hamilton's ability as a campaigner before the populace, they bear directly on the question of his mastery of the subject matter of his speeches delivered at Poughkeepsie. For the whole occasion of persuasion, possibly one of the most significant results of *The Federal-*

---

[79] Copies of *The Federalist* were subscribed for in quantity by men of substance in New York, Albany, and Montgomery County. McLean to Stephen Rensselaer, April 10, 1788. Huntington Library.

[80] *Supra,* p. 52.

ist was the preparation of the orator. Certainly the author of *The Federalist*, even if he were not able to persuade, would be able to command the respect of a selected parliamentary group. Certainly Hamilton's contribution to *The Federalist*, with his service in the constitutional convention, must have furnished his brilliant and inquiring mind with an invaluable education in the issues involved in creating a Federal union. Be that as it may, the history of oratory reveals no more striking instance of a speaker's demonstration of his authority to speak than Alexander Hamilton's contribution to *The Federalist* in advance of his speeches to the convention at Poughkeepsie. Before beginning to address the convention, the speaker had set down, with the assistance of able colleagues and for the education of the public, a complete treatise on the whole subject for discussion, an exhaustive study of the major issues, a detailed consideration of the facts at hand. He had unquestionably gone far toward meeting Quintilian's requirement that the orator shall have "every excellence of mind." [81]

THE SPEAKER'S EXPERIENCE IN SPEAKING

The first public speech of record made by Alexander Hamilton was delivered while he was still a student in King's College, at "the meeting in the fields" on July 6, 1774. The occasion was a mass meeting for the drafting of a resolution against the Boston Port Act. Tradition has it that the speaker, placed on the platform by persons who overheard his remarks on the other speeches, was momentarily struck with stage fright, but recovered to deliver a moving speech.[82] Shortly after the meeting in the fields, Hamilton addressed a meeting of the merchants of New York at the Coffee House and, according to Edward Lawrence, who was present, spoke clearly and impressively.[83]

[81] Quintilian, *Institutes of Oratory*, John Selby Watson, ed., I, 4.
[82] John Church Hamilton, *History*, I, 55. See also Nevins, *op. cit.*, p. 56.   [83] Shea, *op. cit.*, p. 361*n.*

On May 10, 1775, the young orator spoke in a situation which throws more light on his attitudes than on his manner of speaking. Dr. Myles Cooper, the Tory president of King's College, having already received a threatening letter, awoke on the night of May 10 to find a patriot mob outside his lodgings. Alexander Hamilton, the student with whom Cooper had recently exchanged opinions in Holt's *Journal*, was addressing the crowd on their folly, urging them to desist from carrying out their intentions on President Cooper. While Hamilton was speaking, the president managed to escape, scantily clad, to the banks of the Hudson. After some hours, he made his way to the home of a friend and on the following evening slipped aboard a sloop bound for England. Afterwards, President Cooper referred to the young orator in commemorative verse as

> A heaven directed youth,
> Whom oft my lessons led to truth.[84]

Hamilton seems consistently to have opposed irregular and riotous actions of every sort, nor was his defense of President Cooper his only appearance before a mob. He defended a merchant named Thurman against the so-called Travis mob.[85] And it is related that Hamilton, on another occasion, headed a body of men to suppress a mob aroused to riot because of body snatching carried on by young medical students.[86] In the quelling of the riot, John Jay, who was a member of Hamilton's party, was severely injured.[87]

[84] *A History of Columbia University: 1754-1904*, p. 48.

[85] John Church Hamilton, *History*, I, 100.

[86] The effect of speaker on audience has often been the subject of study; not often has much thought been given to the effect of audience on speaker. Hamilton's experiences before mobs afford an opportunity for conjecture concerning the effect of those experiences in the forming or fixing of his attitudes toward the human race and its government.

[87] Lossing, *Pictorial Field Book of the Revolution*, I, 384 *n*. Allan McLane Hamilton (*op. cit.*, p. 81) is in error in attributing to Lossing the statement that Hamilton was injured. Lossing refers to Jay, the

So far as there is record, however, Hamilton had comparatively little experience in addressing large audiences or popular assemblies, either before or after 1788. He was interested in the campaign of Yates for governor against Clinton in 1789; but speeches made during the campaign were evidently not recorded.[88] On July 4, 1789, he delivered a eulogy on his friend and comrade, Nathaniel Greene.[89] But there is no convincing evidence that Hamilton either endeavored to be or was successful as a ceremonial speaker or as a popular orator. His talents, so far as they were exercised, were forensic and parliamentary.

THE SPEAKER'S FORENSIC EXPERIENCE

Having been admitted to the bar in 1782, Hamilton for six years prior to the Poughkeepsie convention had been engaged in legal practice; and, following the custom of the time, he had taken all kinds of cases. While Hamilton's most celebrated case,[90] that in which he defended Croswell, Federal editor, against a prosecution for libel, occurred near the close of his life, the six years' experience as an attorney had required him to address judge and jury and had established him as one of the leaders of the New York Bar.

In the case of *Rutgers vs. Waddington*, tried in the Mayor's Court before Richard Varick in 1784, Hamilton held a brief

author of *The Federalist*, Nos. 5 and 64, rather than to Hamilton. See also Duer, *Reminiscences of an Old New Yorker*.

[88] Nevins, *op. cit.*, p. 297 *et seq.*

[89] Alexander Hamilton, *Works*, Lodge, ed., VIII, 63.

[90] Chancellor Kent, who heard many of Hamilton's pleas, thought his argument in the Croswell case "the greatest forensic effort he ever made." Kent, *An Address Delivered before the Law Association of the City of New-York*, Oct. 21, 1836, p. 27. Barnard, in his discourse on Spencer, thought the "great argument, however, for the defence was made by Hamilton—the greatest, I suppose, no doubt, of his own professional life, and probably, taken in all its aspects and character . . . the greatest ever made at the Bar in this state by any body." Barnard, *A Discourse on the Life, Character, and Public Services of Ambrose Spencer*, p. 27.

for Waddington, a wealthy brewer, against Mrs. Rutgers, a widow, who claimed arrears of rent for her property held by Waddington during the period of the British occupancy of New York City. The immediate circumstances made the case a particularly difficult one. Mrs. Rutgers had suffered obvious injury from the British occupancy. Waddington, a Tory, found no sympathy among the patriots. To give a judgment to Mrs. Rutgers, however, would break the treaty of peace with Great Britain. The treaty had settled all claims and specifically prohibited actions against the late loyalists. As a breach of the treaty of peace, a judgment in favor of Mrs. Rutgers would involve also a breach of the Articles of Confederation, which, Hamilton argued, should take precedence over the laws of any single state. Hamilton was successful in gaining a decision for his client, but the decision of the court aroused deep resentment among the people.[91]

In another case, *Livingston vs. Hoffman*, Hamilton met with an antagonist of merit, for Chancellor Livingston argued his own case. Livingston was a man of presence, and his argument was eloquent. During Livingston's plea, Hamilton was intent on preparing an answer, and as soon as Livingston had closed, Hamilton spoke for about two hours in an exhaustive, searching, and learned reply that was "fluent, argumentative, ardent, and accompanied with great emphasis of manner and expression." [92]

Unfortunately, there appear to be no transcripts of Hamilton's forensic speeches; and those interested in his forensic speaking must therefore depend upon his briefs and upon the statements of his contemporaries. The available briefs furnish ample evidence of the range and scope of Hamilton's argumentative attack on legal problems,[93] and the statements of two

---

[91] Nevins, *op. cit.*, p. 271.   [92] Kent, *Address*, pp. 23-24.
[93] The Library of Congress has a great many of Hamilton's briefs in manuscript. The Library of Hamilton College, Clinton, New York, possesses a manuscript of Hamilton's brief on the Trespass Act.

judges who heard him in court offer testimony concerning his effectiveness as a trial lawyer. Chancellor Kent [94] once undertook an estimate of all those members of the bar in New York "who took a leading share in business for some years after the close of the American War." [95] In those days, everything in law was in a sense new, and circumstances required talents of a high order.[96] Chancellor Kent found one or more of the required talents in each one of the men whom he deemed to be a leader of the bar. Brockholst Livingston was noted for his fluency, Robert Troup for his good sense, and Samuel Jones for his knowledge of the law of real property. Richard Harison was a master of equity jurisprudence, and Egbert Benson knew best the logic of special pleading. Aaron Burr was acute, quick, terse, and polished. "But among all his brethren," Chancellor Kent believed, "colonel *Hamilton* was indisputably pre-eminent." The sources of Hamilton's power, in the Chancellor's opinion, were his "profound penetration, his power of analysis, the comprehensive grasp and strength of his understanding, and the firmness, frankness, and integrity of his character." [97] At the time of Hamilton's practice, the Chancellor was impressed also with Hamilton's gentle, kind, and courteous manner, and with his clear and fluent style.[98] These qualities of

[94] James Kent (1763-1847), the author of *Kent's Commentaries on American Law*, was professor of law in Columbia College from 1793 to 1804, judge and chief justice of the supreme court of New York from 1798 to 1807, and chancellor of the state of New York from 1814 to 1823. Although his account appears to be judicious, Kent was a Federalist, and if he had any weakness as an observer, it came from his Federalist predilections, rather than from his youth; for he was hardly, as Spaulding notes (*New York in the Critical Period*, p. 296) "the boy Kent" in 1788. Actually, he was nearly twenty-five years old, the head of a household, and a practicing lawyer, the partner of Gilbert Livingston. Kent, *Memoirs*, p. 23 *et passim*.   [95] Kent, *Address*, p. 17.
[96] Barnard, *op. cit.*, p. 23.   [97] Kent, *Address*, p. 20.
[98] A survey of the New York Bar at the time when Hamilton was in practice was also undertaken by Daniel D. Barnard, *op. cit.*, p. 24. Barnard characterized Richard Harison, Brockholst Livingston, Edward Livingston, Aaron Burr, Josiah Ogden Hoffman, Abraham Van Vechten, and William

mind, manner, and style, together with Hamilton's dignity of
deportment and melodious voice, caused Hamilton, in the
Chancellor's opinion, to soar "far above all competition" at
the bar of his time.[99]

The high opinion which Chancellor Kent maintained of
Hamilton's forensic abilities was held also by another jurist,
Ambrose Spencer, who served as counsel opposing Hamilton
and as a judge in cases where Hamilton appeared as attorney.[100]
Spencer, like Kent, estimated Hamilton's forensic abilities by a
comparison, but his comparison differs in kind from that of
Kent; for Spencer, having presided, on different occasions, over
actions at law which engaged the talents of Alexander Hamilton and Daniel Webster, chose to compare the forensic abilities
of the two statesmen.

In power of reasoning [Judge Spencer said], Hamilton was the
equal of Webster; and more than this can be said of no man. In
creative power Hamilton was infinitely Webster's superior. . . . He,
more than any other man, did the thinking of the time.[101]

THE SPEAKER'S PARLIAMENTARY EXPERIENCE

Alexander Hamilton's talents in persuasion, like those of
Daniel Webster, were exercised in parliamentary assemblies, as
well as in the court room. Unlike Webster, Hamilton did not
serve in the United States Senate, though he could have done

W. Van Ness, "and, finally, the great Hamilton—great at the Bar, as he was
great every where else—who moved along with the weight of the heaviest
causes on his shoulders, with as much ease as Atlas, standing still, bears up
the world."

[99] Kent to Mrs. Hamilton, Dec. 10, 1832. Kent, *Memoirs*, p. 291.

[100] Ambrose Spencer (1765-1848), graduate of Harvard College, was
the attorney for the prosecution in the famous Croswell case. He was
elected to the New York assembly in 1793 and to the New York senate
in 1795. From 1804 to 1823 he was a judge; the latter four years of the
period he was chief justice of the supreme court of New York. See
Barnard, *op. cit., passim.*

[101] Quoted from Lodge, *Alexander Hamilton*, p. 277.

so had he wished.[102] Prior to 1788 Hamilton had served with distinction in five parliamentary posts. In 1782 Robert Morris appointed Hamilton receiver of taxes for New York. The position really involved negotiation between Hamilton, as agent of the Continental Congress, and the legislature of New York, acting for the state. The work to be done was that of conference, of continuing through negotiations with the state legislature the effort to support the national government which Hamilton was already making unofficially. In his report to Morris, Hamilton revealed the difficulties he had encountered and the extent of his success. The New York legislature, in addition to granting to Congress an appropriation of £18,000, had unanimously passed the resolution proposing a convention of the state to enlarge the powers of Congress and had, at Hamilton's instance, appointed a recess committee to devise a more effective system of taxation. The legislature had, moreover, elected Hamilton, the continental receiver of taxes, to be delegate from New York to the Continental Congress.[103]

The Continental Congress in which Hamilton now took part had before it matters of importance: the restoration of the public credit, the reduction of the public debt, the disbanding of the army, the concluding of a treaty of peace with Great Britain, and the organization of a peace-time government.[104] In all of these matters Hamilton was active in setting forth his views, always with the central purpose of furthering a strong national government. His chief endeavor was to secure to the Confederation the right to tax individuals so that the Continental Congress would not be absolutely dependent upon the mercy of the several states. But the voting in the Continental Congress was by states, and only Connecticut, New York, New Jersey, and Pennsylvania were willing to support a reso-

[102] Jay to Hamilton, April 19, 1798. Alexander Hamilton, *Works*, John Church Hamilton, ed., VI, 281.
[103] John Church Hamilton, *History*, II, 293 *et seq.*
[104] *Ibid.*, III, 323.

lution favoring greater powers for the central American government.[105]

The same essential idea of enlarging the powers of the central government dominated Hamilton's thinking in the convention at Annapolis in 1786. It was Hamilton who carefully phrased the resolutions to the legislatures of Virginia, Delaware, Pennsylvania, and New York, proposing a convention of delegates "to take into consideration the situation of the United States." [106]

In the same year, 1786, Hamilton was elected to the assembly of the state of New York from New York City and took his seat in January, 1787.[107] In the assembly, Hamilton again pursued his favorite object of a firmer union. The state of the nation furnished one of the leading arguments in his famous speech delivered to the assembly on behalf of the independence of Vermont. Prior to the Revolution, Vermont had quarreled with New York and, during the war, had set up a government of its own. The means of settling the question furnished a puzzling problem to national leaders, as well as to politicians in New York.

The present situation . . . [Hamilton observed], appears to me peculiarly critical. . . . I am, therefore, the more solicitous to guard against danger from abroad.[108]

Hamilton served also in the succeeding session of the legislature, which met in January, 1788, but in the meantime, from May to September, 1787, he was a member of the constitutional convention in Philadelphia. Hamilton's part in the deliberations of the constitutional convention has been variously estimated, the character of the estimate depending upon the point of view of the narrator. That he was not the leading figure in

[105] John Church Hamilton, *History*, II, 570.
[106] *Infra*, p. 70. John Church Hamilton, *History*, III, 166.
[107] John Church Hamilton, *History*, III, 180.
[108] "Speech on Acceding to the Independence of Vermont," Alexander Hamilton, *Works*, Lodge, ed., VIII, 42-62.

the company is generally admitted; that he was not merely a figurehead is beyond question. In his speech of June 18, 1787, Hamilton explained his previous silence as coming "partly from respect to others whose superior abilities, age, and experience, rendered him unwilling to bring forward ideas dissimilar to theirs; and partly from his delicate situation with respect to his own state, to whose sentiments, as expressed by his colleagues, he could by no means accede." [109] Whatever his reasons for keeping silent, except for the single occasion on June 18, 1787, he had little to say.

Hamilton's speech of June 18, however, set forth his views completely.[110] Two plans were before the body. One, the Virginia plan, proposed a Federal government with a balance of powers, the states maintaining a large measure of responsibility. The other, the New Jersey plan, retained the chief features of the Confederation, leaving the states essentially sovereign. Hamilton was opposed to both plans. He wished the executive to be given more power and he wished the several states to have less. Though Hamilton's speech was admired, his ideas were not acceptable to the group. As Johnson, of Connecticut, said, Hamilton was "praised by everybody" but "supported by none." [111] It is not necessary to suppose, however, that the speech was without effect. It had at least the result of making the essential features of the Virginia plan, which was finally adopted, appear less radical than they would have seemed otherwise. Hamilton's five-hour speech, a bold advocacy of a single great American state, shifted the center of controversy considerably toward national union. The Virginia

[109] "Madison's Notes," in Elliot's *The Debates in the Several State Conventions . . . Together with the Journal of the Federal Convention . . . etc.* (Philadelphia, 1891), V, 198.

[110] Hamilton's plan for a Federal government, and the outline for the speech of June 18, 1787, will be found in Alexander Hamilton, *Works*, Lodge, ed., I, 347-78.

[111] Max Farrand, *The Framing of the Constitution of the United States*, p. 89.

plan was no longer the extreme nationalist position. It became, after Hamilton's speech, a middle ground between the nationalism of Hamilton and the separatism of New Jersey.

Whatever effect the speech of June 18 may have had in changing the center of controversy, it was evidently well presented, for Gouverneur Morris, himself an eloquent speaker, thought Hamilton's address of June 18 the ablest and most impressive speech he had ever heard. And if one may judge by the brief of the speech, it provided one more evidence of that excellence of mind which is requisite in the genuine orator. Indeed every event in Hamilton's forensic and parliamentary experience up to June, 1788, appears in retrospect not only to have been an event in itself but also to have served as a preparation for the convention at Poughkeepsie. Following the convention of 1788, the Clintonians defeated him in his candidacy for reelection to the old Congress. Later, when he was Secretary of the Treasury of the United States, he was required to present his reports to the national legislators in writing. In Poughkeepsie, on July 26, 1788, at an age when most young men have hardly been heard in public, Alexander Hamilton closed his career as a parliamentary speaker.

IV. THE OCCASION

IN FINE, any discussion of human affairs is carried on by human beings in a given time and place, and each participant is governed by some conception of things, derived from some interest or some combination of interests.—CHARLES A. BEARD

A SPEECH of past times is often thought of as coextensive with its text in book or pamphlet. Even those persons who criticize the text by the canons of oral style sometimes fail to reconstruct the setting of the speech. Yet every speech is delivered among a people, at a time, in a place; and the persuasive speech can hardly be understood without reference to its occasion, to the conditions of location, and to the sequence of events concerning the participants.

THE TIME

Looking backward, one sees the future of the orator as one's own settled and historic past. The occasion of a given speech tends to become a point intermediate between one's own present and a past even more remote than that of the orator. But for the orator and his audience that particular future which has since become a past was not an intermediate point. Save for the most sophisticated persons of any age, the immediate present is the end to which every act has converged since the beginning of time. Every past event has moved to consummate the present, not some future moment; for the future is a hypothesis which remains to be proved.

In the attempt to comprehend the problems of persuasion

of an earlier time, one must forget what comes after and, with the orator and his audience, know the future as conjecture. To do otherwise is to fail to capture the point of view of rhetoric, which deals characteristically not with facts but primarily with unknowns and probable courses of action. It is necessary thus to view the occasion from which Alexander Hamilton looked at the future.

When, on June 17, 1788, a group of sixty-five men met in Poughkeepsie, New York, to consider the ratification of a recently proposed draft of a constitution to replace the existing central government of the thirteen American states, they were dealing with time in terms of an immediate past which they knew and of a future which was only an inference. Therefore it is June 17, 1788, with the day-by-day progression until July 26, 1788, and the past immediately preceding June 17, which form the time element of the occasion here considered.

The selection of any point at which to begin the consideration of the time of an occasion is a purely arbitrary act. The antecedents of the Poughkeepsie convention may conceivably be traced to the Assembly at Runnymede or to an earlier time. By exercise of choice, however, one may view the sequence of events leading up to the convention as dating from the signing of the treaty of peace on September 3, 1783.[1] The colonial system was thus formally disenacted, after having been abjured since 1776, and the loose union of sovereign states, which had sufficed for the waging of a war and the making of a peace, was put to a new test. The League of Friendship, as the Confedera-

---

[1] For the course of historical events narrated in this chapter, the writer is chiefly indebted to contemporary newspapers and to secondary sources, of which the following are most important: Channing, *History of the United States*, III; McLaughlin, *The Confederation and the Constitution, 1783-1789*; McMaster, *History of the People of the United States from the Revolution to the Civil War*, Vol. I; Nevins, *American States during and after the Revolution, 1775-1789*; Wilson, *History of the American People*, Documentary Edition, Vol. V; and Winsor, ed., *Narrative and Critical History of America*, Vols. VI and VII.

tion was familiarly known, was not well equipped to meet the new test.

Every day proves the inefficiency of the present Confederation [Hamilton wrote in the very year of the peace]; yet the common danger being removed, we are receding instead of advancing in a disposition to amend its defects. The road to popularity in each State is to inspire jealousies of the power of Congress, though nothing can be more apparent than that they have no power.[2]

The Confederation's lack of real authority, its complete dependence upon the state governments for requisitions, and its failure to secure the right to levy imposts resulted in difficulty in paying the army, in the failure to carry out the peace treaty in such a manner as to free the western posts, and in the inability to deal with interstate strife. The evidences of the weakness of the Confederation impressed many men of substance besides Alexander Hamilton with the necessity for a change in the national order. Clearly one of the factors at work was the desire of commercial men for the protection and convenience of a strong national government; and another was the hope of holders of the public debt that they might profit by a new régime.

The people generally did not demand a new national organization. The ordinary business of government, as it affected the citizen, was carried on by the officials of the several states; and when the people complained about the lack of currency or about restrictions in trade between the several states, they did not trace the origin of their troubles to the general governmental structure. The agitation for a Federal union was predominantly an upper-class movement, led by men of wealth or position, of whom the most influential was George Washington.

On resigning his command of the Army of the Revolution on December 23, 1783, Washington had retired to Mount Vernon, where he interested himself, among other matters, in plans for

---

[2] Hamilton to Jay, July 25, 1783. Alexander Hamilton, *Works*, Lodge, ed., IX, 381-82.

the navigation of the Potomac. In 1785 he became president of the Potomac Company and shortly afterwards entertained at his home commissioners from Maryland and Virginia, who met for the purpose of arranging joint action of the two states concerning the Potomac. The ratification of the Maryland-Virginia compact was followed, in the Virginia legislature, by Tyler's motion to invite each of the thirteen states to send commissioners to a commercial conference to be held at Annapolis, Maryland, in September, 1786.

New York, New Jersey, Pennsylvania, Delaware, and Virginia appointed the only representatives who attended the convention. However, before the meeting adjourned for want of a quorum, Alexander Hamilton, who came from New York, urged a resolution for a general convention which would not be limited to the consideration of matters of trade and commerce, but would meet "to devise such further provisions as shall appear to them necessary to render the Constitution of the Federal Government *adequate to the exigencies of the Union.*" [3]

THE QUESTION FOR DEBATE

The Federal convention, thus initiated outside of the framework of the constituted national government, received the reluctant sanction of the Congress. It met in May, 1787, went into session behind closed doors, and on September 17 adjourned, after having provided for the transmission of the draft of a new constitution to the Congress. The draft constitution,[4] a short and simple document, proposed a new national government of greatly enlarged powers, the powers to be divided among executive, legislative, and judicial divisions. Far from limiting their task to revising the plan of government in force,

[3] The Annapolis Resolutions, *ibid.*, I, 339.

[4] The term "draft constitution" as used in this study refers to the document approved by the convention at Philadelphia in 1787 in its status during the debates in the several state conventions prior to its establishment as the fundamental law of the land in 1789.

the convention actually proposed to abolish the Congress which
had created it, in order to establish a new authority. The proposed new Federal government was to derive its increased powers primarily from control of the sword and the purse. The
right of the sovereign states to levy and collect impost duties
was denied them; their power to declare and wage war against
other nations was destroyed; their exercise of authority over
their own citizens was diminished.

The people soon discovered that the draft did not include
any specific guarantee of the civil rights of assembly, petition,
press, speech, and religion. The Congress, not without opposition, referred the proposed new constitution to the legislature
of each of the states, with the recommendation that it be passed
on by a convention of delegates of the people.

Thereupon the debating began. In Delaware, Pennsylvania,
and New Jersey the matter was disposed of in short order, each
of these states ratifying before the beginning of the New Year.
Georgia ratified the proposal on January 2 and Connecticut on
January 9, 1788. The supporters of the new government had
thus obtained five victories without suffering any defeats and
were under the necessity of securing the adherence of four
more states before the required nine acceptances would enact
the proposed constitution. On the very day that Connecticut
ratified the draft constitution, the legislature of the state of
New York met in its regular session, and on January 31, 1788,
Egbert Benson introduced in the Assembly a resolution calling
for a ratification convention. The resolution was passed and
concurred in by the Senate, after determined resistance, and a
convention for the consideration of the draft constitution was
assured in New York.

The organization of Federal and Antifederal forces, already
under way, proceeded now in dead earnest. During the heat of
the partisan campaign for the election of delegates to the New
York convention, the Federalists won three more victories.
Massachusetts ratified on February 6, Maryland on April 28,

and South Carolina on May 23. At the time of polling in New York, therefore, eight states had already ratified the proposal for a new national government; and so the situation remained when the convention assembled on June 17, 1788.

THE PLACE: WITHIN NEW YORK

The state of New York should be located, at the time of the election of delegates to the convention for the consideration of the draft constitution, with reference to internal units and to external areas. The political subdivisions were the city and county of New York, the city and county of Albany, and the counties of Clinton, Columbia, Dutchess, Kings, Queens, Montgomery, Orange, Richmond, Suffolk, Ulster, Washington, and Westchester.

Three pertinent facts with reference to the internal units appear to be fairly well established. First, on the question of the new constitution, the state was divided into two well-defined geographic areas—Federal and Antifederal.[5] Second, since the apportionment of delegates to the convention was determined by representation in the state assembly, and since the Antifederalist area was not adequately represented in the assembly, the Federal area had a larger and the Antifederal area a smaller representation in the convention than was justified.[6] Third, the area of support for the proposed new constitution coincided generally with the area of relatively greater density in population.[7] Beard,[8] in quoting Libby, suggests the coincidence of ownership of property with density of population, noting that the city of New York, the center of the Federal

---

[5] Spaulding, *New York in the Critical Period: 1783-1789*, pp. 200 *et seq.*

[6] Spaulding, *op. cit.* Miner, *Ratification of the Federal Constitution by the State of New York.*

[7] Libby, *The Geographical Distribution of the Vote of the Thirteen States on the Federal Constitution, 1787-8*, p. 18.

[8] Beard, *An Economic Interpretation of the Constitution of the United States*, p. 269.

area, was not only the center of population but manifestly the center of ownership of wealth in personal property as well.

Although the studies of Libby and Beard are directed toward establishing the socio-economic background of the occasion, they serve also to indicate the dependence of the persuasive occasion on the method of election. Had the delegates been elected as a single body from the state at large, they would have represented either one party or the other, and the question of ratification would doubtless have been settled in convention with little or no debate. Since the delegates were elected from districts, however, opportunity was provided for the representation of both the Federal and Antifederal areas within the convention. Hence the problem in persuasion which had been presented to the Federal and Antifederal leaders in the election returned in somewhat different form in the convention, and the debates ensued in consequence.

THE PLACE: OUTSIDE NEW YORK

The location of New York within the Federal Union is definitely related to the factors of persuasion bearing on the occasion. One of the concerns of Madison, in *The Federalist,* was "to take notice of an objection, that may be drawn from the great extent of the country which the union embraces." [9] Although Madison was able to offer plausible refutation to the argument that the vast areas of existing states offered a barrier to a more complete union, he appreciated the difficulty of union with other areas in the Northwest, and suggested that "arrangements . . . must be left to those whom further discoveries and experience will render more equal to the task." Indeed, though Madison recognized "the natural limit of a republic" as "that distance from the center, which will barely allow the representatives . . . to meet as often as may be necessary for the administration of public affairs," [10] the problem of area remained,

[9] *New-York Packet,* Nov. 30, 1787.   [10] *Ibid.*

particularly with distance as measured in time rather than in space. For a government founded on the principle of free discussion, there could be no dismissing the problem of distance, when the time required for travel overland between the extremities had to be measured in months and the time for travel between the chief cities—Boston and Philadelphia—was measurable in days. To be sure, the majority of the people lived along the seaboard, and sailing vessels provided a means of travel for them. But accessibility to the sea exposed the seaboard to the navies of Europe and, what was more important, tended to encourage ties between Europe and the seaboard, rather than between the seaboard and the interior. At the same time, a water boundary on the west, the Mississippi, had, so Washington thought,[11] a tendency to draw the western settlers away from seaboard connections.

The Mississippi was more a nominal than an actual boundary. Between the seaboard and the Mississippi was the frontier, an area or condition of life that may be designated as that immediately exposed to the Indian, an enemy whose attacks were directed not toward armies or trained forces alone, but toward women as well and thus toward any expanding order. Military operations during the Revolution had largely removed the threat of the Indian from New York; but in other states the conflict between frontier families and Indian tribes went on spasmodically; it was a part of the atmosphere which pervaded the area at the time, so that problems in political persuasion were in some ways involved in it. Indeed, the members of the New York legislature which voted the ratification convention would have been aware, if they had read their newspapers, that, as they made preparation to open the session of the legislature, one of the personal disasters characterizing the time had taken place on the Georgian frontier. Under the dateline of "Savanna, January 17," the dispatch read:

[11] Washington to La Fayette, July 25, 1785. George Washington, *Writings*, Ford, ed., X, 477.

On the evening of Wednesday the 6th inst. two men, named Rogers and Queeling, and a lad named Bennett, were killed and scalped by a party of 13 or 14 Indians, in Midway settlement, about twelve miles on the other side of Great Ogechee ferry; the horses on which the two men rode were also shot dead, and two negro boys are missing, supposed to be carried off by the savages.[12]

Furthermore, Great Britain, a recent enemy, held Canada; and Spain, a potential enemy, was in possession of Florida. The complete area thus appears bounded on the north by a recently hostile Canada, on the west by hostile or dubiously friendly Indians, on the south by Spanish Florida, and on the east by the navies of France and Britain.

THE POSITION OF NEW YORK

The location of New York within this total area may best be described as strategic. Washington had early recognized the state's military importance, and the control of the Hudson, chief river of the settled territory, had been his prime tactical objective during the Revolution. Without being the leading state either in wealth or in population, New York, by its very location, was nevertheless admittedly indispensable to a completely successful union. For one thing, since the state included within its boundaries the magnificent harbor of the city of New York, which served as an entrepôt not only for the state but also for the region generally, the state could tax the commerce of its neighbors and free itself of heavy taxes on land. Furthermore, the territory of New York, alone of all the states, stretched from the Atlantic to the Lakes. A union without her would leave the South, made up of New Jersey, Delaware, Pennsylvania, Maryland, Virginia, North Carolina, South Carolina, and Georgia, wholly shut off by land from the North, composed of New Hampshire, Connecticut, Rhode Island, and Massachusetts. As Hamilton foresaw, the New England states

[12] *Country Journal and Poughkeepsie Advertiser*, Feb. 12, 1788.

would be completely shut off from the West as well as from the South.[13] New York's strategic position was recognized by the Federalists within the state in the address of R. R. Livingston, delivered before the ratification convention in Poughkeepsie; [14] it was recognized by Federalists without the state in the suggestion that coercion might be employed to bring New York into the union.[15] In the background of the occasion was at least the remote possibility of such a European alliance for New York as Gunning Bedford had suggested for the smaller states in the constitutional convention at Philadelphia.[16] The possibility of war between New York and other sovereign states is suggested by the attention which Hamilton gave the question in *The Federalist*.[17] The further possibility of internal strife within the state is attested by the references to secession of the Federalist areas from the state of New York in case the state as a whole should fail to come into the proposed Federal government.[18]

All of these possibilities—of state independence, of coercion, of war between the states, of alliance abroad, and of secession —were related directly to the factors of location, as well as to other factors of the occasion, and all of them bear upon the problem of persuasion here considered.

[13] In a conversation with Abraham Yates, Hamilton used, though with no immediate effect, the argument that New York's failure to adhere to the new system would divide the Union into northern and southern branches. Abraham Yates to Abraham G. Lansing, May 28, 1788. New York Public Library.

[14] Address of R. R. Livingston, in Elliot, ed., *The Debates in the Several State Conventions on the Adoption of the Federal Constitution*, II, 211.

[15] "A separation of the Southern District from the other parts of the State, it is perceived, would become the object of the Federalists and of the neighboring States." Hamilton to Madison, June 8, 1788. Alexander Hamilton, *Works*, Lodge, ed., IX, 433.

[16] Elliot, *op. cit.*, V, 268. See also *The Federalist*, especially paper No. 4.

[17] See *The Federalist*, particularly papers Nos. 6, 7, and 8.

[18] *Daily Advertiser*, June 14, 1788.

A thoughtful criticism of any persuasive occasion will require some reflection concerning population. It is necessary first of all to differentiate between occasion and audience.

The Aristotelian rhetoric is concerned with people as audience, and, indeed, the hearer forms the very basis of the Aristotelian classification of rhetorical forms. Hearers are of three types: the judges of future events, such as members of assemblies; hearers of past events, such as judges of courts of justice; and hearers who are unconcerned with courses of events, such as the judges of an orator's abilities. The unconcerned hearer, like the member of the assembly and of the court of justice, is fulfilling, in a sense, an audience function, a function discussed in a later chapter of this study. But since Aristotle's *Rhetoric* is a didactic and philosophic survey, rather than a treatise in criticism, the silent, nonparticipating portion of the populace receives only incidental treatment. Yet the onlookers, conceived of as persons unable or unwilling to participate actively in a given controversy, cannot be entirely uninfluential; for to live is to exert pressure, that is, to have influence of a kind. Perhaps the significant figure concerning the nonparticipants in an occasion is not so much one expressing their number as it is one expressing their ratio to the whole group making up the society. This ratio of nonparticipants to participants in controversy is, of course, not static or fixed, for it will vary with the nature of the questions considered. At the same time, populations over a period of time can be observed to show a fairly stable general level, high or low, of interest and participation in occasions of controversy. The onlookers, then, comprise that part of a population whose primary impact on the occasion arises out of their mere being, rather than out of any thinking or feeling within the occasional limits.

It may be objected that the correct point of view would contemplate the whole of a given population as audience, subject to available means of persuasion; and doubtless the orator in the act of persuasion must view the whole populace as available to his art. Nevertheless, the critic will observe that there is a varying normal expectancy of nonparticipation in occasions of controversy and will thus be prepared to view the onlookers as a part of the background of persuasion and will deal with them and with their relation to the whole situation as a part of the occasion not rising to the audience level.

To what extent the population of the state of New York was of the audience level in 1788 is a question which warrants reflection, even though quantitative data are not available. The liability of anyone engaged in rhetorical criticism to seize upon those events having a clear rhetorical significance, to the exclusion of a great host of other activities, should be observed in the beginning. But such a factor as the Federalist control of the mails, as described by Spaulding,[19] is directly related to the problem of persuasion and should not pass unnoticed.[20] Furthermore, if the occasion is to be rightly understood, it must be against a background of matters having little or no discernible relation to the immediate interests of the critic.

A great part of the people during the campaign for the election of delegates and even during the period of the Poughkeepsie convention itself were necessarily concerned about matters

---

[19] Spaulding, "The Ratification of the Federal Constitution," in Flick, ed., *History of the State of New York*, V, 55. See also Spaulding's *New York in the Critical Period, 1783-1789*, p. 259.

[20] On June 27 Richard Henry Lee, of Virginia, wrote to John Lamb, "It is but this day I received the letter that you did me the honor to write to me on the 10th of May last." Lee to Lamb, June 27, 1788. New York Historical Society. On June 23 Aedanus Burke, of South Carolina, wrote to John Lamb concerning Lamb's letter of May 19, "That it came not to hand sooner, I cannot account for; however, it came too late; for our Convention had acceded to the new Constitution on the 24th of May." Burke to Lamb, June 23, 1788. New York Historical Society. That the lack of early and effective correspondence between the Antifederalists in the several states should be considered as one of the important factors in the occasion of the Poughkeepsie convention is clear, without reference to the question whether communication was impeded by the Federalists.

other than ratification. William Arnold, Esq., for example, was
doubtless less interested in knowing that the legislature of the
state of New York was meeting than he was in reading that
". . . on Thursday night a fire broke out at the store of William Arnold, Esq; in East Greenwich which was consumed,
with a quantity of Goods and 800 Quintals of Codfish." [21] In
the milieu, the problems of rhetoric and politics which gave rise
to the occasion of the ratification convention, competed, on a
day, with the knowledge that "at the hon. Court of Common
Pleas, JOHN PEARCE was convicted for horse stealing, sentenced
to pay a fine of 10£, whipped 35 stripes, and ride the wooden
horse"; with the news of the Sheriff's sale of the real and
personal estate of Thomas Carman, of Rumbout precinct; with
the information that "The Social Society of Dutchess County
will meet at the home of Timothy Beadle, on Tuesday, the
5th day of February next . . . on special business."

The citizen, if he interested himself in what the legislature
might do about calling a ratification convention, possibly found
himself interested also in knowing that the wife and son of
Francis Van Dyke had run him considerably into debt and that
Van Dyke was determined to pay no more debts of their con-
tracting; or perhaps he was glad to learn that public securities
and soldier's pay were bought by William Bly at Pleasant Val-
ley, in Clinton Precinct.

Notwithstanding the necessary allowance for other interest
factors than that of the public business, however, there was a
substantial audience in the state of New York before and during
the Poughkeepsie convention. The election of the delegates by
manhood suffrage, as an exception to the limited suffrage prevailing at the time, was in itself a bid for popular interest. The
great numbers of pamphlets, of which the papers comprising
The Federalist were only a few, the items in the newspapers,
the accounts of electioneering, speeches, and celebrations—all

[21] *Country Journal and Poughkeepsie Advertiser*, Jan. 16, 1788. The
quotations following are from the same source.

these offer testimony to the existence of an audience and to one of considerable political sophistication. James Duane referred to this audience in his speech favoring a free convention for the consideration of the draft constitution, delivered in the New York legislature:

. . . this is not a question to be decided here; every man has a right to judge for himself; people out of doors are as well informed as we are; they are not hoodwinked; do they want us to open their eyes by the miricle of our wisdom? This subject has been canvassed with diligence, by all ranks of Americans; the papers have abounded with the most clear and important discussions; and there is no resolution, no new thing the Senate can hand them.[22]

Even with proper allowance for Duane's enthusiasm for his own position in debate, he could not greatly have exaggerated the circumstances in such a situation. Furthermore, his inferences are supported by the observation of a brilliant young man, who, though not a member of the ratification convention, was living in Poughkeepsie and attended the sessions daily. "The intense interest with which the meeting of the convention was anticipated and regarded can hardly be conceived at this day [1836]," he said, "and, much less, adequately described." [23] Apparently, there was, in addition to the persons who can be most accurately described in terms of the background of the occasion, a body of active participants in public affairs.

In summary, the occasion of Hamilton's speeches should be considered in terms of time, place, and population as the election of a group of sixty-five men by the alert members of a population containing apathetic members as well; and the functioning of that chosen group in a meeting at Poughkeepsie, New York, in June and July, 1788, for the purpose of deciding whether, after five years of living at peace under a national confederation of doubtful efficiency, the strategically located state of New York should accept or reject the new national order.

[22] *Country Journal and Poughkeepsie Advertiser*, Feb. 12, 1788.
[23] James Kent, *Memoirs and Letters*, William Kent, ed., p. 30.

V. THE AUDIENCE

FOR OF *the three elements in speech-making—speaker, subject and person addressed—it is the last one, the hearer, that determines the speech's end and object.*—ARISTOTLE

A THOUGHTFUL view of the audience immediately discloses problems related not only to rhetoric but also to the other arts and sciences, including economics, psychology, and philosophy. The economic interpretation of history is of particular relevance and should be considered forthwith. To the idea of Seligman,[1] who is apparently concerned with a kind of economic atmosphere prerequisite to life, it is hardly possible to state a reasonable objection. Neither is it necessary to question the highly particularized form in which the economic interpretation appears in Beard's study of influences affecting the adoption of the American Constitution.[2] But whenever the economic interpretation of history becomes an economic determinism, the student of rhetoric should make direct objection. Anyone who wishes to understand speakers and audiences must free himself from the simplifications of pure economic determinism, for the theorist who construes human activity to be the simple reflex of an economic stimulus minimizes or overlooks the process of major interest to those who concern themselves with persuasion. Even if it should be true that man is generally dominated by economic self-interest, the primary problem of men facing futurity is not that of end at all, but of means. The hearer's question in a given instance is not so much, "Should I act in my

[1] Seligman, *The Economic Interpretation of History,* pp. 93 *et seq.*
[2] Beard, *An Economic Interpretation of the Constitution of the United States.*

own best interest?" as it is, "What are my best interests and how can they be achieved?"

The statement of the foregoing questions involves the acceptance of an idea of choice. The historian, wise after the event, can perhaps show that an economic interest has been registered in a political society; but the plain man at a given moment, acting without benefit of a history of the future, generally solves his problems in the supposition that he is free to choose, even though he be mistaken. What concerns the student of rhetoric is the process by which men make choices, a process which cannot be adequately explained in terms of economic determinism. From the point of view of the student of rhetoric, the economic determinist makes too easily the assumption that a social order possesses an unerring instinct for knowing its own interests. But how can one be sure that the American Tories followed their own best interests in preferring British to American citizenship? How can one be sure that the South Carolina audiences in 1860 were acting in their own best interest when they went with their orators into secession? Actually, there would appear to be no complete and infallible connection between a hearer's own interest and his knowledge of it. The hearer's conception of his interest is formed or influenced, wisely or unwisely, by the rhetorician, just as the rhetorician's conceptions are formed or influenced in part by the nature of his audience. The apparent economic interest of his hearers is thus simply one of the speaker's available means of persuasion.

It is by no means implied that choices are made free from immediate economic factors. Governor Clinton, writing as "Cato," offered the citizens of New York the practical advice that the "disposal of your reputation, and of your lives and property, is more momentous than a contract for a farm, or the sale of a bale of goods." [3] And Beard's documentation serves to justify contemporary suspicion that the men who sought the ratification of the Constitution were "largely concerned in the

[3] *New York Journal and Weekly Register*, Sept. 27, 1787, *et seq.*

monied transactions of the United States." [4] Neither is it necessary to suppose that the accomplished fact of persuasion offers
final evidence that the choices made were the best ones; nor
is it necessary to enter the debatable ground of whether they
could have been other than they were. What is stated here is
simply that, for the student of public speaking, the sophisticated
structure of the determinist is less helpful than the naïve out-
look of the plain man, who believes himself to respond somewhat freely as a person rather than to react as an economic
automaton.

THE AUDIENCE DIVISION

For the New York convention of 1788, as for any other parliamentary speech occasion, there were two audiences: the people
out of doors and the members within.[5] The immediate audience
was the elected representation of an interested constituency. The
people out of doors made the initial decision when they chose
their representatives, and their influence did not cease when
their ballots were cast.

[4] "A Republican" used the contemporary economic interpretation of
the Constitution shrewdly as an argument: "You have been informed, in
a speech made in favor of the new Constitution by one of its advocates,
and who, (if credit can be given to common fame) took a principal lead
in the business, that 'it is the nature of man to pursue his own interest in
preference to the public good;' and as it is well known, that there were
gentlemen in the Convention of great weight and influence, who have, in
divers characters, been most largely concerned in the monied transactions
of the United States, and whose accounts remain unsettled—is it therefore
uncharitable to conclude that they were influenced by the above sentiment
of their friend and colleague, and consequently solicitous to establish a
principle, which would effectually preclude a settlement of their accounts?
And is this not rendered the more probable, by the consideration that
their agents and connections throughout the States are the warmest advocates for its precipitate adoption, even before the people could have time
to understand its principles, and reflect upon the resulting consequences."
Daily Advertiser, Dec. 27, 1787.
[5] The term "people out of doors" was used in 1788 to identify the
remote audience.

THE ORIGIN OF THE AUDIENCE

A great body of the people in the state of New York, like those of the other sovereign American states, appear always to have been awake to public affairs; and it is hardly possible to suggest a time when a conscious audience was created. "A Republican Soldier," expressing himself in Mr. Childs's paper, found more than one reader sympathetic with his dictum that "it is the privilege, nay, it is the duty, of every freeman to animadvert *publicly* on every *public* measure." [6] It is fair to say, nevertheless, that the issue created by the failure of New York to grant the right of impost to the Confederation was directly contributory to the creation of an audience prepared to hear the discussion of arguments for and against a firmer national union. The Impost Act, designed to effect the surrender by the several states to the Confederation of the right to collect port duties, was in considerable measure the result of the labors of citizens of New York, including Alexander Hamilton, who had worked both within and without the state to secure an opinion favorable to the grant of power required. [7] But Hamilton did not have the confidence of Governor Clinton, who entertained somewhat different notions about the surrender of state prerogatives from those held by the mercantile interests of the city of New York, the group which Hamilton largely represented. Accordingly, the state legislature, which was under the influence of Clinton, on May 4, 1786, passed the Impost Act in so ambiguous a fashion as to force its return by the Continental Congress on August 4 following. Although the Congress requested Governor Clinton to call a special session of the New York legislature to reconsider the Impost Act, he refused. When the legislature met in the regular session of January 2, 1787, he thought it necessary to explain "that a regard to our excellent constitution, and an anxiety to preserve unimpaired the right of free delibera-

[6] *Daily Advertiser*, Dec. 5, 1787.
[7] John Church Hamilton, *History*, III, 168.

tion on matters not stipulated by the confederation, restrained me from convening you at an earlier period." [8] The whole matter of the impost was referred to a committee which included Alexander Hamilton, a member of the assembly from the city of New York. The committee reported without approving Governor Clinton's refusal to call a special session of the legislature, whereupon an amendment from the floor offered the entire approbation of the house to the governor's conduct. Prolonged and heated debate ensued, in which Samuel Jones, "strenuous for the amendment," drew a comparison between the king of England and any Congress empowered to collect imposts. Alexander Hamilton immediately "entered largely upon the debate, with an intention to prevent the members being biassed by Mr. Jones's sentiments, which he conceived dangerous"; and before he concluded he offered an exhaustive statement for the impost. Mr. Jones, very lengthy in reply, finally concluded, in reference to Hamilton that *"we differ more in words than any thing else!"* [9]

If one were required to note a single origin for the greater audience which participated in the discussions of national versus state sovereignty in New York, it would be at this point. Here are the major protagonists: George Clinton, shrewd, able, stubborn, and genuinely concerned not only for his own prerogatives but also, as he thought, for the sovereignty of his state; and, on the other side, Alexander Hamilton, of the reporting committee, brilliant, personally charming, persistent, and genuinely concerned for the welfare of the mercantile class which he represented but also, as he thought, for the interests of national unity. Here the issue is clearly drawn: Shall the state surrender more power to the general government? Here the audience out of doors begins to "animadvert publicly on a public matter," with some, like Cimon, pointing to the machinations of local men to preserve themselves in power and urging people to

[8] *New York Journal and Weekly Register*, Jan. 18, 1787.
[9] *Ibid.*, Jan. 25, 1787.

listen to the "unawed eloquence of a Hamilton," [10] and with others viewing with alarm the encroachments of a tyrannical super-government. Here also begins the bitter and personal debate which characterized the continuing discussions of national policy in New York. And, significantly enough, the legislature, in spite of all Hamilton could do in opposition, adopted the amendment approving Clinton's recalcitrance by a vote of thirty-six to nine.

But the debate had just begun. The question of the impost had still to be settled. Cimon and Candidus, Republican and Rough-Hewer, began to fill the columns of the newspapers, and were shortly joined by Patrioticus and Thersites, with many others. Within the legislature, the debate proceeded, with the opponents of the impost quick to point to the dangers of the grant. Hamilton's exhaustive reply, exposing all the aspects of the question, was dealt with by the simple process of ignoring it; and the impost was definitely and finally killed.

Nevertheless, an audience had been prepared by the discussion of the issue, and debaters had come to terms.[11] Some of them had resorted to the lie direct. "Pray Candidus," asked Cimon, "did you never lie?—And have you not Candidus borne false witness against your neighbour?" [12] Others had offered the personal affront. The correspondent calling himself "An Admirer of Cimon" reported the substance of a dream in which he saw "Cimons venerable shape . . . changed . . . into a bladder of wind, which laid before the fire of criticisms, instantly burst, and left nothing but small stink and garbage behind!—" [13]

---

[10] *Daily Advertiser*, Jan. 31, 1787.

[11] Melancton Smith complained that the better sort had means of convincing those who differed with them with which he was unacquainted. "And how prevalent these kind of means may be," he wrote, "I cannot pretend to say." Smith to Abraham Yates, Jan. 28, 1788. New York Public Library.

[12] *Daily Advertiser*, Feb. 21, 1787.

[13] *Ibid.*, March 1, 1787.

Neither the audience nor the debaters died with the impost, and the continued agitation for a national union, which necessarily resulted when New York's failure to ratify the act finally signaled the defeat of the Confederation, found an audience aroused if not greatly informed by the previous discussion.

THE CONSTITUTIONAL CONVENTION

In singular contrast to the lively and acrimonious debating on the Impost Act, the question of participating in the proposed convention for revising the Articles of Confederation received comparatively little attention, at least in the public press. To be sure, there was an attempt within the legislature to limit the powers of the proposed convention; but it did not succeed. And on March 6, 1787, the assembly cast ballots for three delegates, with the result that Robert Yates received 52 votes, Alexander Hamilton 49, John Lansing 26, James Duane 23, Robert R. Livingston 4, John Taylor one, and Melancton Smith one. Yates, Hamilton, and Lansing, on the agreement of the Senate, were declared delegates, and thus the matter was closed for the time being.[14]

The state of comparative calm which characterized the acceptance of the idea of a Federal convention did not long continue. From May to September, 1787, while the convention was in session, the newspapers gave space to such matters as reflections on Governor Clinton's "currently reported and believed" reprobation of the constitution,[15] to an expression that the "conduct of several leading men, among us, has, of late, given the friends of liberty much uneasiness,"[16] and to strong pleas in weak verse for a better union, as in *The Anarchiad*:

> Shall lordly Hudson part contending powers?
> And broad Potowmack lave two hostile shores?

---

[14] *Ibid.*, March 8, 1787.   [16] *Ibid.*, July 26, 1787.
[15] *Ibid.*, July 21, 1787.

Must Allegany's sacred summits bear
The impious bulwarks of perpetual war?

.   .   .

Ere death invades and night's deep curtain falls,
Thro' ruin'd realms the voice of Union calls
Loud as the trump of heaven thro' darkness roars
When gyral gulfs entomb Caribbean towers,
When nature trembles thro' the deeps convulst,
And ocean foams, from craggy cliffs repulst,
On you she calls! Attend the warning cry,
'YE LIVE UNITED, OR DIVIDED DIE'.[17]

At the same time, the observations of "A Foreign Spectator"
on the character of the people who were deliberating their national future offered a candid criticism of some of their habits
and customs, albeit from a single and not-too-sympathetic point
of view. "A degree of indolence is perhaps a trait in the American character," observes the spectator, "owing in some degree
to the climate." To this quality of indolence, the spectator attributes the failure to pay taxes when due, the neglect of public
bridges to the point where wayfarers are in great danger, and
that lack of concern for even the most frequented roads which
makes them impassable in winter. European travelers, the spectator notes, find a certain ease and mildness in the American
character, see Americans to be less turbulent than other peoples.
Unfortunately the "infamous doctrine that *every man has his
price*" is current, but "contempt for religion is by no means general in America." The spectator's severest strictures are reserved for the politics of the day, for

the people in general know too much, and too little. The wretched
dialogues on politics, so frequent in taverns and elsewhere, please
the mirthy not less than the novels of Peregrine Pickle, while they
enrage the splenetic, and grieve the serious patriot.

---

[17] *Daily Advertiser*, May 31, 1787, *et seq.*

The spectator is himself perturbed that these "political tinkers think themselves capable of governing a universal monarchy; speak with contempt of their legislators as *the servants of the public;* and declaim with more than royal pride on *the majesty of the people.*" [18]

While the political tinkers were talking in the taverns in New York, the respectable characters were talking in a convention in Philadelphia, trying to agree on a draft of a constitution. The secrecy which veiled the convention's actions lent force to the suspicions of it, and the Clinton party was not slow to make the most of them. The responses from the friends of national unity were, in the great American tradition, *ad hominem.* Lacking any real information concerning the progress of matters in Philadelphia, the nationalists perforce resorted to personal attacks on Governor Clinton or to generalities favoring a central government.

FOLLOWING THE PHILADELPHIA CONVENTION

On September 27, 1787, just one week after the convention at Philadelphia had adjourned, the first of a series of articles by Governor Clinton appeared in the *New York Journal and Weekly Register,* over the pseudonym of Cato. The article, mild in tone, advised caution and deliberation and a wariness of those "who wish to influence your passions, and to make you dupes to their resentments and little interests." [19] On October 1 Alexander Hamilton, using the unfortunate pen name of Caesar, began a series of answers to Cato, and the issue was joined. Caesar's position was not left in doubt, for he wrote ". . . with all deference to Cato's penetration, I would recommend to him, instead of entering into fruitless discussion of what has come from so many *clear heads, and good hearts,* to join his Fellow-Citizens, and endeavour to reconcile this *excellent Constitution*

[18] *Ibid.,* Aug. 13, 1787, *et seq.*
[19] *New York Journal and Weekly Register,* Sept. 27, 1787.

to the *weak*, the *suspicious*, and the *interested*, who will be chiefly opposed to it . . . as soon as possible." [20] Finally, with a remarkable lack of consideration for any principle of persuasion, Caesar threw out the suggestion, sufficiently ambiguous to serve Cato's purposes, that Washington should rather be induced to accept the presidency of the new government than solicited again to accept the command of an army. Cato's answer to Caesar was a forthright attack on the draft constitution, with pointed reference to the dangers of a standing army, of a powerful government, and of an aristocratic court. In reply, Caesar again exhibited a singular lack of even elementary tactfulness.

For my part [he said candidly], I am not much attached to the *Majesty of the multitude*, and therefore wave all pretensions (founded on such conduct) to their countenance. I consider them in general as very ill qualified to *judge* for themselves what government will best suit their peculiar situations; nor is this to be wondered at:—The science of Government is not easily understood.[21]

Cato prefaced his second paper with a stanza of verse:

Remember, O my friends! the laws, the rights,
The generous plan of power deliver'd down,
By your renown'd Forefathers;
So dearly bought, the price of so much blood!
O let it never perish in your hands!
But piously transmit it to your children.[22]

The argument follows out the line of the verse.

For what [Cato asks] did you open the veins of your citizens and expend their treasure? For what did you throw off the yoke of Britain and call yourselves independent? Was it from a disposition fond of change, or to procure new masters?

---

[20] *Daily Advertiser*, Oct. 1, 1787. (The essays of Caesar are reprinted in P. L. Ford, *Essays on the Constitution of the United States.*)
[21] *Ibid.*, Oct. 17, 1787.
[22] *New York Journal and Weekly Register*, Oct. 11, 1787.

And in this paper, Cato states succinctly the burden of the argument against the proposed constitution. "This Convention," he exclaimed, not without some warrant, "have exceeded the authority given to them, and have transmitted to Congress a new political fabric . . . in which the different states do not retain separately their sovereignty and independency." [23] The papers of Cato reflect, as a matter of fact, the prevailing distrust of any kind of rulers, republican or otherwise, and the distaste of the people in general for that energy in government which was the ideal of Alexander Hamilton.

Cato was soon assisted in the war of words by Brutus, who brought another line of attack. Brutus observed with misgivings that the "territory of the United States is of vast extent; it now contains near three millions of souls." [24] The differences in climate, manners, and habits among the peoples inhabiting the region were commented on, as was the inability to execute laws with promptitude in so vast an area. Brutus greatly feared the encroachments of a standing army, the aggrandizement by great officers of government, and the supremacy of Federal over state judiciary.

Clearly the line of argument being followed by Clinton required the immediate attention of the proponents of national union. Hamilton, wisely abandoning both the pseudonym and the tactics of Caesar, began, with the assistance of Madison and Jay, a series of addresses to the people of the state of New York over the name of Publius and under the shrewdly chosen title *The Federalist*. Designed to present the whole case for the new system, the writings of Publius were enthusiastically received by those inclined toward Federalism; but they were read without favor by those predisposed against the new order. The "Countryman" thus complained that he really could not find what Mr. Publius "would be at"; [25] but a gentleman from

[23] *Ibid.*
[24] *New York Journal and Weekly Register*, Oct. 18, 1787.
[25] *Ibid.*, Jan. 10, 1788.

South Carolina, whose letter was printed in the *Daily Advertiser* for the edification of New Yorkers, averred that *The
Federalist* "does honor to your city, and indeed to the United
States. All our patriots and literati, in the year 1773, did not
understand the principles of Government as well as that single
writer." [26]

Cato, having driven Caesar from the field, was not disposed
to surrender easily to Publius. Continuing his explanation and
attack, he viewed with suspicion the length of the terms of
office under the proposed government, bringing Montesquieu
to witness that any term longer than one year is dangerous to
a people's liberties. The area of ten square miles to be ceded as
a Federal state was also a source of danger, Cato thought, and
the establishment of a vice-presidency was not only dangerous
but unnecessary. All in all, he was convinced, "this government is no more like a true picture of your own, than an Angel
of darkness resembles an Angel of light." [27] Neither Cato nor
Publius was without assistance. Indeed, as Hamilton wrote
Washington, "The constitution proposed has in this State warm
friends and warm enemies." [28] Americanus seconded Publius,
while Cincinnatus now joined with Brutus in helping Cato to
destroy the proposed constitution, that "iron trap that is prepared, and *bated with some illustrious names, to catch the
liberties of the people.*" [29] "A Citizen," "An Old Customer,"
and "A Constant Reader" were heard from; and letters to the
editor were printed in great number. The editors were considerate and gave first place in their columns to the issues of the
political debate.[30] One editor, having been obliged to omit a

[26] *Daily Advertiser*, July 7, 1788.
[27] *New York Journal and Weekly Register*, Nov. 8, 1787.
[28] Hamilton to Washington, Oct. 30, 1787. Alexander Hamilton,
Works, Lodge, ed., IX, 425.
[29] *New York Journal and Weekly Register*, Nov. 1, 1787.
[30] There were private complaints against the newspapers. Abraham G.
Lansing wished that someone would "disconcert these White Livers by
publishing an impartial paper." Lansing to Abraham Yates, Jan. 31, 1788.

number of pieces from the previous week's paper, excused himself because of the "expediency, in a free and independent country, of transmitting to the public cool and well written discussions on both sides of a subject that is closely connected with . . . fredom and independence." [31] Further, he thought it fortunate that "there is a dearth of news this week—for the few paragraphs prepared for this paper have also given place to more important political animadversions." [32] Extended play of fancy, carried out in great detail, evidently found favor, as in the contribution by Lunarian, who gave a full report of the reception accorded to the weekly productions of Brutus and Cato among the inhabitants of the moon.[33] Satire, in prose and bad verse, spared no contenders. The disparagement of an opponent with uncomplimentary references was the stock in trade of many disputants. The entrance of Samuel Bryan's arguments into Connecticut was thûs noted for neighboring New Yorkers in the statement, "Broke into the State of Connecticut on the Evening of the 12 ult. a large overgrown Creature, marked *and branded* CENTINEL." [34] If one were to believe uniformly the public and printed statements [35] of each side about

---

New York Public Library. The Antifederalists in Albany were willing to advance money to establish "an impartial printer" in that city. John Lansing, Jr., Jeremiah Van Rensselaer, Peter W. Yates, Henry Oothoudt, Richard Lush, Matthew Visscher, and Abraham G. Lansing to Melancton Smith. March 1, 1788. New York Public Library.

[31] *New York Journal and Weekly Register*, Oct. 18, 1787.

[32] *Ibid.*, Dec. 19, 1787.

[33] *Daily Advertiser*, Dec. 20, 1787.

[34] *Ibid.*

[35] Low opinions of members of the opposition were also expressed in private. Abraham G. Lansing desired Abraham Yates to send him certain confidential information by a "Skipper who has the Character of an *Honest Man and is Anti.* Disappointed Federalists," he observed, "will do anything." Lansing to Yates, June 1, 1788. New York Public Library. Robert Livingston complained to James Duane of those members of the opposition who went about to "poison" the tenants, admitting that they did considerable mischief "among the Ignorant." Livingston to Duane, April 30, 1788. New York Historical Society. Hugh Williamson de-

the other, there could be no doubt that the issue was joined between rival sets of rogues, miscreants, and evil-doers. "Nothing," complains a correspondent, "can equal the meanness of the Anti-Federal junto in America, but the low arts of our enemies during the war." A specific item in the indictment is that, like the late enemies, "the Anti-Federal men are circulating handbills, fraught with sophistry, declamation and falsehoods." [36]

On the one hand, if all charges were to be given credence, was a group of aristocrats, plotting the establishment of a monarchy and the destruction of the liberties of the people; on the other, if the countercharges were taken at face value, was a complete set of demagogues, interested in their own welfare and bound eventually to destroy the liberties of the people. Fortunately for the people's liberties, both charge and countercharge were largely either the exaggeration of the debater or the self-hypnosis of the politician. Fortunately for the people's sanity, the citizens were evidently not without a sense of humor. A parody of the *News-Mongers' Song* pokes sly fun at the opinionated gentlemen of the press:

> Come on brother scribblers, 'tis high time ye learn,
> The calf must be catch'd thats got out of the barn;
> A feast boys is cooking, the whiskey is good,
> We've fire and molasses, we ve honey and wood.
>
> Of Holland the Orange, of Canaan the goards,
> Of Greece the law-sophists, of Britain the lords;
> American Shayites, antifederals and laws,
> All fine twisting matters adopted to flaws.
>
> Much joy to ye, printers, ye'll now get your part,
> The *law* and *land-jobbers* are losing the start;

clared that the Antifederalists had in many cases carried their elections by imposing false representations on their constituents and propagating impudent lies. Williamson to James Iredell, July 26, 1788. New York Public Library.

[36] *Daily Advertiser*, Dec. 4, 1787.

The *New Constitution* has still to undo her,
In front the sly CATO—in rear the ROUGH HEWER.[37]

And Roderick Razor takes off the orators of the day in a fine
bit of raillery when he begs

to put *myself up* (as we do some times for Semblymen) for Norotor
General. . . . Thank Heaven I have good lungs, and I have kept
company so long, with our most learned and most virtuous, and most
wisest men; that I can say off about standing armies and juries
without trial, and the extinguishing the liberty of speaking and printing, and excise, and all them things, as well as my betters; whose
betters I expect one of these days to be.[38]

Because of vocabulary difficulties, the issues of the day were not
altogether clear to Roderick. Therefore, he says,

I asked *Squire Sour Crout* (who was one of our head men) what
this same *Stocracy* was? and he told me "it meant the same as tho'
you should say, such a one is *not of our side.* He said it was a mar-
velously useful word." [39]

Despite the sanative influence of humor, however, the fever-
ish state of mind of the participants continued throughout the
process of resolving the issue; so that near the conclusion of the
whole matter there was still reason for expressing the hope that
"each party will be ready to receive whatever may be the result,
with great calmness." [40]

THE LEGISLATURE OF 1788

The legislature met in its regular session on January 2, 1788,
with the air filled with controversy over the proposed constitution. The parole of the day, so it is said, was *New Constitution,* the countersign was *State Conventions,* and the rage of

---

[37] *Ibid.,* Dec. 11, 1787.   [38] *Ibid.*   [39] *Ibid.*
[40] *Country Journal and Poughkeepsie Advertiser,* July 22, 1788.

the season was "Hallow, damme, Jack, what are you, boy, FEDERAL or ANTI-FEDERAL?" [41] In such circumstances, the item of first importance before the session was obviously that of deciding what to do about a convention for considering the proposed national constitution, even though Governor Clinton would gladly have dispensed with the question. But the question being forced, the issue was clear: Shall the proposed constitution be referred to convention with or without recommendation? There was never any real doubt concerning the nature of the recommendation that might be made. A favorable one was out of the question. Among the papers communicated to the legislature by the governor was a report by Robert Yates and John Lansing, the majority members of the delegation sent to Philadelphia, explaining their conduct in leaving the meeting before it had adjourned. The convention, so the report read, had exceeded its powers. "A general government. . . ," the delegates informed the legislature, "must unavoidably, in a short time, be productive of the destruction of the civil liberty of such citizens who could be effectually coerced by it." [42] Since there must be a convention, the Clinton party heartily desired to prepare for the voters a statement prejudicial to the acceptance of the proposed constitution, an official record that the Philadelphia convention had exceeded its authority. The issue was closely contested, with Benson leading the Federal forces in the assembly, against the Antifederal forces, led by Schoonmaker; and with Duane captaining the Federal group in the senate against the opposition led by Abraham Yates. After exhaustive debate and delay to the point of filibuster, the Federalists finally gained their point, but by the narrowest of margins. The prejudicial amendment was defeated by a vote of 27 to 25 in the assembly and by one of 12 to 7 in the senate. The Federalist victory, though a modest one, was nevertheless significant, for it placed the proposed constitution squarely be-

[41] *New York Journal and Weekly Register*, Dec. 27, 1787.
[42] *New York Packet*, Jan. 15, 1788.

fore the adult male citizens of the state of New York, without
prejudice or equivocation, without official advice or comment.
The people, as the Federal forces desired, were left by their
choice of delegates to a state convention to decide whether they
wished New York to approve or to disapprove the new plan of
government.

THE ELECTION

Both parties continued to provide the people with the means
of arriving at their decision. Not all the Federalists had that
nicety of taste which caused one Federal correspondent to de-
plore the practice of issuing handbills. On April 30, 1788, an
election handbill, circulated in the city of New York, held up
the citizens of Philadelphia as unfortunate examples of lethargy
and urged the citizens of New York to vote in numbers. Since
the handbill included invidious comment on the amount·and
source of Governor Clinton's private fortune, it was hardly the
work of the Antifederalists.[43] On April 28 "A Flatbush
Farmer" answered the "King's County Farmer" with a handbill, stating that he "has trod again in the same dirty path in
which he first set out, as if he expected to carry his point by
mere abuse." [44] As the election days approached, the recrimina-
tions, personal references, charges of falsehood, and appeals to
fear and prejudice continued unabated, along with clear and
well-reasoned discussions. One of the factors in the decision was
the old, reliable hard-times argument, which had been resorted to early in the campaign by one disputant. The times, he
observed, are bad for shopkeepers, for whig merchants, for
butchers, for farmers, and for actors in the playhouse. But since
the peace, times were never better for brokers, usurers, alder-

[43] Handbill. "To the Citizens of New-York, New-York, April 30,
1788. One of Yourselves." Broadside Collection, New York Public Library.
[44] Handbill. "A Flatbush Farmer, Flatbush, 28th April, 1788." Broadside Collection, New York Public Library.

men, constables, and coiners of circulating coppers. The remedy? "A Constitution," says Poor S—m.[45]

It was clear, even before the election, that the city of New York would send a Federalist delegation, but the rest of the state was in doubt. All doubt concerning the popular decision vanished when the returns were completely available. The people of New York had clearly indicated, by their choice between slates of Federal and Antifederal delegates, that they wanted none of the new "tyrannical constitution." Only the city of New York, with the territory immediately contiguous, was indisputably Federalist. Of the whole body of sixty-five members, only nineteen could be counted for the proposed constitution. It was a triumph for the Antifederalists. Cato was victorious over both Caesar and Publius. The arduous labors of Clinton had succeeded where the brilliant endeavors of Hamilton had failed. The people had heard debate and discussion for nearly two years, they had read pamphlets and newspapers, they had talked in taverns and written letters to the editor; and, after full opportunity for deliberation, they had made up their minds. They were against the government of larger powers offered under the new constitution.

THE POSITION OF HAMILTON

All this was clear to Hamilton. "They have a majority of about two-thirds in the Convention," he wrote, "and, according to the best estimate I can form, of about four-sevenths in the community." But Hamilton refused to surrender to the popular verdict. Even before the full extent of the loss at the polls was known, he had considered what to do and had outlined his plans to Madison.

As Clinton is truly the leader of his party [he wrote], and is inflexibly obstinate, I count little on overcoming opposition by reason.

---

[45] *New York Packet,* Feb. 12, 1788.

Our only chances will be the previous ratification by nine States, which may shake the firmness of his followers; and a change in the sentiments of the people,[46] which have, for some time, been travelling towards the Constitution.[47]

Acting on his assumption that the event in other states would affect the judgment of Clinton's party,[48] Hamilton asked Madison to send word at once of any favorable action in Virginia; and he urged on John Sullivan, president of the state of New Hampshire, ". . . the *great advantage* of a speedy decision in your State if you can be sure of the question, and a prompt communication of the event to us." [49] There the matter remained when the convention assembled at Poughkeepsie on June 17.

THE MEMBERS WITHIN THE HOUSE

The audience addressed by Hamilton at Poughkeepsie was essentially different from his audience for *The Federalist*.[50]

[46] Hamilton's estimate of the shift in public opinion receives some corroboration from the correspondent who noted as "a circumstance highly favorable to the federal cause, that in this county there should be at least one third of the votes for members in favor of the Constitution . . . at the beginning of the year it was the better opinion that there were hardly one twentieth of the Electors inclined to the federal side." *Country Journal and Poughkeepsie Advertiser*, June 3, 1788.

[47] Hamilton to Madison, May 19, 1788. Alexander Hamilton, *Works*, Lodge, ed., IX, 430.

[48] That Hamilton's assumption was sound is indicated by the attitude Melancton Smith expressed toward the decision in Massachusetts. Smith to Abraham Yates, Jan. 23, 1788. New York Public Library. Abraham Yates observed that New York City was all in a panic with the adoption by Massachusetts. Yates to Abraham G. Lansing, Feb. 28, 1788. New York Public Library.

[49] Hamilton to Sullivan, June 6, 1788. Alexander Hamilton, *Works*, Lodge, ed., IX, 432.

[50] Concerning the membership of the Poughkeepsie convention, the present writer is indebted, as every student of the period must be since the publication of *New York in the Critical Period*, to E. Wilder Spaulding, not only for his text but also for the suggestions offered by his helpful bibliography and documentation. Spaulding, *op. cit.*, pp. 232-48.

Whereas, with *The Federalist*, his problem had been that of writing an appeal to a large group of persons of varying abilities, in large measure unused to exercising the franchise, his problem at Poughkeepsie was that of immediate and direct address to a group which included, with a few exceptions, the prominent political leaders of New York.[51] The delegates were distinctly not a cross-section of the population. In attainments, in prestige, in education, in experience, and in abilities, the sixty-five members of the convention were far above the average for the state.[52] While the more brilliant Federalist minority has received greater attention from historians and biographers, the Antifederalist majority was made up of solid men who, though less articulate than their Federalist opponents, were nevertheless shrewd in the management of their own affairs and experienced in public business. The common people were not present; and, since the great majority of them had failed to vote, they were not directly represented.[53] The whole arena of conflict was shifted, and Hamilton, having fallen short of complete success in addressing a popular audience, focused his attention on ways and means of getting the voters' representatives to do what the voters had, in essence, instructed them not to do.

The situation Hamilton faced was not a typical one. In most audience situations, even in parliamentary groups, an audience can be classified by degrees of friendliness, hostility, and neutrality. Most parliamentary audiences, moreover, are elected on general party issues or for terms of office; but the audience with which Hamilton had to deal was elected for no term, and each member was chosen not so much for party affiliation as for his announced stand on the one issue before the body. There was thus no neutral section; there were no groups with whom bargains could be made; there were presumably no leaders

---

[51] Spaulding notes among the absentees "Colonel Willet, Egbert Benson, the Schuylers, Peter Van Schaack, Abraham Ten Broeck, and General Lamb." *Op. cit.*, p. 232.

[52] Kent, *Address*, p. 28.   [53] Spaulding, *op. cit.*, p. 230.

with whom compromises could be effected, even if compromise were possible. Furthermore, there were no future issues to come before the body; hence the promise of future support could not be traded for support on present issues. Hamilton saw just two groups: eighteen men, besides himself, who were pledged to the draft constitution; and forty-five men (Governor Clinton being in the chair), who had been elected to the convention because they opposed the draft constitution.

Hamilton had two audience problems. The first was that of keeping his own force intact; the second was that of securing enough votes or absences from the Antifederalists to allow ratification. Fortunately for Hamilton, the first problem gave him little concern; the group of which he was the acknowledged leader was united by one single purpose—that of securing the unqualified ratification of the proposed constitution. Although the members of the Antifederalist group were agreed in opposing the draft constitution, the extent and nature of their objections varied; and it was the divergence of views among the members of the opposition that Hamilton endeavored to exploit.[54]

THE AUDIENCE ANALYSIS

In contemplating his audience, Hamilton saw that of the thirteen district delegations, four were Federalist and nine Antifederalist. He could count on Peter Lefferts and Peter Vandervoort, of Kings County, on Abraham Bancker and Gozen Ryerss, of Richmond County, on Thaddeus Crane, Richard Hatfield, Philip Livingston, Lewis Morris, Lott W. Sarls, and

[54] The divergence of views was not fully recognized when the convention opened but became more apparent as new issues were created during the session. On June 18 James Hughes reported that unanimity and harmony reigned among the Antifederalists. The promptitude with which they assembled, their concurrence in sentiment, and their determination to bend their force to the same point appeared to Hughes to "shut out the Shadow of Hope, in the Federalists, of creating Divisions." Hughes to John Lamb, June 18, 1788. New York Historical Society.

Philip Van Cortlandt, of Westchester County, as well as on his
own delegation from the city and county of New York, which
included, besides himself, John Jay, Richard Morris, John Sloss
Hobart, Robert R. Livingston, Isaac Roosevelt, James Duane,
Richard Harison, and Nicholas Low.[55]

The members of his own group, Hamilton knew, represented wealth and distinction. They were prevailing Epis-
copalian in religion, as they were Federalist in politics. As
landholders or speculators in land,[56] they could understand
Hamilton's doctrine of the ordered state, of a strong central
government. Hamilton also knew that some of his colleagues were men of formal education. John Jay, Philip
Van Cortlandt, and Robert R. Livingston had studied, before
Hamilton's days there, at King's College; [57] and Lewis Morris,
John Sloss Hobart, and Richard Morris were graduates of Yale
College.[58] The Federalist group included some of the leading
lawyers and jurists of the time: Chancellor Robert R. Living-
ston, Chief Justice Richard Morris, Justice John Sloss Hobart,

[55] The membership roll, including the rendering of the names, is taken
from *Journal of the Convention of the State of New-York Held at
Poughkeepsie, in Dutchess County, the 17th of June, 1788. Poughkeepsie:
Printed by Nicholas Power, a few rods East from the Court-house.* Referred to hereafter as *Journal.* Information concerning the delegations,
given in contemporary newspapers, is conveniently summarized by Spaulding, *New York in the Critical Period,* pp. 285-87. It should be noted,
however, that Spaulding has fallen into error in listing Jesse Woodhull as
voting against the Constitution. The final vote was 30-27, as Spaulding
notes correctly in his text (*op. cit.,* p. 267), and not 29-28 as his table
would read.

[56] Hamilton may not have known that besides himself, at least nine of
his party were holders of public securities. It is not likely that the knowl-
edge would have surprised or greatly concerned him. Beard lists John Jay,
Gozen Ryerss, Richard Harison, Robert R. Livingston, Philip Livingston,
James Duane, Philip Van Cortlandt, Nicholas Low, Isaac Roosevelt, and
Alexander Hamilton as holders of public securities. Beard, *An Economic
Interpretation of the Constitution of the United States,* p. 270.

[57] Spaulding, *New York in the Critical Period,* pp. 243, *et passim.*
Monaghan, *John Jay: Defender of Liberty,* p. 31.

[58] Spaulding, *op. cit.,* p. 246, *et passim.*

and the eminent attorneys, Richard Harison, James Duane, and John Jay.[59]

Among the eighteen members of the friendly section of his audience, Hamilton could observe Richard Harison, who had been a Tory in the late war. But Philip Van Cortlandt had served Washington with distinction as lieutenant colonel; and other members of his party, Hamilton knew, had rendered invaluable service to the patriot cause. James Duane, Mayor of New York, had served on the Committee of One Hundred in 1775. At the outbreak of the Revolution, Governor Tryon had removed Robert R. Livingston from office because of his patriotic activities. The loyalty of Jay, Hobart, Roosevelt, and, indeed, the Federalist group as a whole, was beyond question.[60]

The friendly section of Hamilton's audience, as he saw it, was a group of eighteen lawyers, merchants, and landholders, all men of learning, ability, or distinction, holding in general sound religious and political views, and bound to his idea of a firmer union both by their convictions and by their economic interests. And all of them, Hamilton doubtless observed, came from the city of New York or areas adjacent to it.

THE HOSTILE GROUP

When he viewed the group from which his converts must come, Hamilton saw nine solid Antifederalist delegations. The city and county of Albany, which the Federalists had hoped to carry, had sent instead a delegation of Antifederalists: Robert Yates, John Lansing, Jun., Henry Oothoudt, Peter Vroman, Israel Thompson, Anthony Ten Eyck, and Dirck Swart. Suffolk County had sent Henry Scudder, Jonathan N. Havens, John Smith, Thomas Tredwell, and David Hedges. Queens County had returned Samuel Jones, John Schenck, Nathaniel Lawrence, and Stephen Carman.

Governor Clinton himself, with his brother, James Clinton,

[59] *Ibid.*   [60] *Ibid.*, p. 244, *et passim.*

and John Cantine, Cornelius C. Schoonmaker, Ebenezer Clark, and Dirck Wynkoop, represented Ulster County. Orange County, south of Ulster, had sent John Haring, Jesse Woodhull, Henry Wisner, and John Wood; and Dutchess County, to the East, had sent Zephaniah Platt, Melancton Smith, Jacobus Swartwout, Jonathan Akins, Ezra Thompson, Gilbert Livingston, and John D'Witt.

Montgomery County, Antifederalist stronghold in the new western part of the state, had returned William Harper, Christopher P. Yates, John Frey, John Winn, Volkert Veeder, and Henry Staring. Washington and Clinton Counties, on the northern border, had returned Ichabod Parker, John Williams, Albert Baker, and David Hopkins; [61] and Columbia County had sent Peter Van Ness, John Bay, and Matthew Adgate.

As Hamilton saw his opposition, they represented the ruling political force within the state; for the Antifederalists were not only in the majority in the convention but also, under the leadership of Governor Clinton, they had controlled New York state since 1777, when George Clinton defeated Philip Schuyler for governor.[62] The patronage of the state was, Hamilton observed, in the hands of Governor Clinton.

Acquainted with the politics and politicians of his day, Hamilton doubtless knew most of the members of his opposition. Certainly he knew the leaders. The members of his opposition, Hamilton understood, were not to be despised. Although they were not men of genius, those who were not notable were at least local leaders allied with the Clinton party. Most of them had seen service in legislative halls, and some had opposed Hamilton's Federalism on other occasions. Indeed, of Hamilton's opposition at least thirty-four men, in addition to the governor, are known to have had one or more terms of legisla-

[61] David Hopkins, Peter Van Ness, John Bay, and Matthew Adgate arrived late and were ordered seated after the convention opened. *Journal*, p. 7.
[62] Spaulding, *op. cit.*, p. 99.

tive experience, either in the Provincial Congress or in the state legislature or in the constitutional convention of New York.[63] Furthermore, Melancton Smith, Zephaniah Platt, and John Lansing at one time or another had been members of the Continental Congress; and John Lansing and Robert Yates had been members of the constitutional convention at Philadelphia.[64]

While the legislative record of Hamilton's opposition was its chief distinction, certain members of the group were well known for other reasons. James Clinton, hardy patriot, had served against the British and against the Indians.[65] John Lansing was mayor of Albany. Thomas Tredwell, graduate of Princeton, was a distinguished lawyer; and John Williams, physician, was a member of the first Board of Regents of the University of the State of New York. Although the Antifederalist group included men of small or moderate means, it also included, in addition to the Clintons, who were at least well-to-do, such men of wealth and property as Samuel Jones, Melancton Smith, Gilbert Livingston, John Williams, and John Lansing.[66]

[63] In Spaulding's account, state or provincial legislative service is noted for the following men: James Clinton, John Cantine, Ebenezer Clark, Cornelius C. Schoonmaker, Dirck Wynkoop, Henry Wisner, John Haring, Gilbert Livingston, Jacobus Swartwout, Zephaniah Platt, John D'Witt, Samuel Jones, John Schenck, Stephen Carman, John Lansing, Robert Yates, William Harper, Christopher Yates, John Winn, David Hedges, Jonathan N. Havens, John Smith, Thomas Tredwell, Albert Baker, David Hopkins, Volkert Veeder, Ichabod Parker, John Williams, Matthew Adgate, Israel Thompson, Peter Vroman, Dirck Swart, Anthony Ten Eyck, Peter Van Ness. Spaulding's note reads: "The legislative records of . . . members of the convention . . . are based upon the *Journals* of the legislature." Spaulding, *op. cit.*, p. 232, *et passim.*

[64] It is difficult to reconcile the legislative records of Hamilton's opposition with Monaghan's statement that "these rustics and village lawyers sat with mouths agape as the 'Titans' of the convention unleashed their thunder." Monaghan, *op. cit.*, p. 295.

[65] Pound, "James Clinton," in *Native Stock: The Rise of the American Spirit Seen in Six Lives*, p. 155.

[66] Beard lists John D'Witt, Jonathan Havens, Samuel Jones, John Smith, Melancton Smith, and Jesse Woodhull. *An Economic Interpretation of the Constitution of the United States*, p. 270.

Among the Antifederalists, Samuel Jones and John Schenck, both of Queens County, had been Loyalists during the Revolution. But the Antifederalist group, like the Federalist, was made up largely of men who had been active for the colonies in the late war. Melancton Smith, John Williams, Anthony Ten Eyck, and Henry Scudder, with the Clintons, had seen active service.[67] Indeed, the patriotism of Federalist and Antifederalist was not called into question during the course of the debates, each group apparently accepting as axiomatic the fundamental loyalties of the other.

To Hamilton, then, his opponents doubtless appeared to be a group of citizens of established patriotism, but of deplorably narrow views, largely under the domination of George Clinton, who was himself, so Hamilton thought, lacking in insight and slow to see the obvious advantages of a strong central government. As he saw his opponents, Hamilton sensed that no persuasion could affect George Clinton. If converts were to be won, they must come from Clinton's followers by argument, by persuasion, and by the logic of events.

SPEAKERS AND NONSPEAKERS

The group with which Hamilton had to deal was unusual not only for its strict division on a single issue but also, as a parliamentary audience, for the marked differentiation between speakers and listeners. Of the sixty-five members of the convention, fifty-two, so far as the reports go, had not a word to say during the period of strenuous debate reported for the period of June 17 to July 2. The entire debate for the period was carried on by thirteen men, six Federalists and seven Antifederalists; and of the thirteen who spoke, two men, Melancton Smith and Alexander Hamilton, did more speaking than all the other eleven speakers together. Indeed a page count of the transcript indicates that Hamilton did almost one-third and Smith one-

[67] Spaulding, *op. cit.*, p. 233, *et passim*.

fourth of all the speaking reported.[68] Smith was assisted in debate by Lansing, Jones, Gilbert Livingston, Tredwell, and Williams. Jay, Duane, Harison, and Richard Morris, with Chancellor Livingston, all of the New York delegation, upheld the Federalist cause.

THE LISTENERS

Care should be exercised, however, in arriving at judgments about the relative worth to the group of speakers, and non-speakers. There are, of course, no transcripts of negotiation and no records of conversation off the floor. The silent members may have kept silent for the sufficient reason that, since the subject had been thoroughly discussed, there seemed to be nothing sensible for them to say. Perhaps more than one of the listeners shared the vexation of William Harper, who complained, after the convention had been sitting for nearly a month, that the members have spent "three days doing nothing but talk." [69] Harper wanted the question put and the matter settled.

It is worthy of note that when Thomas Tredwell, usually one of the listeners,[70] finally broke his silence on July 2, to deliver

[68] The estimates given are based on the debates for the first period of the convention as reported by Francis Childs, *Debates and Proceedings*. During the final period of the convention, July 14 to July 26, John Bay, Matthew Adgate, John Sloss Hobart, William Harper, Nathaniel Lawrence, Zephaniah Platt, Henry Wisner, and Dirck Wynkoop, in addition to the earlier speakers, took the floor one or more times. But, except for Hobart's resolution, their speeches were evidently neither extended nor very important. The participation by Hamilton and Smith for the final period seems to have followed the ratio for the first two weeks. The newspaper accounts for the unreported period, July 3 to July 13, add no new names to the group except that of Robert Yates, who replied to questions. Throughout the convention, two-thirds of the members, apparently, were listeners, one-third were speakers, and two men, in point of participation at least, were outstanding. See also Gilbert Livingston, "Reports of the Poughkeepsie Convention," New York Public Library.

[69] Speech of William Harper, July 14. Gilbert Livingston, "Reports of the Poughkeepsie Convention."

[70] Tredwell prefaced his speech with the following apology: "Sir, little accustomed to speak in public, and always inclined, in such an assembly as

the only address of length reported for him, he gave a speech which, in content at least, did him credit. Tredwell closed his speech with a simple statement of the position of the Antifederalists: "There are no advantages that can possibly arise from a union which can compensate for the loss of freedom, nor can any evils be apprehended from a disunion which are as much to be dreaded as tyranny." [71] No comments on the delivery of the speech are available, and there are no references concerning its reception by the convention. But in its careful organization, its thorough analysis of the course of debate to date, in its logical structure, rhetorical plan, and simplicity of language, the speech merited the attention of Hamilton and his party. Certainly Tredwell's address suggests the necessity of observing a proper caution in characterizing the silent contingent of the assembly. [72]

THE SPEAKERS

Nevertheless, since by custom and usage leadership in a parliamentary assembly is commonly associated with the exercising of the privileges of the floor, some special attention should be given to those of Hamilton's opponents and colleagues who were willing to speak in behalf of their opinions. A letter written by an observer during the early progress of the convention is of interest at this point, even though it offers more indiscriminate admiration than specific description:

. . . Col. H———— stands the political porcupine, armed at all points, and brandishes a shaft to every opposer: A shaft, powerful to

---

this, to be a hearer rather than a speaker, on a less important occasion than the present I should have contented myself with a silent vote." Speech of Thomas Tredwell, July 2, 1788. Elliot, *Debates on the Adoption of the Federal Constitution*, II, 396.

[71] Speech of Thomas Tredwell, July 2, 1788. Elliot, *op. cit.*, II, 406.

[72] Tredwell's speech causes one to question, so far as Hamilton is concerned, Spaulding's statement that it "is hard to imagine the pompous Chancellor Livingston or the eloquent Hamilton listening attentively to these rustics and village lawyers." Spaulding, *op. cit.*, p. 241.

repel, and keen to wound. The C————r pours a stream of eloquence deep as the Ganges, and irresistible as the Cadaraqui. Mr.
J————y's reasoning is weighty as gold, polished as silver, and strong
as steel. Mr. H————n's harangues combine the poignancy of
vinegar with the smoothness of oil: His manner wins attention—his
matter proselytes the judgment.

Mr. S————h, the Anti champion, adds the subtilty of Locke to
the candour of Sydney. If his elocution is hesitating, it is still eloquent;
and the exertions of his mind exhibit a man formed for investigation
and debate. G————r C————n has spoken but seldom; but his
silence does not proceed from a consciousness that he has not powers
to persuade or arguments to convince.

Mr. L————g is often upon the floor, and has that respect paid him
by his auditors, which none but men of abilities can obtain: He is
heard with attention. Besides these, Mr. J————s, Mr. G————
L————n and Mr. W————ms have made remarks, and Judge
M————s observations, very pertinent to the occasions on which
they were delivered. . . . Upon the whole I believe, that in no
state in America has the new constitution been fairer canvassed,
abler defended, or more powerfully opposed. What will be the result
I dare not divine.[73]

THE HONORABLE GENTLEMAN FROM NEW YORK

Of the six Federalists who shared the burden of debate with
Hamilton, Richard Morris and James Duane were least active.[74] Morris, the chief justice, Hamilton believed to be "a
well-meaning man." [75] But Morris, despite his qualifications

[73] The description is here quoted from the *Country Journal and
Poughkeepsie Advertiser*, July 1, 1788. It is quoted also in Miner, *The
Ratification of the Federal Constitution by the State of New York*,
pp. 108-109, and credited to the *New York Journal*, July 4, 1788.

[74] Hugh Ledlie, Antifederalist, believed that the Federalists had almost
all the best writers and speakers on their side. The Antifederalists, he
thought, overbalanced the Federalists in point of honesty and integrity.
Ledlie to John Lamb, Jan. 15, 1788. New York Historical Society.

[75] "Genl. Alexander Hamilton's confidential letter to Robert Morris on
the government of New York, and his estimate of the leading men of

in the law, was not a debater and he had the good judgment to leave the speaking to other members of his party.[76]

James Duane, mayor of New York, was a conservative revolutionary, a man who had sided with the rebel patriots in New York possibly as much in an attempt to control them as in any great zeal for the cause. However, he "hewed wood and drew water for American independence" and earned the respect of the American patriots.[77] Duane fully appreciated the advantages of a strong government in the protection of property and was relied on as a right-thinking person, but he was not one to enrapture an audience. One of his hearers in Poughkeepsie wrote that "Mr. Mayor of New York . . . in an harangue of two hours and an half, which consisted chiefly of declarations of his intended brevity of exordium and peroration, raised into view the devastations of the late war." [78]

Justice John Sloss Hobart was, in Hamilton's opinion, "solemn and sententious." [79] But Hamilton approved of Hobart, whom he knew to think "rightly in the main as to the imperfections of our present system." [80] Destined to achieve a solid career as a judge, Hobart never acquired a reputation as a public speaker.

Richard Harison was an accomplished scholar,[81] a sound lawyer, and "a plausible, if not a pleasing speaker; though at times, the native acidity of his temper would effervesce in pithy sallies and petulant contradiction." [82] Any inclinations to contra-

---

that state," Aug. 13, 1782. Transcript; Alexander Hamilton Papers, New York Public Library.

[76] Morris is not mentioned by Kent. See *Memoirs*, p. 304; *Address*, p. 29.

[77] Edward P. Alexander, "James Duane, Moderate Rebel," *New York History*, XVII (No. 2, April, 1936), 123-34. See also Alexander, *A Revolutionary Conservative: James Duane of New York.*

[78] *New York Journal and Weekly Register*, July 10, 1788.

[79] "Genl. Alexander Hamilton's confidential letter," Aug. 13, 1782.

[80] *Ibid.*

[81] Duer, *Reminiscences of an Old New Yorker*, p. 24.

[82] *Ibid.*

diction the scholarly lawyer may have had were restrained at
Poughkeepsie. His speeches were uniformly mild and concilia-
tory in tone. That Hamilton valued Harison is indicated by
Harison's appointment to be the first District Attorney of the
United States in New York, an appointment given on Hamil-
ton's recommendation.[83]

Robert R. Livingston, the chancellor of the state of New
York, was one of the most noted members of the convention.
As a member of the Second Continental Congress, as a member
of the committee which drafted the Declaration of Independence, and as secretary for foreign affairs,[84] he had created for
himself prestige throughout the state and the nation. This personal prestige, added to that of his family, one of the first in
the country, gave weight to his words.[85] The chancellor,
moreover, had long been an orator. Even as a youth he had
delivered "an oration in *praise of liberty*" [86] and in his maturity
he had become known for "polished address and elegant erudi-
tion." [87] But the worthy chancellor, for all his polished oratory,
was not an effective debater. His very eminence, with perhaps
his own consciousness of it, worked against him at Poughkeepsie. Even Melancton Smith, noted for his manners and moderation,[88] was so irritated by the chancellor as to give the gentleman a lesson in persuasion.[89]

When he [Livingston] attempts to explain my ideas [Smith de-
clared], he explains them away to nothing; and, instead of answer-

[83] Duer, *op. cit.*, p. 25. Dixon Ryan Fox, *The Decline of Aristocracy
in the Politics of New York*, p. 12.
[84] Spaulding, *op. cit.*, p. 244.
[85] Sedgwick, *A Memoir of the Life of William Livingston*, p. 426, *et
passim*.
[86] See Rivington's Gazette. Cited in Sedgwick, *op. cit.*, p. 426.
[87] Kent, *Address*, p. 29.
[88] Duer, *op. cit.*, p. 7.
[89] Williams compared the chancellor to a windmill. Gilbert Livingston
charged him with ridiculing the Bible. De Witt Clinton to Charles
Tillinghast, July 2, 1788. Columbia University Library.

ing, he distorts, and then sports with them. But he may rest assured that, in the present spirit of the Convention, to irritate is not the way to conciliate.[90]

But the chancellor did not learn his lesson well. A few days later Gilbert Livingston, his kinsman, accused the orator of departing "from the line of propriety" in order to display his own powers of ridicule,[91] and John Williams spoke even more to the point.[92] While the honorable gentleman, he said, "may . . . by his . . . ridiculing powers, excite laughter and occasion smiles . . . they will, instead of having the desired effect . . . be considered with contempt." [93]

What Hamilton missed in Livingston as a collaborator, he doubtless found in Jay. John Jay enjoyed no great reputation as an orator, but he spoke with dignity, candor, and strength [94] and he was, if anything, even more distinguished than the chancellor.[95] Jay's part in writing the New York constitution and in organizing the first state convention of New York was well known. He had served with distinction in the Continental Congress, and though it was not common knowledge, he had been largely responsible, as one of the peace commission, for the liberal concessions granted to the colonies by Great Britain.[96] But Hamilton knew of Jay's service in making the peace, and

[90] Speech of Melancton Smith, June 23, 1788. Elliot, op. cit., II, 280.
[91] Speech of Gilbert Livingston, July 2, 1788. Elliot, op. cit., II, 391.
[92] De Witt Clinton, who witnessed an interchange between Livingston and Smith, thought one of Smith's observations so appropriate to Livingston's character that he could not refrain from reporting it to Charles Tillinghast. Smith observed that he had no objections to giving the Congress the sword but he was for restricting their power over the purse, because some people who had no great inclination to handle the sword were notwithstanding very fond of thrusting their hands into the purse. De Witt Clinton to Charles Tillinghast, July 2, 1788. New York Historical Society.
[93] Speech of John Williams, July 2, 1788. Elliot, op. cit., II, 392.
[94] Kent, Memoirs, p. 304.
[95] Monaghan, John Jay, p. 290, et passim.
[96] Ibid., pp. 198-228.

believed the credit for the successful negotiation should have
gone to him rather than to John Adams.[97] For that matter,
Adams thought the credit properly belonged to Jay rather than
to himself.[98] In any case, the industrious, the thoughtful Jay,
whom John Adams found to be both honest and subtle,[99] was
Hamilton's colleague at Poughkeepsie. Jay's experience in nego-
tiating the British peace, his reputation for probity, and his
quiet manner, all served the Federalist cause. Jay, furthermore,
was as fully enlisted in the campaign for the new constitution
as Hamilton himself.[100] Though his contribution to *The Federalist* had not been great, he had for years been active in pro-
moting national union; and he was the author of *An Address
to the People of the State of New-York* . . . , a pamphlet,
which, as a campaign document, was more effective in design
than *The Federalist*.[101] A writer to Nicholas Power's paper
observed that if the pamphlet attributed to Mr. Jay had

made its appearance a little sooner . . . there would have been a
still more compleat Revolution in the minds of the people. That publication treated the subject as relative to us in its proper light: As the
States one after another came into the measure the great political
controversy gradually changed its ground, and what was once a question on the *merits* of the Constitution now becomes only a question
of public *expediency* and policy.[102]

Jay, as well as Hamilton, attempted to press the question of
expediency to the foreground in the convention, and Jay, the
conciliator, in the closing weeks attempted moderation and
concession.

[97] *The Diary of John Jay during the Peace Negotiations of 1782,*
Frank Monaghan, ed., p. 7.
[98] John Adams, *Works*, C. F. Adams, ed., III, 339.
[99] Adams, *Works*, III, 300. Monaghan, *John Jay*, p. 207.
[100] Monaghan, *John Jay*, pp. 278-301.
[101] *An Address to the People of the State of New-York on the Subject
of the Constitution* (New York, 1788).
[102] *Country Journal and Poughkeepsie Advertiser*, June 3, 1788.

We did not come here to carry points, or gain party triumphs [he said]. We ought not to expect it, or wish it. . . . The laurels of mere party victory, might be bedewed with the tears, or stained with the blood of our fellow citizens.[103]

The attitude of conciliation was not a new one for Jay,[104] nor was his collaboration with Hamilton a recent development. Hamilton and Jay had known each other with respect for at least thirteen years, since Hamilton, in his characteristic fashion, had written Jay a persuasive letter, observing that in troublous times, there are dangers from irregularities which "ought to be checked, by every prudent and moderate mean." [105] Hamilton and Jay shared each other's strong prejudices against any form of disorder; and both were deep in the affections of Philip Schuyler.[106] Hamilton had endeavored without success to have Jay named with himself on the New York delegation to the Philadelphia Convention of 1787.[107] Hamilton valued Jay's collaboration at Poughkeepsie, and both men, with their cause, profited from their mutual assistance.

THE LEADER OF THE OPPOSITION

When Hamilton considered the president of the convention, it was with some respect, but without enthusiasm.[108] For although, in Hamilton's judgment, Clinton deserved credit

[103] Kent, *Address*, p. 36.

[104] Hamilton also had the ability to conciliate. Abraham Yates noted the civilities accorded him by Hamilton in a formal call and in an invitation to Sunday dinner. Yates to Abraham G. Lansing, May 28, 1788. New York Public Library.

[105] Hamilton to Jay, Nov. 26, 1775. Alexander Hamilton Papers, New York Public Library.

[106] Monaghan, *John Jay*, pp. 235, 344.

[107] *Ibid.*, p. 283.

[108] Although Governor Clinton was president of the convention (*Journal*, p. 5) the burden of presiding, since most of the debate was actually carried on in the committee of the whole, fell to Henry Oothoudt, chairman. *Journal*, pp. 24, 36, *et passim*.

for firmness in keeping order in troublous times, nevertheless, Hamilton was certain, "his passions are much warmer, than his judgement is enlightened." [109] Clinton had beaten Hamilton's father-in-law for the governorship, and General Schuyler, in defeat, felt that Clinton had been raised to a position to which his family and connections did not entitle him.[110] Doubtless Hamilton, notwithstanding his own rather humble origins, shared Schuyler's sentiments that Clinton was hardly a person of quality. But Hamilton knew, and had said frankly, that Clinton was a man of integrity.

The people of the state did not altogether share Schuyler's views concerning Clinton. The citizens of Ulster had manifested their confidence in Clinton when, in 1768, they returned him to the Provincial Assembly, where he had consistently supported the patriot cause and lent his enthusiasm, in the later days, toward actual preparation for war.[111] As Clinton viewed the group over which he presided at Poughkeepsie, he saw among his followers men who had served with him in that final tempestuous Provincial Assembly.[112] He saw also men to whom he was related by ties of kinship, either directly or through his wife, Cornelia Tappen. Clinton's wife had brought him not only property, but also the asset of relationship to a substantial Dutch family, one which counted cousinship to remote degrees.[113] But more important, he saw before him men whose spirit he felt and understood; for, while Clinton lacked Hamilton's keen intelligence and insight into abstractions, he had one talent which Hamilton was never fully to acquire— that of inspiring the affections and confidence of the middle classes of men, of the "lower orders," destined soon to replace

[109] "Genl. Alexander Hamilton's confidential letter," Aug. 13, 1782.
[110] Schuyler to Jay, July 14, 1777. *The Correspondence and Public Papers of John Jay*, H. P. Johnston, ed., I, 147.
[111] Spaulding, *His Excellency George Clinton: Critic of the Constitution*, p. 43, *et passim*.
[112] *Ibid.*, p. 38.
[113] *Ibid.*, p. 31.

the "high aristocracy" which Hamilton understood.[114] Although Clinton was not a public speaker of note and allowed other men to conduct the debates for the Antifederalists in the convention, there was never any doubt in anyone's mind concerning his leadership. It was George Clinton in the president's chair—not Melancton Smith, or John Lansing, or Samuel Jones—who headed Hamilton's opposition.

But as chairman, Clinton was fair as well as capable. A constant visitor at the convention, one who had strong political prejudices against the governor,

became very favorably struck with the dignity with which he presided, and with his unassuming and modest pretensions as a speaker. It was impossible not to feel respect for such a man, and for a young person not to be somewhat over-awed in his presence, when it was apparent in all his actions and deportment that he possessed great decision of character and a stern inflexibility of purpose.[115]

THE GENTLEMEN OF THE OPPOSITION

Unfortunately for Clinton's purposes, his followers did not all have his own "decision of character." Indeed, even his leaders in debate were eventually to be found lacking in that inflexibility for which he was noted. But the speakers for the Antifederalists yielded no position without a struggle.

Of the Antifederalist speakers who participated in the debates Robert Yates was least active. The only occasion of record in which he spoke was in answer to questions put to him directly by Hamilton and Lansing, who called him as witness in an altercation concerning statements Hamilton had made in the Philadelphia Convention.[116] All three of them had been dele-

---

[114] D. R. Fox, *op. cit.*, pp. 1-30, *et passim.*

[115] Kent, *Memoirs*, p. 306. The Convention voted that "the thanks of this Convention be given to the President, and Chairman of the Committee of the whole House, for their equal and impartial conduct in their respective stations." *Journal*, p. 86.

[116] Gilbert Livingston, "Reports of the Poughkeepsie Convention." *Daily Advertiser*, July 4, 1788.

gates, and Yates, as Lansing knew, had kept notes of the proceedings. That Yates should have spoken only on request is not surprising, for although he was thought to be an able judge and a man of great legal abilities, he was more noted for his abundant health than for any distinction as an orator.[117]

John Bay, Matthew Adgate, Dirck Wynkoop, and Nathaniel Lawrence made some observations for the Antifederalists, while William Harper contented himself with raising points of order in an attempt to force a vote.[118] Henry Oothoudt did not take part in the debates; but he served faithfully as Chairman of the Committee of the Whole, an office which doubtless required his full attention.

Henry Wisner, of Orange County, who had served ten years in the Provincial Assembly, and had also been a member of the Continental Congress, made, so far as the records show, a single speech, the last one of the convention, in which he pledged himself to abide by the vote of the majority, and to endeavor to have others do so.[119] Judge Zephaniah Platt, who had likewise been a member of both the Provincial Assembly and the Continental Congress, also made a single speech, one explaining his vote, evidently in support of Melancton Smith, his colleague from Dutchess County.[120] Hamilton believed Platt to be "a man of plain sense [who] intends to do well whenever he can hit upon what is right." [121] But neither Platt nor Wisner was a speaker of note.

Thomas Tredwell, whom Hamilton thought to be "esteemed

---

[117] William Pierce, "Character Sketches of Delegates to the Federal Convention," in *The Records of the Federal Convention of 1787*, Max Farrand, ed., III, 90.

[118] Gilbert Livingston, "Reports of the Poughkeepsie Convention."

[119] Spaulding, *New York in the Critical Period*, p. 233. Gilbert Livingston, "Reports of the Poughkeepsie Convention." *Country Journal and Poughkeepsie Advertiser*, July 29, 1788.

[120] Spaulding, *New York in the Critical Period*, p. 235. Gilbert Livingston, "Reports of the Poughkeepsie Convention." *Daily Advertiser*, July 28, 1788.

[121] "Genl. Alexander Hamilton's confidential letter," Aug. 13, 1782.

a sensible and an honest man," [122] limited himself, except for his formal address during the early period of the convention, largely to objections in the procedure. Tredwell was never reconciled to the course of events in the convention, for he firmly believed that the draft constitution "departed widely from the principles and political faith of '76." [123]

John Williams, the physician who had served with distinction throughout the Revolution, had been a member of both the assembly and the senate. He was a friend of Philip Schuyler and the owner of a great deal of land in Washington County.[124] Although Williams maintained a steadfast position against the ratification, his objection to the draft constitution appears to have been expressed chiefly against the central idea of granting the power of taxation to the Federal government.[125] There is no evidence that his speeches were considered to be distinguished in any way.[126]

Gilbert Livingston, who was Governor Clinton's brother-in-law as well as a kinsman of Chancellor Livingston,[127] participated rather fully in the debates of the convention, though how wisely it is difficult to say, for it seems quite possible that Livingston's ambitions as a speaker exceeded his abilities. On one occasion at least, his somewhat florid style amused the house. In a burst of oratory in which he viewed with suspicion the influence which the senators might obtain under the proposed constitution, the speaker declared that the Senators were

[122] "Genl. Alexander Hamilton's confidential letter," Aug. 13, 1782.
[123] Speech of Thomas Tredwell, July 2, 1788. Elliot, *op. cit.*, II, 401.
[124] Spaulding, *New York in the Critical Period*, p. 239.
[125] Speech of John Williams, June 26, 1788. Elliot, *op. cit.*, II, 330.
[126] Morgan Lewis asked Charles Tillinghast who wrote the speech with which Williams opened the session of the convention on June 21. Tillinghast replied that Williams had doubtless written it himself, whereupon Lewis replied that Williams was not equal to it. Griswold, who was standing by, averred that Williams had compiled his speech from the newspapers. Tillinghast to John Lamb, June 21, 1788. New York Historical Society.
[127] Spaulding, *New York in the Critical Period*, p. 235.

provided with the means of securing to themselves a life appointment:

What will be their situation in a federal town? Hallowed ground! Nothing so unclean as state laws to enter there, surrounded, as they will be, by an impenetrable wall of adamant and gold, the wealth of the whole country flowing into it.

Just here a member who had not understood clearly called out to inquire what *wall* the speaker meant, whereupon Livingston turned and repeated "A wall of gold—of adamant, which will flow in from all parts of the continent." The reporter noted that at this "flowing metaphor," there was "a great laugh in the house." [128]

Whatever his effectiveness with audiences, Gilbert Livingston was clearly a man of substance. He had been a member of the Provincial Assembly from 1775 to 1778,[129] and, as a Livingston, he had the prestige of family to assist him. His account of the Poughkeepsie Convention reveals him to have been a man of capacity for orderly analysis, and his final speech delivered before the convention, in which he explained his vote, shows him to have been a person of courage and no little discernment.[130]

Samuel Jones, delegate from Queens county,[131] was an "old-

[128] Speech of Gilbert Livingston, June 24, 1788. Elliot, *op. cit.*, II, 287.

[129] Spaulding, *New York in the Critical Period*, p. 235.

[130] Gilbert Livingston's speech of July 26, 1788, is not mentioned in Childs's *Debates and Proceedings*. In his own "Reports," Livingston set his initials, without comment, to indicate the order in which his speech was made. An available source for the speech is what appears to be a fairly adequate reporting in the *Country Journal and Poughkeepsie Advertiser*, July 29, 1788. Nicholas Power, the editor of the paper, was official printer to the convention.

[131] Samuel Jones and Alexander Hamilton served together as counselors and solicitors representing the state of New York in a controversy with Massachusetts. See "Notice of Appointment of Alexander Hamilton and Samuel Jones to act as Counsellors and Solicitors on behalf of the State of New York." New York, June 9, 1785. Huntington Library.

fashioned, black-letter lawyer" [132] and the friend of Governor Clinton.[133] Although he spoke but little during the early part of the convention, Jones was active in offering amendments.[134] During the closing days, also, he took part in the debates.[135] But Samuel Jones was doubtless valued more for his "sound judgment" [136] than for his forensic powers, for to "the reputation of an orator . . . he never pretended." [137]

John Lansing, the mayor of Albany, was a man of considerable wealth. He had been secretary to General Schuyler, and had served in the assembly, having been speaker in 1786.[138] As one of the members of the New York delegation to the Philadelphia Convention of 1787, Lansing probably felt justified in speaking extensively, and for that reason he was doubtless given attention, though, since he suffered from "a hisitation [sic] in his speech," [139] his contributions must have been welcome more for his "plausible deductions" [140] than for his eloquence. Hamilton, who was of about the same age as Lansing, thought him "a good young fellow, and a good practitioner of the Law." [141] But Hamilton also thought Lansing's "friends mistook his talents when they made him a statesman." [142] At the same time, however, Hamilton acknowledged that Albany County was not of the same opinion in the matter as himself.[143]

---

[132] Duer, *op. cit.*, p. 23.

[133] Spaulding, *New York in the Critical Period*, p. 236.

[134] Elliot, *op. cit.*, II, 406.

[135] Gilbert Livingston, "Reports of the Poughkeepsie Convention."

[136] Kent, *Address*, p. 29.

[137] Duer, *op. cit.*, p. 24.

[138] Spaulding, *New York in the Critical Period*, p. 237.

[139] Pierce, "Character Sketches of Delegates to the Federal Convention," in *The Records of the Federal Convention of 1787*, Max Farrand, ed., III, 90.

[140] Kent, *Memoirs*, p. 304.

[141] "Genl. Alexander Hamilton's confidential letter," Aug. 13, 1782.

[142] *Ibid.*

[143] Hamilton thought well enough of Lansing to recommend his services as an attorney to Schuyler. Hamilton to Schuyler, Nov. 20, 1786. Huntington Library.

There was at least one man among the Antifederalists, however, who deserved and received the respect of Alexander Hamilton. That man was Melancton Smith, self-educated lawyer and merchant. Former soldier of the Revolution, former member of the Continental Congress, and former sheriff of Dutchess County, Melancton Smith was a man of substantial wealth [144] and considerable intellectual attainments.[145] Interested in politics and, as his speeches reveal, in religion and metaphysical speculation, he was a formidable antagonist in debate or discussion. Although Smith's usual manner of speaking was plain, dry, and syllogistic,[146] he was not without talent as a popular speaker.[147] The most prominent and responsible debater on the Antifederalist side of the House, Smith was acknowledged to be his party's foremost leader in acute and logical discussion; [148] and even by his political opponents, Melancton Smith was well liked as a man of genuine simplicity of character,[149] of genial, liberal, and amiable disposition, and of remarkable candor.[150] He gave the impression of speaking with earnestness, dignity, and great sincerity.[151] As a speaker, Melancton Smith "possessed that just and enviable influence, which arises from the experienced confidence of an intelligent people, in the integrity of their representatives." [152] First brought to the status of a celebrity [153] by his opposition to the Constitution,[154] Smith did

[144] Spaulding, *New York in the Critical Period*, p. 234.

[145] De Witt Clinton observed on June 27 that Judge Smith opened the debate today "with his usual good sense." Clinton to Charles Tillinghast, June 27, 1788. Columbia University Library.

[146] Kent, *Memoirs*, p. 306.   [149] *Ibid.*, p. 306.
[147] Duer, *op. cit.*, p. 7.   [150] *Ibid.*
[148] Kent, *Memoirs*, p. 305.   [151] *Ibid.*
[152] Duer, *op. cit.*, p. 7.

[153] Smith's preëminence among the Antifederalist speakers was anticipated by Tillinghast, who wrote, "Smith before the Convention breaks up *will shine.*" Tillinghast apparently wished to praise both Smith and Lansing in writing, "I can assure you that Mr. Smith and Mr. Lansing keep close to Hamilton." Tillinghast to John Lamb, June 21, 1788. New York Historical Society.

[154] Duer, *op. cit.*, p. 7.

not, after its adoption, pursue a public career; but he long maintained the interest in debate and the discussion of public affairs which he exhibited at Poughkeepsie. Ten years after the adjournment of the convention, he was heard by a debating society to argue with ingenuity and sincerity for the negative of the question "Whether the *carrying trade* is advantageous to the United States or not?" [155] It was this plain man of disarming but dangerous simplicity, this self-educated dialectician, this lawyer and merchant interested in discussion for its own sake, who led Hamilton's opposition from the floor.

As a matter of fact, the two men were not direct opposites in character. Concerning two important matters—the nature of human beings and the proper ordering of the state—on which both Smith and Hamilton had decided opinions—they agreed in some measure on the former and disagreed completely on the latter. For Melancton Smith was hardly more a believer in the natural goodness of the human race than Alexander Hamilton; and, believing in a natural aristocracy, he certainly accepted no equalitarian ideas of democracy.

Every society [Melancton Smith observed] naturally divides itself into classes. The Author of nature has bestowed on some greater capacities than others; birth, education, talents, and wealth, create distinctions among men as visible, and of as much influence, as titles, stars, and garters.[156]

To these ideas Hamilton certainly offered no objection. But from their common premise, the men moved to opposite conclusions, for Smith, unlike Hamilton, believed that the "superior degree of respect" which accrues to the natural aristocracy will so incline the government into their hands as to make expedient the provision of some special measures to insure active participation in government by the "middling class"; and, by corollary, his idea of the properly ordered state, quite different

[155] Duer, *op. cit.*, p. 8.
[156] Speech of Melancton Smith, June 21, 1788. Elliot, *op. cit.*, II, 246.

from Hamilton's, was one in which the government is kept so simple and diffused that the yeomanry can deal with it.[157] Smith suspected all central tendencies just as he opposed great energy in government. Indeed, even before the convention opened, Smith, writing under the pseudonym of Plebeian, had expressed himself fully and competently in an address to the people of the state of New York. As well as any other man, Smith expressed the prevailing American fear not of kings and nobles only, but of all kinds and conditions of government:

Besides, when a government is once in operation, it acquires strength by habit, and stability by exercise. If it is tolerably mild in its administration, the people sit down easy under it, be its principles and forms ever so repugnant to the maxims of liberty.—It steals, by insensible degrees, one right from the people after another, until it rivets its powers so as to put it beyond the ability of the community to restrict or limit it. The history of the world furnishes many instances of a people's increasing the powers of their rulers by persuasion, but I believe it would be difficult to produce one in which the rulers have been persuaded to relinquish their powers to the people.[158]

In all his arguments Hamilton had to meet this shrewd suspicion of government, present not only in Melancton Smith but also in Smith's colleagues both within the convention and without.[159] Obviously there were economic aspects, personal equations, and political necessities related to Hamilton's audience; but, insofar as the audience mentality reached a conscious level, its dominant and pervading quality was a great distrust of the leviathan state.

[157] *Ibid.*
[158] Melancton Smith, *An Address to the People of the State of New York*, pp. 4-5.
[159] Melancton Smith appears to have understood the possibilities of judicial powers better than Hamilton ever expressed them. Smith feared that the judicial powers were so framed as to extend to all the other powers of government in a silent and imperceptible manner, while the court vested with those powers was independent and uncontrollable. Smith to Abraham Yates, Jan. 23, 1788. New York Public Library.

Leaving lesser matters to other men, Hamilton attempted personally to deal with his fundamental audience problem; and he attacked the problem immediately by addressing himself directly to his most formidable antagonist, Melancton Smith. For days the other members of the parliamentary group, speakers and listeners, Federalists and Antifederalists alike, really constituted an audience, almost one would say a background, for the continued Hamilton-Smith debate.

THE PEOPLE OUT OF DOORS

Meanwhile, the people out of doors had not adjourned. The doors of the convention were open to the public, and throughout the session the newspapers gave their readers accounts of the action of the body in Poughkeepsie, together with letters from partisans, reflections on points at issue, and occasionally some good advice. On the day that Hamilton and his party left New York for Poughkeepsie, for example, Mr. Childs's paper gave attention to a "query . . . daily discussed by many of our citizens, viz. Whether this City had not better become a free and independent Town?" Mr. Childs was quick to advise his readers that "unless the question is properly stated, it is highly *treasonable*." [160] It is doubtful whether the readers paid much attention to the advice; and discussion concerning the secession of the southern from the northern part of the state was still further aroused by the news that Virginia had ratified the Constitution. The news, which reached New York City at 2:37 A. M. on Wednesday, July 2, was the occasion of a celebration in the city. Not long after the news reached the city, Col. William S. Livingston rode off in a great hurry for Poughkeepsie, where he arrived shortly after noon, having covered the eighty-two miles "with more expedition than has heretofore been known" in seven and a quarter hours.[161]

[160] *Daily Advertiser*, June 14, 1788.
[161] *Country Journal and Poughkeepsie Advertiser*, July 8, 1788.

But the news from Virginia, while it aroused the populace, did not bring the Poughkeepsie convention to an end. Two weeks after Livingston rode into Poughkeepsie with the news of Virginia's ratification, the *Daily Advertiser* in New York had still to report from a Poughkeepsie correspondent that it is impossible to tell what the "final decision will be: I cannot even conjecture with plausibility." [162]

The people were not so calm and collected as their representatives. During the first week in July the papers described a "disagreeable fracas" in the city of Albany. The Albany Federalists, determined to use the Fourth of July to celebrate Virginia's accession to the Union, were met with opposition by the Antifederalists; and in the ensuing battle with swords, bayonets, clubs, and stones one man was killed and eighteen men were injured.[163]

In the city of New York, on behalf of Virginia, the celebration was more elaborate and fortunately more peaceful, for the Antifederalists remained at home. As soon as the favorable news from Virginia had been received, following close upon that from New Hampshire, the Federalists in New York City began to plan a grand procession in honor of the Constitution of the United States.[164] On July 23, while the convention at Poughkeepsie was still debating, the grand procession, making "a very pompous appearance," paraded in the fields at eight o'clock in the morning, and at ten o'clock, after a salute of thirteen

[162] *Daily Advertiser*, July 24, 1788.

[163] *Ibid.*, July 10, 1788. Abraham G. Lansing maintained that the quarrel was unintentional on the part of the Antifederalists and would not have occurred had not both sides been heated with liquor. Lansing to Abraham Yates, July 9, 1788. New York Public Library. See also letter, De Witt Clinton to Charles Tillinghast, July 12, 1788. New York Historical Society.

[164] In a letter to St. George Tucker, young John Randolph described the celebration in detail. ". . . it put me in mind," he wrote, "of the great Preparations which were made, in *Don Quixote*, for the wedding of Camacho the rich and the fair Quiteria." Randolph to Tucker, July 30, 1788. New York Public Library.

guns fired from the Federal procession ship, began to move down Broadway. On the parade grounds all during the day there was great feasting and drinking,[165] two bullocks and a sheep having been roasted whole.

The persons of distinction occupied an elevated position in the center of the grounds, where they could see and be seen; but everyone, whether of high or low degree, was protected from the rain which fell intermittently throughout the day. Six or seven thousand people gathered and, at the corner of Wall Street, an object of interest for all of them was a circle of about two feet in diameter, exhibiting thirteen stars. Ten stars were bright; one, designed to represent New York, was only half illuminated; and two others, initialed for recalcitrant Rhode Island and North Carolina, were almost obscured.[166]

But the day of rejoicing was not without an untoward circumstance, perhaps one of some symbolic significance. At the launching of the Federal ship, chief object of the grand procession, "she *bilged*, and the right arm of Col. *Hamilton* (the head of the ship) holding the constitution" was broken off, whereupon a bystander "exclaimed with some humour 'gentlemen; there is certainly room for amendments.' "[167]

[165] Randolph thought it greatly to the honor of New York that among the 8,000 people who were said to have dined together on the green, there was not a single drunken man or fight to be seen. Randolph to St. George Tucker, July 30, 1788. New York Public Library.

[166] *Daily Advertiser*, July 26, 1788. *Country Journal and Poughkeepsie Advertiser*, July 29, 1788.

[167] *Daily Advertiser*, July 26, 1788.

VI. THE SPEECHES

I PRESUME *I shall not be disbelieved when I declare, that the estab-*
lishment of a republican government, on a safe and solid basis, is an
object of all others the nearest and most dear to my heart.—ALEX-
ANDER HAMILTON

IN HIS ISSUE for June 24, 1788, Nicholas Power, the editor
of the *Country Journal and Poughkeepsie Advertiser*, reported concerning the convention in progress at Poughkeepsie
that the second section of the first article of the proposed constitution had given rise to a very long and interesting debate.
"It is not to be expected," he added, "that we can give our
readers the arguments in detail that were used; we can only
say that it was attacked on the one side, with much spirit and
ingenuity, and advocated on the other, with equal ability and
address." [1]

Since Power, as the official printer to the convention, was
required to print the *Journal* for the use of its members, and
since he had unusual opportunity to hear all that went on,
his hesitancy in undertaking to report the speeches might well
have encouraged other printers to beware of the task; and,
indeed, although news items and descriptions of the speeches
are found in the current newspapers generally,[2] only one
printer, evidently, was ambitious enough to undertake a reporting of them.[3] Francis Childs, the editor of the *Daily Advertiser,*

---

[1] *Country Journal and Poughkeepsie Advertiser,* June 24, 1788.
[2] See the *Country Journal and Poughkeepsie Advertiser,* the *Daily Advertiser* (New York), the *New York Packet,* the *New York Journal,* and
the *Albany Journal* for the period June 17 to July 26, 1788.
[3] In a paper entitled "Thomas Lloyd: Reporter to the First House of

began to run full reports of the speeches in his New York paper; and his columns for June 24 and June 27, 1788, gave transcripts of the speeches to date. But Childs soon desisted in his publishing of the speeches in the *Daily Advertiser*. Perhaps he was moved by the letter of the citizen who complained of the abandonment of a series of articles by Colonel Morgan on the control of the Hessian fly.[4] Or perhaps he found no advantage in printing in his paper reports which were promptly pirated by other editors.[5] Or it may be that the convention was protracted many days beyond his early expectations.[6] At any rate, after June 27 he desisted from printing full reports of the speeches in his newspaper; but in December he printed a volume under the title *Debates and Proceedings of the Constitutional Convention* . . . , in which he provided reports of the speeches from June 17 to July 2. In the advertisement to his volume, the editor offers an apology and explanation:

Though the EDITOR has taken great pains to render the publication as perfect and satisfactory as possible, and believes, that the substance of what was said in Convention has been justly stated, yet he thinks an apology due to the Gentlemen concerned, for the imperfect dress in which their arguments are given to the Public. Not long accustomed to the business, he cannot pretend to as much accuracy as might be expected from a more experienced hand;—and it will easily be comprehended how difficult it must be to follow a copious and

Representatives," Martin J. Griffin lists Lloyd as a reporter for the New York convention at Poughkeepsie. Lloyd's other reportorial experiences are described in some detail, but the reports of the Poughkeepsie convention are merely listed. I have been able to find no evidence substantiating Griffin's note. See Records of the *American Catholic Historical Society of Philadelphia*, III, 1888-91; 221-40. See also *The American Catholic Historical Researches*, VII (No. 1, Jan., 1890), 17-32.

[4] *Daily Advertiser*, July 2, 1788.

[5] See the letter, presumably from a correspondent, objecting to another printer's reprinting the debates verbatim from Childs's paper. *Daily Advertiser*, June 27, 1788.

[6] Childs, Francis, ed., *The Debates and Proceedings of the Constitutional Convention of the State of New-York* . . . (New York, 1788), p. i.

rapid Speaker, in the train of his reasoning, much more in the turn of his expression.[7]

There are two circumstances, however, which suggest that the advertisement may have been a bit more modest than the facts required. The first is that Childs had reported a famous speech by Alexander Hamilton made during a legislative session some months previously; [8] the second is that Childs, evidently careful in his work, transcribed in the evening the notes he had taken during the day.[9] Furthermore, Childs's reports have an internal consistency and they agree in point of fact, where parallel reports are given, with current newspaper accounts. For Hamilton's speeches made during the period covered by Childs's notes, June 17 to July 2, 1788, there are thus records which, if they are not excellent, are at least adequate and even incomparably better than the records of the speeches of certain other men, notably Charles James Fox.[10] Nevertheless, since the transcript shows evidence of condensation, it is wise not to rely on it too heavily for any considerations concerning fine points of Hamilton's style, but to restrict conclusions largely to the lines of argument, since they are not so directly affected by the transcription.[11]

The transcript has the further disability that, while the convention extended from June 17 to July 26, Childs provides a text only for the initial periods of the convention, from June 17 to July 2, restricting the account for the period from July 3 to

[7] *Ibid.*, p. ii.
[8] Kent, *Memoirs*, p. 297.
[9] *Ibid.*, p. 300.
[10] Reid, *Charles James Fox: A Study of the Effectiveness of an Eighteenth Century Parliamentary Speaker*, p. 34, *et passim*.
[11] "From a letter in the Lamb papers (New York Historical Society) it appears probable that at least Hamilton, Jay, and Lansing revised their speeches, though Francis Childs, the reporter, virtually, in his preface, says that no such revision took place." P. L. Ford, *Bibliography and Reference List. . . . Relating to the Adoption of the Constitution of the United States*, p. 36.

July 26 to a bare record of proposals for amendment.[12] However, the deficiency at this point has been partially remedied by Dr. V. H. Paltsits's discovery, in 1932, of a portion of the "Reports of the Poughkeepsie Convention" written by Gilbert Livingston, who was a member from Dutchess County.[13] Livingston's "Reports," which are notes rather than transcription, provide a brief description of the lines of argument and trends of discussion in the convention for the closing weeks, July 14 to July 26. For the period from July 3 to July 13 inclusive there appears to be neither adequate description nor transcript, except for notices in contemporary newspapers and references in correspondence; but these serve to establish that the period was one of comparative inactivity so far as debates are concerned.[14] The convention had reached something like a stalemate.[15]

[12] The source most commonly cited for the debates in the convention in New York is Jonathan Elliot's *The Debates in the Several State Conventions*, in various editions. (See P. L. Ford, *Bibliography and Reference List of the History and Literature Relating to the Adoption of the Constitution of the United States*, p. 14. In his title-page, Elliot notes that his publication is "collected and revised from contemporary publications," but the sources are not specified. Spaulding notes Childs's *Debates and Proceedings* as the source for Elliot's matter (*New York in the Critical Period*, p. 292). The texts of Childs and Elliot are not identical. There are minor textual discrepancies. Compare, e.g., Elliot, II, 207, with Childs, p. 5; and Elliot, II, 246, with Childs, p. 32. Furthermore, Elliot, II, 413-14, appends the circular letter from the convention of the state of New York to the governors of the several states; Childs does not. And while Elliot reports the extended speech of Thomas Tredwell of July 2, 1788, Childs does not. The two accounts are, however, substantially parallel; and for convenience in reference, citations herein are to Elliot, second or later editions, the more easily available source for most readers.

[13] Spaulding, *op. cit.*, p. 303.

[14] The McKesson papers (New York Historical Society) are useful without providing an adequate text. Hamilton's own "Sketch of Journal Convention of N. Y." (Library of Congress) is interesting as regards Hamilton, for it appears to be a record which he kept for making refutation; but it is not useful as a text.

[15] Elliot, *op. cit.*, II, 410.

The divisions into which the available texts and reports of the convention appear to fall seem, by coincidence, to parallel closely the divisions or periods into which the convention can be analyzed. In a parliamentary sense, the first period of the convention may be thought of as that extending from the call to order on June 17 to the notice of New Hampshire's ratification, which was taken in convention by Chancellor Livingston on June 25.[16] The second period extended from June 25 to July 2, when the news of Virginia's ratification was received.[17] These two periods are the ones covered by Francis Childs's transcript. The third period of the convention began on July 2 and closed on July 16, when Hobart's motion to adjourn brought matters to a crisis.[18] The fourth and final period, that covered by the extant portion of Gilbert Livingston's "Reports," began on July 16 and closed on July 26, with the adjournment *sine die*.[19] The first two periods, it will be observed, are reported; the last period is described, but not reported; and the third period is neither reported nor systematically described. But the convention, during its whole sitting, was the subject of news items in the papers, including descriptions of some of the speeches, and the official *Journal* provides an adequate record of all official actions.[20]

HAMILTON'S ACTIVITY

Hamilton was the active leader of his party during the four periods of the convention and he made many speeches, short and long. Furthermore, Hamilton, with his colleagues, was

[16] *Ibid.*, p. 322.
[17] *Country Journal and Poughkeepsie Advertiser*, July 8, 1788.
[18] Elliot, *op. cit.*, II, 411.
[19] *Ibid.*, p. 413.
[20] Dunlap's *History of the New Netherlands, Province of New York, and State of New York* includes a discursive chapter on the Poughkeepsie convention, with excerpts from the speeches; but the chapter adds nothing to Elliot's *Debates*.

busy off the floor in discussion, conciliation, and argument.[21] Three speeches, or series of speeches, which he made during the course of the convention were thought at the time to be outstanding,[22] and a careful study of the text furnishes no reason for disagreeing with the contemporary opinion.[23] The first speech, that on the principles of union, was delivered on June 20 and 21; the second, on the powers of the senate, on June 24 and 25; the third, on taxation and the rights of the states, on June 27 and 28.[24]

Following the principle that it is fair criticism to give chief attention to a man's outstanding performances, and the observation that Hamilton's characteristic speaking habits and attitudes are manifest in his major speeches, the analysis in this chapter

[21] Spaulding, *op. cit.*, p. 253.

[22] Kent, *Memoirs*, p. 305.

[23] Unfortunately, while Gilbert Livingston's "Reports of the Poughkeepsie Convention" and available newspaper reports describe a fourth speech of considerable interest, the descriptions available are hardly sufficient to justify extensive criticism.

[24] There seems to be no question concerning the date or the reception accorded the three outstanding speeches. Concerning a fourth, however, there is some question as to when it was delivered. Spaulding supposes the "speech which was enthusiastically praised by young James Kent and which caused the reporter, Childs, to regret his temporary absence from the hall" to have been delivered on July twenty-fourth. (*New York in the Critical Period*, p. 267.) Yet the speech which Kent describes (*Memoirs*, p. 309) must be that described also by Gilbert Livingston as of July 17, unless, as would appear most unlikely, Hamilton repeated himself on July 24. Furthermore, Kent himself dates the speech as "in the midst of that gloomy period" of three weeks during which the convention continued their sharp debate subsequent to the ratification by New Hampshire. (*Memoirs*, p. 309.) The newspaper accounts, moreover, set the date of a powerful and significant speech by Hamilton on July 17. The reference in Dunlap (*op. cit.*, II, 281) to which Spaulding refers is, as Spaulding observes, received at thirdhand; and, since it records the impressions of a boy many years after the event, might well be better evidence for impressive circumstances than for specific facts concerning dates. That Hamilton delivered a powerfully effective speech on July 17 is clear; that he delivered a similar speech on July 24 is at least not beyond question.

will be devoted primarily to Hamilton's three outstanding speeches. At the same time, each of the speeches will be presented in its parliamentary context and each of the periods will be considered, so that the analytical discussion will proceed progressively.

THE FIRST PERIOD

The first action taken by the delegates when they assembled in convention on June 17 was to elect Governor George Clinton president of the body, Federalists and Antifederalists joining to make the election unanimous.[25] Immediately after the election of the president, the minor officers were appointed. It was decided that the doors of the convention should be kept open and that the convention should begin each morning with prayer. A committee on rules, composed of three Federalists and two Antifederalists,[26] was appointed to report on the following day, and the meeting adjourned.

On Wednesday, June 18, the convention met and adopted twelve rules of order,[27] heard the reading of the draft constitution proposed by the general convention at Philadelphia, together with accompanying resolutions and letters, and agreed, on the motion of John Lansing, to meet as a committee of the whole house on the following day.

On Thursday, June 19, the convention met, resolved itself into a committee of the whole, and called Henry Oothoudt to the chair. The proposed constitution was read again, and only then did the formal debate and discussion begin.[28]

The first speech of the convention was a carefully prepared oration by Robert R. Livingston, who addressed a hypothetical and nonexistent audience of "gentlemen present, who have yet

[25] *Journal*, p. 5.
[26] Duane, Jones, Richard Morris, Lansing, and Haring were appointed.
[27] It was agreed that the rules should be observed in the committee of the whole as well as in convention. Elliot, *op. cit.*, II, 208.
[28] *Ibid.*, p. 208.

formed no decided opinion." [29] To this audience the chancellor declared that ever since "a pure and perfect religion has lent her mild lights to philosophy, and extended her influence over the sentiments of men, it has been a received opinion that the happiness of nations, as well as of individuals, depends on peace, and that intimate connection which mutual wants occasion." [30] In continuing, the speaker reviewed the unsuccessful efforts in the Old World to set up the basis for a union of nations and urged the advantage, in the New World, of using existent opportunities to fix lasting peace on the basis of a firm national union. At the same time, he pointed out the dangers inherent in a weak confederation of sovereign states and defended a Federal government of enlarged powers as a solution for the problems of New York. The chancellor closed his formal address with an appeal to the state officeholders in the audience to "forget the pride of office" and allow the general good to determine their conduct.[31] However well-meant the appeal may have been, it was not well-considered; for it was taken unkindly by those to whom it was addressed.[32] After concluding his speech, the chancellor offered a resolution, which was carried, deferring the vote upon any question relating to the proposed constitution until the whole had been considered,[33] whereupon the convention adjourned for the day.

On Friday, June 20, the convention met and went at once into committee of the whole. John Lansing rose immediately and delivered an extended reply to Livingston's speech of the previous day. Lansing undertook a defense of the Confederation, and, while he deplored the possible dissolution of the union, he argued that conquest "can do no more, in the state of civilization, than to subject us to be ruled by persons in whose appointment we have no agency." Since government under the proposed constitution, he maintained, would certainly

[29] Elliot, *op. cit.*, II, 209.
[30] *Ibid.*
[31] *Ibid.*, p. 216.
[32] *Ibid.*, p. 221.
[33] Childs, *op. cit.*, p. 11.

have such a result, he preferred the possible evil of statehood to the certain one of union.[34] Chancellor Livingston replied to Lansing at some length, whereupon Melancton Smith objected to the general observations being made and desired that the proposed constitution should be read by paragraphs.[35] The convention being agreeable to the consideration *seriatim*, the first section of the first article was read without any comment; but on the reading of the second section of article one, Smith made an extended speech, partly in refutation of Livingston and partly in attack on the plan of representation provided in the article.[36]

At the conclusion of Smith's speech, Hamilton took the floor to reply in the first of his three notable speeches delivered during the convention.[37]

The Principles of Union.—Technically, Hamilton's speech on the *Principles of Union* was delivered in committee, a committee of the whole house, and to the question of the second section of the first article of the proposed constitution. Actually, it was delivered on the larger proposition that was before the convention during the first period of its sitting. That larger proposition is so simple as almost to state itself in the form of the resolution "That New York should assist the several states in forming a new national government." In the parliamentary situation, the burden of the argument necessarily fell on Hamilton and his colleagues, for the existing Confederation provided union of a sort, however inadequate it might be thought by some of the Federalists; and it was Hamilton, not Smith, who proposed a change.

The line of discourse.—In the beginning of his *Principles of Union* speech, Hamilton acknowledged his affirmative position by aligning himself with Livingston and opposing Smith and Lansing.[38] Agreeing with Livingston on the weaknesses of

[34] Elliot, *op. cit.*, II, 219.
[35] *Ibid.*, p. 222.
[36] *Ibid.*, pp. 222-30.
[37] *Ibid.*, pp. 230-39; 251-59.
[38] *Ibid.*, p. 230.

New York, he nevertheless deprecated the idea, doubtless with reference to the opposition, that it was necessary to sacrifice liberty in order to secure union. He attacked the old Confederation directly, insisting that it could never be an effective means to union, since it applied to the states in their corporate capacity rather than to individual citizens. The fundamental principle of the old Confederation, with its dependence on requisitions subject to the scrutiny of thirteen different legislatures must, he insisted, be entirely discarded. He referred to historic instances of the failure of federated states and warned against placing too much dependence on the favorable outcome of the war with Britain. He continued by analyzing the Union into its different interest-classes: navigating and non-navigating states; large and small states; and slave and free states. Compromise, he declared, was necessary to union; and any convention would have clashing interests to reconcile. The Committee at Philadelphia had tried to deal with disputed matters in that spirit of accommodation without which no union could have been formed.

He considered the matter of representation, and the expediency of allowing representation to be based partly on slave populations, and he continued the discussion of representation by taking up the question of a proper number of representatives for the whole country. He concluded by pointing to the strength of the state governments and their ability to look after their own interests.

The organization.—In organization, the speech is remarkable for its union of constructive argument with refutation and for its direct reference, on the one hand, to Livingston's earlier speech and, on the other, to specific arguments advanced by Melancton Smith.

The speech was broken by adjournment. After speaking at length on June 20, Hamilton closed by saying,

Many other observations might be made on this subject, but I cannot now pursue them; for I feel myself not a little exhausted. I beg leave, therefore, to waive, for the present, the further discussion of the question.[39]

He concluded the speech on June 21, after Williams and Smith had spoken in answer to that part of the speech delivered on June 20.

In its structure, the speech reveals the author's acquaintance with the Aristotelian concept of organization. In Aristotle's view, there are only two strict requirements of the orator: that he state his case and that he prove it.[40] It is only as a concession to the deficiencies of the audience that the speaker must have also an introduction and a conclusion.[41] Nevertheless, audiences being what they are, the introduction and the conclusion must be given full consideration. In the introduction, the speaker will attempt to secure the attention of the hearers and to give them a good impression of himself.[42]

Since Hamilton's speech on the *Principles of Union* was broken by adjournment, he made two introductions and two conclusions; but each was brief, the speaker's time being spent almost exclusively with the body of his argument. In the first introduction, he referred to Chancellor Livingston's speech and to the arguments advanced against it.

Gentlemen [he said] have this day come forward to answer him. He has been treated as having wandered in the flowery fields of fancy; and attempts have been made to take off from the minds of the committee that sober impression which might be expected from his arguments.[43]

And continuing, he said, "Let us consider the Constitution calmly and dispassionately, and attend to those things only

[39] *Ibid.*, p. 239.
[40] Cope has explained clearly both Aristotle's point of view and the legitimate criticism of it. Cope, *Introduction to Aristotle's Rhetoric*, pp. 139-47.
[41] Aristotle, *Rhetoric*, 1414a.
[42] *Ibid.*, 1415b.
[43] Elliot, *op. cit.*, II, 230.

which merit consideration." [44] Such an introduction was calculated to produce the sober state of mind which Hamilton
wished; at the same time, Hamilton knew as well as any man
the value of the appeal to reason as ethical proof in such an
assembly as he addressed. The brief introduction to the second
portion of the speech is limited to an outline of the arguments
presented on the previous day; the conclusion on the first day
was a bare statement of the wish to continue at another time;
and the conclusion on the second day was a summary and
rebuttal.

In the body of the argument, Hamilton is always careful to
make transitions unmistakably clear. If the progress of the
speech is not evident from the language, he introduces an express phrase such as: "Without dwelling any longer on this
subject, I shall proceed to the question immediately before the
committee." [45] Or again: "Another circumstance ought to be
considered." [46] Or "But, dismissing these reflections, let us consider how far the arrangement is in itself entitled to the approbation of this body. We will examine it upon its own merits." [47]
Or, "I now proceed to consider the objection with regard to
the number of representatives, as it now stands." [48]

Hamilton's care exercised in transition is an evidence of his
following strictly the Aristotelian injunction to *state* the case.
In the *Principles of Union* speech, there are no doubts about
the reference of the argument; and even in spite of the inter-
ruption of adjournment the speech is an organic whole, unified
within itself.

The purpose.—Hamilton's basic purpose in the speech is quite
clear, even though it is implicit rather than explicit. He is endeavoring to get to some fundamental premise upon which all
can unite. He is attempting to lay the foundation for a discussion of the question. In no other speech does he more fully
justify Pierce's contemporary description of his method: "Colo.

[44] Elliot, *op. cit.*, II, 230.   [46] *Ibid.*, p. 237.   [47] *Ibid.*
[45] *Ibid.*, p. 235.   [48] *Ibid.*, p. 238.

Hamilton . . . enquires into every part of his subject with the searchings of phylosophy, and when he comes forward he comes highly charged with interesting matter, there is no skimming over the surface of a subject with him, he must sink to the bottom to see what foundation it rests on." [49]

The preparation.—In his search for the foundations of his subject, Hamilton had no opportunity for immediate preparation. Livingston, on June 19, had delivered a prepared oration; and Lansing and Smith had been able, overnight, to consider their reply; but insofar as his refutation was concerned, Hamilton had no time for special study. He was limited to his immediate knowledge of the subject. Fortunately for his presentation, Hamilton, having for years studied the question of national union and having recently written the major portion of *The Federalist*, had considered in advance every argument likely to be brought against the proposed constitution. His problem was therefore not one of finding arguments. It was simply one of adjustment and organization.[50]

Special characteristics.—It has been noted that the state of the text precludes the making of extensive observations concerning the finer points of Hamilton's style.[51] Nevertheless, some characteristics are so clearly marked as to warrant notice. The first is Hamilton's tendency to amplify. An idea is so stated and restated with amplification and extension that there

[49] Pierce, "Character Sketches of Delegates to the Federal Convention," in Farrand, ed., *Records of the Federal Convention*, III, 89.

[50] Hamilton kept careful notes of important speeches delivered during the convention. His most careful attention was given to the speeches of his opposition, particularly to those of Melancton Smith, and his summary of Smith's speech on taxation, delivered on June 27, 1788, for example, constitutes a précis of the argument, Smith's points being listed in numbered order. Hamilton's habit of careful attention to the speeches of his opposition will serve to explain his readiness in refutation. See Alexander Hamilton, "Sketch of Journal Convention of N. Y." Alexander Hamilton Papers, Library of Congress, Vol. VII, 1787-89.

[51] *Supra*, p. 129. In this connection, it should be noted that James Kent, who heard the *Principles of Union* speech, alludes to illustrations not found in the text. Kent, *Memoirs*, p. 307.

is every opportunity for the listener to understand. The purposeful repetition with variation which characterizes Hamilton's discourse should not be confused with mere verbiage. His attack on a problem of persuasion, rather than being merely lengthy, is thorough and diversified.[52]

A second marked characteristic is the use of the rhetorical question. "Would it have been wise and prudent in that body," he inquires, "in this critical situation, to have deserted their country?"[53] And again he asks rhetorically, "Would it be just to impose a singular burden, without conferring some adequate advantage?"[54] The notable use of the rhetorical question is significant in characterizing Hamilton's oral style as one of direct appeal to the audience.

There are other evidences, also, of Hamilton's consistent use of direct address. He calls on his hearers as witnesses. Concerning the noncompliance with requisitions, for example, he inquires, "Have not all of us been witnesses to the unhappy embarrassments which resulted from these proceedings?"[55] Again and again, he identifies himself with the group. His use of the personal pronoun obviously goes beyond the mere adherence to the formality of the speaker. Like Melancton Smith, but in contrast with Livingston and with Harison, for example, Hamilton is inclined to use the plural rather than the singular first personal pronoun. "Amidst all our distresses, *we* have fully complied," he says referring to New York's record in supporting the Confederation.[56] Again, in stating a premise which could easily have been worded impersonally as the principle that national objects require national revenues, Hamilton worded the premise in terms of participation: "if we have national objects to pursue, we must have national revenues."[57] And the directness of the premise is reënforced immediately by a direct

---

[52] See, for example: Elliot, *op. cit.*, II, 238; *ibid.*, p. 254.
[53] *Ibid.*, p. 236.
[54] *Ibid.*, p. 237.
[55] *Ibid.*, p. 231.
[56] *Ibid.*, p. 232.
[57] *Ibid.*

question to the hearers, "If you make requisitions, and they are not complied with, what is to be done?" [58]

Hamilton does not weaken his emotional proof by use of a descriptive third person. He makes his point in terms of his hearers. In stating the perilous condition of New York, it is *your* capital, not *the* capital, and *you*, not *they:*

This is a weak state, and its relative state is dangerous. Your capital is accessible by land, and by sea is exposed to every daring invader; and on the north-west you are open to the inroads of a powerful foreign nation. Indeed, this state, from its situation, will, in time of war, probably be the theatre of its operations. [59]

Hamilton's *Principles of Union* speech, marked by direct address, is notable also for the almost complete lack of rhetorical adornment. The speech is matter-of-fact, not metaphorical; it attempts, for the most part, to be fact-giving rather than argumentative; and, indeed, the style suggests that the mind and manner of the speaker at the moment of delivery were often expository rather than persuasive. Although the primary object of the speech is that of persuasion, the style and method of the speaker are expository. He is endeavoring to make things clear.

There are thus no purple passages in Hamilton's discussion of the principles of union; and the lack of purple passages is hardly to be fully accounted for as a condition of the text, for the ebullience of other speakers was reported both in the New York and in other conventions of the time. [60] But Hamilton's style was Attic rather than Asiatic. There is nothing in his speech, for example, to compare with the apostrophe of Nason, who addressed the Massachusetts convention:

And here, sir, I beg the indulgence of this honorable body to permit me to make a short apostrophe to Liberty. O Liberty! thou greatest good! thou fairest property! with thee I wish to live—with thee I wish to die! Pardon me if I drop a tear on the peril to which she is

---

[58] *Ibid.*   [59] *Ibid.*   [60] *Ibid.*, pp. 225, 287.

exposed: I cannot, sir, see this brightest of jewels tarnished—a jewel worth ten thousand worlds; and shall we part with it so soon? O no.[61]

The modes of proof.—Aristotle, in his *Rhetoric*, sets up a tripartite division of proof. The division is based upon the ways in which an audience can be persuaded. The first mode of proof depends on the personal appeal of the speaker to the audience; the second, on putting the audience into a disposition or state of mind favorable to the speech; and the third, on the speech itself.[62] The three divisions, referred to here as ethical, emotional, and logical proof, cannot properly be considered as separate entities. In the Aristotelian system they are rather the divisions of a single art.[63] They represent merely a convenient means of considering a complete process in which each is part.

Hamilton's ethical proof in the Principles of Union speech.— In any given act of persuasion, the reputation of the speaker is of great importance. Whether the speaker will be able to convince his hearers in any specific instance will perhaps depend primarily on his acceptance by the group. The unconscious attitude of most audiences is expressed overtly in the saying that one should beware even of the truth from the mouth of an evil man. That Alexander Hamilton was admired by the friendly section of his audience and at least respected by those who differed with him has already been shown.[64]

What attempt did Hamilton make, in his *Principles of Union* speech, to present himself favorably to his hearers? It is not difficult to find examples. Early in his speech, he said, "I trust, sir, that observations of this kind are not thrown out to cast a light air on this important subject, or to give any personal bias on the great question before us." [65] And later, in the second

[61] Elliot, *op. cit.*, II, 133.
[62] Aristotle, *op. cit.*, 1356a.
[63] Baldwin, *Ancient Rhetoric and Poetic*, p. 11.
[64] *Supra*, p. 61.
[65] Elliot, *op. cit.*, II, 230.

portion of his speech, he declared, "Sir, we hear constantly a great deal which is rather calculated to awake our passions, and create prejudices, than to conduct us to the truth, and teach us our real interests." [66] And again, in his conclusion, he asserted in refutation, "Sir, I am confident that such remarks as these are rather occasioned by the heat of argument than by a cool conviction of their truth and justice." [67]

In the first place, it will be observed that Hamilton's ways were carefully considered. His ethical proof is genuinely associated with the substance of his argument. His methods of establishing himself with his audience do not differ from those which he habitually employed in his speech-making. He appeals to the audience to exercise judgment and reason, in the problems to be considered,[68] and thus establishes himself as one who attempts persuasion on a high level; he asks that consideration be given to all arguments and professes and fulfills an intention to deal with them all; [69] and, unlike Chancellor Livingston, he refrains from the ridicule of any argument, however puerile, or any speaker, however ill-prepared. For such an audience as Hamilton had at Poughkeepsie, there was obviously high ethical value in the attempt to place the discussion on a judgment basis, particularly since the speaker consistently demonstrated his ability to keep his speeches on the plane of reasoned discourse.

Hamilton's emotional proof in the Principles of Union speech.—Hamilton consistently fortifies his enthymemes with emotional proof. In the *Principles of Union* speech, as a matter of fact, he appeals to one of the basic emotions, that of fear; but the emotional is so closely integrated with the logical proof, and the specified instances of appeal to fear are so firmly rooted in the logic of the case as to make it easy to overlook the employment of the emotional mode of proof at all. Hamilton's use of emotional proof in the speech is an appeal to "reasonable

[66] *Ibid.*, p. 256.
[67] *Ibid.*, p. 258.
[68] *Ibid.*, p. 230.
[69] *Ibid.*

fear," if such a category can be said to exist. He sets up no artificial bogey men, and he does not attempt the improbable; but in presenting what should be proved, he resorts to the method of antecedent probability, reasoning from present to future. Early in his speech he declares:

Although I am persuaded this Convention will be resolved to adopt nothing that is bad, yet I think every prudent man will consider the merits of the plan in connection with the circumstances of our country, and that a rejection of the Constitution may involve most fatal consequences. I make these remarks to show that, though we ought not to be actuated by unreasonable fear, yet we ought to be prudent.[70]

Hamilton's attempt to secure a solid foundation for his emotional proof can be noted in still another instance:

I will not agree with gentlemen who trifle with the weaknesses of our country, and suppose that they are enumerated to answer a party purpose, and to terrify with ideal dangers. No. I believe these weaknesses to be real, and pregnant with destruction.[71]

Perhaps the most impressive use which Hamilton made of emotional proof in the *Principles of Union* speech involved the use of past and present circumstances known to his hearers in reasoning to a future probability:

Of this truth we have the most solemn proof on our records. In 1779 and '80, when the state, from the ravages of war, and from her great exertions to resist them, became weak, distressed, and forlorn, every man avowed the principle which we now contend for —that our misfortunes, in a great degree, proceeded from the want of vigor in the Continental government. These were our sentiments when we did not speculate, but feel. We saw our weakness, and found ourselves its victims. Let us reflect that this may again, in all probability, be our situation.[72]

Hamilton's logical proof in the Principles of Union speech.— But, however useful Hamilton may have found his appeal

---

[70] Elliot, *op. cit.*, II, 230.   [71] *Ibid.*   [72] *Ibid.*, p. 232.

to "reasonable fear," his speech is predominantly of logical rather than of ethical or of emotional structure. He relies primarily, as he professes to do, on the kind of persuasion which is brought about through proving "a truth or an apparent truth by means of the persuasive arguments suitable to the case in question." [73] In the development of his speech, Hamilton uses logical proof both in constructive argument and in refutation. Since his refutation becomes an integral part of the developed speech, there is no sharp distinction between refutation and constructive argument.[74] Both are developed largely through the logical mode of proof; both exhibit Hamilton's acquaintance with the various methods of proving a proposition; and both illustrate his chief dependence on the establishing of causal relation as a means of getting at the truth. It is common for him to appeal to the knowledge or experience of his audience, and frequently he states a premise which is thought to be acceptable and reasons from it. He uses the dilemma, the analogy, and the refutatory methods of exposing inconsistency and reducing to absurdity, and, in one instance, the argument *a fortiori*.

Hamilton's analogies were developed by comparing the American states with those of the Amphictyonic League,[75] the Dutch Republic,[76] the German Confederacy,[77] and the Lycian and Achaean Leagues.[78] Although the analogies are vulnerable on logical grounds by reason of the dissimilarity of the objects

---

[73] Aristotle, *op. cit.*, 1356a.

[74] Hamilton's characteristic method of dealing with the problem of logical proof in speech composition was apparently the construction of an extensive topical outline of all available arguments, each numbered and supported by statements which were likewise numbered. Occasionally, his topical outline included a question to which numbered statements are given in answer. The topical outline evidently served Hamilton both as a logical brief and as a rhetorical plan for presentation. The briefs of his cases at law offer consistent evidence of his method; and the available notes of his speeches delivered at Poughkeepsie confirm it. See Alexander Hamilton, "Notes of Speech in Convention of N. York," Alexander Hamilton Papers, Library of Congress, Vol. VII, 1787-89.

[75] Elliot, *op. cit.*, II, 234.
[76] *Ibid.*
[77] *Ibid.*, p. 235.
[78] *Ibid.*

compared, they apparently escaped attack from the opposition. The development of the analogies obviously follows the line of *The Federalist*.

Hamilton's stating of a dilemma likewise escaped adequate rejoinder. The dilemma concerned the most fundamental question of the Union:

But can we believe that one state will ever suffer itself to be used as an instrument of coercion? The thing is a dream, it is impossible. Then we are brought to this dilemma—either a federal standing army is to enforce the requisitions, or the federal treasury is left without supplies, and the government without support. What, sir, is the cure for this great evil? Nothing, but to enable the national laws to operate on individuals, in the same manner as those of the states do. This is the true reasoning upon the subject, sir. The gentlemen appear to acknowledge its force; and yet, while they yield to the principle, they seem to fear its application to the government.[79]

The occasion for the argument *a fortiori* was that which dealt with compliance with requisitions. Hamilton's argument was offered in refutation of the statement that "non-compliance of the states had been occasioned by their sufferings."[80] Yet, Hamilton argued, "Amidst all our distresses, *we* have fully complied," and continued with the implication that states not having suffered from the war should have been even better able than New York to comply in part, at least, with the requisitions of the Congress.[81]

Early in the speech Hamilton resorted to the time-tried device of exposing an inconsistency between the diverging attacks of two advocates of a single cause.

This day, sir [he noted], one gentleman has attempted to answer the arguments advanced by my honorable friend; another has treated him as having wandered from the subject. This being the case, I trust I shall be indulged in reviewing the remarks that have been made.[82]

---

[79] Elliot, *op. cit.*, II, 233.
[80] *Ibid.*, p. 232.
[81] *Ibid.*
[82] *Ibid.*, p. 231.

And, immediately thereafter, he used again the device of exposing inconsistency, but to another purpose:

Sir, it appears to me extraordinary, that, while gentlemen in one breath acknowledge that the old Confederation requires many material amendments, they should in the next deny that its defects have been the cause of our political weakness, and the consequent calamities of our country. I cannot but infer from this, that there is still some lurking favorite imagination, that this system, with correctness, might become a safe and permanent one.[83]

Hamilton's use of the device of reducing to absurdity involved an answer to the charge that the number of representatives provided in the proposed national legislature was insufficient to secure the liberties of the people. His method was to exhibit the varying practices among the several states and to inquire whether the inhabitants of any state felt their liberties to be endangered by their having too few representatives in the state assembly.[84]

Hamilton uses all available evidence to point to the conclusion at which he is to arrive. Often he depends upon common knowledge which he believes to be accepted by his hearers, or calls on them to witness facts from their experience; and only infrequently does he call on formal authority, as when he says, "The best writers on government have held that representation should be compounded of persons and property." [85] And even then, he adds immediate reference to a fact within the direct observation of his audience: "This rule has been adopted, as far as it could be, in the constitution of New York." [86]

"Have not all of us," he asks, "been witnesses to the unhappy embarrassments which resulted from these proceedings?" [87] And, in another instance, with full knowledge of his audience, he sought confirmation by inquiry: "Has not every man who has been in our legislature experienced the truth of

[83] *Ibid.*
[84] *Ibid.*, p. 254.
[85] *Ibid.*, p. 237.
[86] *Ibid.*
[87] *Ibid.*, p. 231.

this position?" [88] But the appeal is sometimes to experience beyond the immediate range of observation:

It has been observed, by an honorable gentleman, that a pure democracy, if it were practicable, would be the most perfect government. Experience has proved that no position in politics is more false than this.[89]

It is hardly possible to enumerate all the instances in which Hamilton states a maxim or a principle and proceeds from it, attempting to carry his audience with him, to his conclusion. But some of his maxims should be noted, both as examples of his method and as statements of his thought: "All governments," he says, "even the most despotic, depend, in a great degree, on opinion." [90] Again he asserts that "the true principle of a republic is, that the people should choose whom they please to govern them." [91] And he objects to the "harsh doctrine that men grow wicked in proportion as they improve and enlighten their minds." [92]

But Hamilton's mode of logical proof is chiefly distinguished for his use of antecedent probability in projecting from present circumstances to a hypothetical future. Concerning the number of representatives in Congress, for example, he calls into view the developing states:

The Congress is to consist, at first, of ninety-one members. This, to a reasonable man, may appear as near the proper medium as any number whatever, at least for the present. There is one source of increase, also, which does not depend upon any constructions of the Constitution; it is the creation of new states. Vermont, Kentucky, and Franklin, will probably become independent. New members of the Union will also be formed from the unsettled tracts of western territory.[93]

In another instance, he develops a probability which illustrates the difficulty of considering separately his emotional and

[88] Elliot, *op. cit.*, II, 231.   [90] *Ibid.*, p. 252.   [92] *Ibid.*
[89] *Ibid.*, p. 253.   [91] *Ibid.*, p. 257.   [93] *Ibid.*, p. 238.

logical proof. Considering the events likely to follow from a
weak central government, he finds a legitimate use for the appeal
to fear:

Suppose Massachusetts, or any large state, should refuse, and Congress should attempt to compel them, would they not have influence
to procure assistance, especially from those states which are in the
same situation as themselves? What picture does this idea present to
our view? A complying state at war with a non-complying state;
Congress marching the troops of one state into the bosom of another;
this state collecting auxiliaries, and forming, perhaps, a majority
against its federal head. Here is a nation at war with itself. Can any
reasonable man be well disposed towards a government which makes
war and carnage the only means of supporting itself—a government
that can exist only by the sword? Every such war must involve the
innocent with the guilty. This single consideration should be sufficient
to dispose every peaceable citizen against such a government.[94]

Concerning Hamilton's proof in the *Principles of Union*
speech, it appears, then, that his method was primarily logical
and that he used many means of developing his logical proof.
At the same time, he did not neglect expedient means of establishing himself with the audience or of putting the audience in
a favorable disposition toward him and toward his logical
presentation. Ethical, emotional, and logical proof in the *Principles of Union* speech are developed out of the circumstances
of the occasion, the interests of the audience, and the logic of
the case.

The effect of Hamilton's Principles of Union speech.—In
accordance with Livingston's motion of June 19 [95] to defer any
vote until the whole case had been heard, no vote was taken
on the second section of the first article, which was supposedly
the instance of Hamilton's speech. No doubt if a vote had been
taken following Hamilton's speech, it would have fallen along
strict party lines, 46 to 19 against favoring the clause; for there

[94] *Ibid.*, p. 233.   [95] *Ibid.*, p. 216.

was on June 21 no evidence of any change in party sentiment,[96] and, furthermore, Hamilton's speech was delivered not for immediate but for cumulative effect. Whether the speech actually changed any minds, it is impossible to say; but it furnished Hamilton with the solid foundation which he found necessary in all his speech-making and it added to his contemporary reputation as a speaker.[97]

The continuing debate.—The response of the opposition speakers, at any rate, was immediate. Hamilton was replied to in turn by Melancton Smith, John Lansing, and George Clinton. Smith observed that the gentleman might have spared many of his remarks on which they were not in disagreement and then continued in rebuttal.[98] Smith's statement is really testimony to Hamilton's success in arriving at some principles held in common. Lansing contented himself with raising new and further objections. And Clinton made some observations favoring a more comprehensive representation than that proposed in the draft constitution, closing with the conciliatory statement that

I only suggest these observations, for the purpose of hearing them satisfactorily answered. I am open to conviction, and if my objections

---

[96] "I believe there has not been a Time since the Revolution in which, the *Well Born*, who are the Leaders of that [Federalist] Party, have felt and appeared so uninfluential, as they feel and appear at this Time and Place . . ." James M. Hughes, at Poughkeepsie, to John Lamb, June 18, 1788. New York Historical Society. ". . . Our friends here continue firm . . . all the arts of a Hamilton &c will have no effect." Charles Tillinghast, to John Lamb, June 21, 1788. New York Historical Society. "It appears to be the opinion of all those whom I have conversed with that the Constitution will be effectually amended previous to its adoption—or that it will be Totally rejected." Abraham G. Lansing to Abraham Yates, June 15, 1788. New York Public Library.

[97] Young De Witt Clinton, Antifederalist, wrote concerning this speech, "He [Melancton Smith] was answered by Mr. Hamilton in an eloquent speech." Clinton to Thomas Greenleaf, June 22, 1788. Columbia University Library. See also Kent, *Memoirs*, p. 305.

[98] Elliot, *op. cit.*, II, 259.

can be removed, I shall be ready frankly to acknowledge their weakness.[99]

Hamilton answered the three men, in a speech of refutation; a short exchange followed between Clinton and Hamilton; Smith made a few remarks, and the meeting adjourned until Monday, June 23.[100]

On Monday morning the debate was opened by Harison, who was followed by Lansing. Hamilton rose, not to extend the debate, but to state a pertinent fact, and was followed by Lansing. The chancellor spoke at some length and was followed by Melancton Smith, who concluded with the apology that he had troubled the committee too long and would not have spoken had not his ideas been grossly misrepresented.[101] It was Livingston whom Smith accused of misrepresentation. Smith was followed by Jay, who made a speech designed to keep the peace and to emphasize the points held in common by the two groups. In courteous fashion, "he called on Mr. Smith, to know if he had mistaken him," and after receiving an explanation from Smith, continued at length in the vein of reasoned discourse, closing with a statement designed to repair the damage done by Livingston.[102] Jay's conclusion provides an interesting formulation of his stated principle of discourse and a good example of the speech of conciliation:

Sir, I argue from plain facts. Here is no sophistry, no construction, no false glosses, but simple inferences from the obvious operation of things. We did not come here to carry points. If the gentleman will convince me I am wrong, I will submit. I mean to give my ideas frankly upon the subject. If my reasoning is not good, let them show me the folly of it. It is from this reciprocal interchange of ideas that the truth must come out. My earnest wish is, that we may go home attended with the pleasing consciousness that we have industriously and candidly sought the truth, and have done our duty.[103]

---

[99] *Ibid.*, p. 262.
[100] *Ibid.*, p. 268.
[101] *Ibid.*, p. 282.

[102] *Ibid.*
[103] *Ibid.*, p. 285.

After Jay had concluded, Smith spoke briefly and the meeting adjourned for the day.

The convention assembled on Tuesday, June 24, to consider the clause (Article I, Section 3, Paragraph 1) concerning the number of senators and their length of office. Gilbert Livingston arose to a forthright attack upon the whole concept of a senate embodied in the clause. The proposed Senate, the speaker maintained, was a dangerous body. It was given too much power. He therefore moved that the committee "adopt the following resolution as an amendment to this clause":

Resolved, That no person shall be eligible as a senator for more than six years in any term of twelve years, and that it shall be in the power of the legislatures of the several states to recall their senators, or either of them, and to elect others in their stead, to serve for the remainder of the time for which such senator or senators, so recalled, were appointed.[104]

Gilbert Livingston was followed immediately by John Lansing, who spoke in favor of the motion to amend; and Lansing was followed by R. R. Livingston, who opposed the resolution. Lansing, R. R. Livingston, Richard Morris, Gilbert Livingston, and Harison spoke in turn; Chancellor Livingston again spoke briefly and was answered by Melancton Smith and John Lansing. At this point on Tuesday, June 24, Hamilton arose to deliver his speech on the *Powers of the Senate.*

The Powers of the Senate.—Like his *Principles of Union* speech, Hamilton's address on the *Powers of the Senate* was delivered in debate; and it was likewise broken by adjournment and by intervening speeches made by other members of the convention. Nevertheless, the speech has unity and is systematically developed. Technically the speech was delivered to Gilbert Livingston's motion concerning the tenure of senators; but, although the address did deal more specifically with the question before the House than the *Principles of Union* speech

[104] Elliot, *op. cit.,* II, 289.

had done, it was also delivered to the general proposition before the body during the first period of the convention.

The line of discourse.—In his speech on the *Powers of the Senate*, Hamilton advocated stability and vigor in the Federal government, holding that the amendment offered was calculated to weaken the proposed republic. Every republic, he believed, should have a permanent body to check the democratic one. The body should not be too large, it should not be too directly responsible to the people, and it should be a repository of political wisdom. Particularly wise, he thought, was the provision for the senate's participation in foreign affairs.

But since the proposed amendment made senators ineligible for immediate reëlection, it would deprive the senate of permanency and hence of the advantages of seasoned counsel. It would tend to defeat the usefulness of the senate in combatting local prejudices and in destroying cabals and popular fluctuations in opinion. It would produce that instability in government which has always been the bane of republics. The republic proposed under the constitution offered an opportunity to remedy the evils of instability.

The organization.—The speech on the *Powers of the Senate* has a discernible organization into introduction, body, and conclusion; but the introduction and conclusion are abbreviated, both in the first and in the second part of the speech. The introduction proper, which was delivered on June 24, is designed to note modestly that the speaker has not yet addressed the house on the question before it, to attribute good intentions to all the members of the house, and to set forth the speaker's own personal commitment to the policy of strong government. Although the introduction is short, it served to establish the speaker with his audience:

I am persuaded, Mr. Chairman, that I, in my turn, shall be indulged in addressing the committee. We all, in equal sincerity, profess to be anxious for the establishment of a republican government on a safe and solid basis. It is the object of the wishes of every honest man in the United States; and I presume I shall not be disbelieved, when I declare that it is an object, of all others, the nearest and most dear to my own heart. The means of accomplishing this great purpose become the most important study which can interest mankind.[105]

The second part of the speech, delivered on June 25, is largely refutatory. The introduction is simple, but calculated to conciliate the opposition and to establish the speaker as a man of fairness and judgment:

Mr. Chairman, in debates of this kind, it is extremely easy, on either side, to say a great number of plausible things. It is to be acknowledged that there is even a certain degree of truth in the reasonings on both sides. In this situation, it is the province of judgment and good sense to determine their force and application, and how far the arguments advanced on one side are balanced by those on the other.[106]

The conclusion to the first part of the speech is deliberately pointed to the new opportunity for establishing stability. It involves emotional proof, and, unusual in the records of Hamilton's speeches, a rather extended figure of speech:

This sir, is the first fair opportunity that has been offered of deliberately correcting the errors in government. Instability has been a prominent and very defective feature in most republican systems. It is the first to be seen, and the last to be lamented, by a philosophical inquirer. It has operated most banefully in our infant republics. It is necessary that we apply an immediate remedy, and eradicate the poisonous principle from our government. If this be not done, sir, we shall feel, and posterity will be convulsed by, a painful malady.[107]

The conclusion to the second part of the speech, involved in refutatory material, is limited to the observation that the operation of the proposed amendment "might be extremely inconvenient, if not fatal to the prosperity of our country." [108]

The body of the speech shows progressive development from

---

[105] Elliot, *op. cit.*, II, 300.

[106] *Ibid.*, p. 315.

[107] *Ibid.*, p. 307.

[108] *Ibid.*, p. 321.

idea to idea, always with adequate transition, so that the reference throughout is clear. When a point of the opposition is to be refuted, the point is always fully stated before any refutation is offered. Thus concerning the responsibility of the senator, he says, "The gentleman observes, that there is a fallacy in my reasoning, and informs us that the legislatures of the states, not the people, are to appoint the senators." [109] And concerning an alleged inconsistency, he replies fully only after an initial statement of the point to be refuted: "It has been remarked, that there is an inconsistency in our admitting that the *equal vote in the Senate* was given to secure the rights of the states, and at the same time holding up the idea that their interests should be sacrificed to those of the Union." [110] Again, with reference to the senatorship, he states his opponent's point clearly as the first step in refutation: "It has been observed, that it is not possible there should be in a state only two men qualified for senators." [111]

In the body of his speech, Hamilton's great care to state fairly the point to be refuted, together with his attention to transition, indicates that the development of the speech was sound and the progression clear. It was organized in terms of the hearers.

The purpose.—The direct purpose of the speech was to kill the specific amendment offered by Gilbert Livingston providing for certain limitations on the United States senators. More generally, of course, Hamilton was opposed to any amendment which might be urged as a condition for ratifying the constitution. Hamilton used the occasion, also, as a means of pleading for that energy and stability in government which he believed Livingston's amendment would tend to subvert.

The preparation.—The first section of Hamilton's speech was delivered near the close of a legislative day. Livingston had made his amendment limiting the office of senator the first business of the day. Hamilton's speech came, from the Federal-

[109] *Ibid.,* p. 317.   [110] *Ibid.,* p. 319.   [111] *Ibid.,* p. 320.

ist point of view, as a summary and conclusion; and his specific preparation was made during the course of the debates. Although the speech was extempore, it was not unprepared. The second part of the speech likewise followed other speeches on the subject of the senate and, largely refutatory, it was directed at specific arguments which only Hamilton's wide reading and writing could have enabled him to meet adequately on short notice.

Special characteristics.—In his speech on the *Powers of the Senate,* Hamilton's style shows the same tendency toward meaningful amplification already noted in his *Principles of Union* speech. Hamilton's characteristic way of dealing with a question is indicated in the following passage: "Sir, when you take a view of all the circumstances which have been recited, you will certainly see that the senators will constantly look up to the state governments with an eye of dependence and affection." [112] It was his object in the speech throughout to "take a view of all the circumstances." [113] The result is that the speech appears to be long and, to the reader, it might even appear too long for effective appeal. But the amplification provided is an assistance to one who hears rather than reads the speech.

The speaker's directness, also, is an assistance to the hearer. The speaker's style in the *Powers of the Senate* speech involves question and answer, give and take between speaker and hearer, direct address and forthright plea. Hamilton often asks the question which a member of the audience might want asked, and then answers it. And this answered question is, as a stylistic device, one of his chief means of holding the group to attention. "Now, sir," he inquires, "what is the tendency of the proposed amendment?" [114] The answer is clear, specific, and to the point. It is obviously addressed to an immediate audience.

Both speaker and hearer are frequently identified with a larger audience, as in the initial injunction:

[112] Elliot, *op. cit.,* II, 306.   [113] *Ibid.*   [114] *Ibid.,* p. 302.

It is our duty to examine all those means with peculiar attention, and to choose the best and most effectual. It is our duty to draw from nature, from reason, from examples, the best principles of policy, and to pursue and to apply them in the formation of our government. We should contemplate and compare the systems which, in this examination, come under our view; distinguish, with a careful eye, the defects and excellences of each, and, discarding the former, incorporate the latter, as far as circumstances will admit, into our Constitution. If we pursue a different course, and neglect this duty, we shall probably disappoint the expectation of our country and of the world.[115]

But the seeker after oratory in the grand manner will not find anything in the text of Hamilton's speech on the *Powers of the Senate* to excite his envy or admiration. Direct, forthright, clear, and purposeful, the speech is communicative rather than exhibitive. It is another bit of evidence bearing out the observation of William Pierce that Hamilton was rather a convincing speaker, than a blazing orator.[116]

Hamilton's ethical proof in the speech on The Powers of the Senate.—Hamilton's formal attempt to establish himself with his hearers was limited to the introduction. Throughout the speech, however, by the level at which he maintained the discourse, and by his attitude of deference to other opinions than his own, the speaker showed himself inferentially to be a man worthy of attention. At the same time, Hamilton's forthright expression of certain opinions concerning the people at large might well have created some distrust among the members of his opposition by tending to substantiate the opinion that Hamilton was an enemy of the people.

Men will pursue their interests [Hamilton said]. It is as easy to change human nature as to oppose the strong current of the selfish

---

[115] *Ibid.*, p. 301.
[116] Pierce, "Character Sketches of Delegates to the Federal Convention," Farrand, ed., *Records of the Federal Convention*, III, 89.

passions. A wise legislator will gently divert the channel, and direct it, if possible, to the public good.[117]

In another instance, a frank statement concerning the people at large was perhaps ameliorated by the implied compliment to his hearers:

It is an unquestionable truth, that the body of the people, in every country, desire sincerely its prosperity; but it is equally unquestionable, that they do not possess the discernment and stability necessary for systematic government. To deny that they are frequently led into the grossest errors by misinformation and passion, would be a flattery which their own good sense must despise. That branch of administration, especially, which involves our political relation with foreign states, a community will ever be incompetent to. These truths are not often held up in public assemblies; but they cannot be unknown to any who hear me.[118]

Hamilton's emotional proof in the speech on The Powers of the Senate.—As in his *Principles of Union* speech, Hamilton relied mainly, in the speech on the *Powers of the Senate*, on an indisputably logical mode of proof. Insofar as he was concerned with emotional proof, he dealt with the basic emotion of fear, being concerned to establish the reasonableness of one fear and the unreasonableness of another. In the former instance, he sought to show that, without the senate as a stabilizing influence, "prejudices would govern the public deliberations, and passions rage in the counsels of the Union." [119] But concerning the fear of the national government which animated Smith and Lansing, Hamilton had an entirely different view:

Gentlemen indulge too many unreasonable apprehensions of danger to the state governments; they seem to suppose that, the moment you put men into a national council, they become corrupt and tyrannical, and lose all affection for their fellow-citizens. But can we imagine that the senators will ever be so insensible of their own advantage as to sacrifice the genuine interest of their constituents? The state

---

[117] Elliot, *op. cit.*, II, 320.   [118] *Ibid.*, p. 302.   [119] *Ibid.*, p. 307.

governments are essentially necessary to the form and spirit of the general system.[120]

The compound of antecedent probability and emotional proof based on a kind of cogent fear is a characteristic of the speech; but the development is careful, as in the instance in which the fear of disapprobation of foreigners is resorted to:

There is another view in which duration in the Senate appears necessary. A government changeable in its policy must soon lose its sense of national character, and forfeit the respect of foreigners. Senators will not be solicitous for the reputation of public measures, in which they had but a temporary concern, and will feel lightly the burden of public disapprobation, in proportion to the number of those who partake of the censure. Our political rivals will ever consider our mutable counsels as evidence of deficient wisdom, and will be little apprehensive of our arriving at any exalted station in the scale of power.[121]

Hamilton's logical proof in the speech on The Powers of the Senate.—Hamilton's typical development of logical proof in his speech on the *Powers of the Senate* is that of causal relation. While he may resort, in refutation, to the device of turning the tables,[122] or to a defense of a supposed inconsistency,[123] his chief reliance is on bringing evidence to bear in support of the relation of cause and effect. In the process, he depends more frequently on what he calls "common sense" or "experience" as a court of last resort than on other authority. His characteristic method appears to be that of starting from an accepted fact, a truism on which all agree, to build a bridge by logical sequence over a stream of doubt to reach an acceptable conclusion. The bridge between the truism and the conclusion is buttressed firmly in the basic assumptions of his hearers.

In one instance he rests his whole case on an appeal to common sense:

[120] *Ibid.*, p. 303.
[121] *Ibid.*, p. 307.
[122] *Ibid.*, p. 305.
[123] *Ibid.*, p. 319.

Whenever, therefore, Congress shall meditate any infringement of the state constitutions, the great body of the people will naturally take part with their domestic representatives. Can the general government withstand such a united opposition? Will the people suffer themselves to be stripped of their privileges? Will they suffer their legislatures to be reduced to a shadow and name? The idea is shocking to common sense.[124]

In another case he appeals to the history of ancient and modern republics; [125] and in another he depends upon the fact, known to his hearers, that such "considerations as these induced the Convention which formed your state Constitution to institute a Senate upon the present plan." [126] Rhode Island, in still another case, is set up as an example of bad government, having been betrayed by the multitude.[127]

Hamilton's enthymemes are thus typically developed out of the immediate experience of his hearers; and his maxims are commonly those which they are willing to accept. "There are two objects," he says, "in forming systems of government—*safety* for the people, and *energy* in the administration." [128] From this principle he goes on to develop a conclusion. Again he supposes "it is a truth sufficiently illustrated by experience, that when the *people* act by their representatives, they are commonly *irresistible*." [129] And again he goes on to his conclusion. He does not hesitate to deal with any point, whether it be weighty or obscure, so long as it helps him to establish his thesis. He calls into account the duty of sixpence per pound on salt in the state of New York,[130] the compromises effected between counties,[131] and the nature of legislatures.[132] Finally, he reasons to the conclusion:

If the members of Congress are too dependent on the state legislature, they will be eternally forming secret combinations from local views. This is reasoning from the plainest principles. Their interest

---

[124] Elliot, *op. cit.*, II, 304.   [127] *Ibid.*, p. 317.   [130] *Ibid.*, p. 318.
[125] *Ibid.*, p. 302.   [128] *Ibid.*, p. 316.   [131] *Ibid.*
[126] *Ibid.*   [129] *Ibid.*   [132] *Ibid.*

is interwoven with their dependence, and they will necessarily yield to the impression of their situation. Those who have been in Congress have seen these operations. The first question has been, How will such a measure affect my constituents, and, consequently, how will the part I take affect my reelection? This consideration may be in some degree proper; but to be dependent from day to day, and to have the idea perpetually present, would be the source of numerous evils.[133]

In general, it may be concluded, Hamilton's speech on the *Powers of the Senate* exhibits characteristics of ethical, emotional, and logical proof quite similar to those shown in his speech on the *Principles of Union*. The speech is remarkable for its directness of appeal to the audience, for the sustained quality of its logical proof, and for its persuasive exposition. How effective it was in the immediate situation is another question.

The effect of the speech on The Powers of the Senate.—In 1788, Hamilton's speech on the *Powers of the Senate* was regarded as the best specimen which the debates at Poughkeepsie afforded "of the ability and wisdom of a consummate statesman."[134] Despite the opinion held concerning the speech, it fell short of complete success in moving the house to agree with the speaker. That it was a persuasive speech is clear; but Hamilton's opposition was made up of men who knew their own minds;[135] and when the recommendatory amendments were finally adopted, Gilbert Livingston's amendment limiting the powers of the senate, the amendment against which Hamilton had called all his abilities, was among them.[136] Even Hamilton's powers of persuasion could not bring the Clintonians to trust the idea of a senate, set off from the people and ensconced in a Federal town.

---

[133] *Ibid.*   [134] Kent, *Memoirs*, p. 307.

[135] In a conversation with Hamilton, Yates declared he would prefer to risk government by Jew, Turk, or Infidel to adopting the new Constitution. Abraham Yates to Abraham G. Lansing, May 28, 1788. New York Public Library.

[136] Kent, *Memoirs*, p. 309.

THE SECOND PERIOD

Melancton Smith replied to Hamilton's address at once, noting that "Few observations have fallen from the gentleman which appear to be new."[137] Yet Smith undertook briefly to refute the arguments advanced. He was followed in debate by Chancellor Livingston, who, on June 25, observed for the first time in the convention that New Hampshire had ratified the Constitution.[138] Livingston analyzed the persuasive and parliamentary situation correctly when he declared that the circumstances of the country were greatly altered and the ground of the debate changed. The Confederation was dissolved, as Livingston observed, and the new government was ratified by the necessary nine states. The question before the New York convention thus became one of expediency. But after his preliminary reference to the establishment of the new Union, Livingston returned to the question of the senate.[139]

As soon as Livingston was seated, Melancton Smith rose to answer him.

With respect [he said] to the change of circumstances which had such a solemn effect upon the honorable gentleman, he confessed it had not altered his feelings or wishes on the subject. He had long been convinced that nine states would receive the Constitution.[140]

Lansing followed Smith, supporting Smith's attempted refutation of the accomplished fact.

It is true [Lansing admitted], we have received information that the *ninth state has ratified the Constitution;* but I contend that no such event ought to influence our deliberations. I presume I shall not be charged with rashness, if I continue to insist that it is still our duty to maintain our rights. We acknowledge that our dissent cannot prevent the operation of the government: since nine states have acceded to it, let them make the experiment.[141]

---

[137] Elliot, *op. cit.*, II, 321.   [139] *Ibid.*, p. 323.   [141] *Ibid.*
[138] *Ibid.*, p. 322.   [140] *Ibid.*, p. 324.

But no kind of reasoning could argue away the basic fact that the house had now to consider a new proposition.[142] Lansing might choose to let the other states experiment; but he could not deny that they had made their decision, that the new federation was operative. Therefore, the real question before the house was no longer, as it had been, "That New York should assist the several states in forming a new national government," with Hamilton and his colleagues bearing the burden of the argument. The background question now became "Resolved: That New York should stay out of the New Union," and the burden was shifted to Lansing and to Smith. The Antifederalists now had to propose action, to find a way out, and to offer a plan of procedure.

Nevertheless, the Antifederalists continued for a while to debate from the old ground. The procedure of reading the Constitution, now the basic law of the new United States of America, was continued. Several paragraphs of the third article were passed over without debate, but when the fourth section of article one, that concerning the time, place, and manner of elections, was reached, Jones rose to offer an amendment protecting the rights of the states. Jay, Richard Morris, Governor Clinton, and Melancton Smith joined in the debate on June 25.[143]

[142] Even so, George Clinton wrote on June 28, "The Anti's are Firm [and] I hope and believe will remain so to the End—." George Clinton to Abraham Yates, June 28, 1788. New York Public Library. On hearing of the ratification by New Hampshire, Abraham Yates, who was at the Continental Congress in New York, was asked by several members what New York would do. Yates answered that his mind was made up and that if all twelve states came in still New York ought not. Abraham Yates to Abraham G. Lansing, June 25, 1788. New York Public Library. On June 29 Lansing wrote to Yates, "The Federalists here plume themselves much on the accession of New Hampshire. . . . We congratulate them and our Friends and express our satisfaction that they can now give the New System an Experiment without Interfering in the politics of the State of New York—Virginia will have a more serious effect I fear upon the Spirits and determinations of our Friends." Abraham G. Lansing to Abraham Yates, June 29, 1788. New York Public Library.

[143] Elliot, op. cit., II, 326.

On the following day, the convention continued to debate
Jones's motion, and to offer additions and emendations. Succeeding sections of the Constitution were read without debate until
the first paragraph of section eight of article one was reached.
To this section, which concerned the power of Congress to lay
and collect taxes, duties, and imposts, John Williams offered
a long speech concluding with an amendment severely limiting
the Congress in the levying of taxes.[144] At the conclusion of
Williams's speech, the convention adjourned until Friday, June
27, when section eight was again read. Thereupon began the
brilliant debate on taxation and the rights of the states which
called forth the best efforts of Smith, Williams, Livingston,
and Hamilton.

The speech on Taxation and the Rights of the States.—Hamilton's speech on *Taxation and the Rights of the States,* like his
other leading addresses in the convention at Poughkeepsie, was
delivered in two parts. The first section of his address was
delivered at the close of the legislative day of June 27; the
second section was delivered at the opening of the legislative
day of June 28, after numerous interruptions having to do with
some papers which Hamilton introduced as evidence.[145] Both
Federalists and Antifederalists well understood that the question of the fundamental rights of the states was inextricably
bound up with taxation; and so in Hamilton's speeches, as in
others delivered on the motion, there is no possibility of divid-
ing the two questions.

In the parliamentary situation, Hamilton's speech was de-
livered in debate to the question of amending a section of the
Constitution in such a way as to limit the taxing power of the
Federal government. But since the speaker knew that no vote

[144] Elliot, *op. cit.,* II, 330.
[145] While Hamilton was delivering this speech, Clinton was writing a
letter to General Lamb. It began as follows: "I steal this Moment while
the Convention is in Committee and the little Great Man employed in
repeating over Parts of Publius to us." George Clinton to John Lamb,
June 28, 1788. New York Historical Society.

of consequence could be taken immediately, he addressed himself directly to his audience, and, it would appear, especially
to one member of his audience, Melancton Smith, in an effort
to further the larger aim of securing a stable union.

The line of discourse.—Near the close of the day, after
extended debate by Smith, Williams, and Livingston, Hamilton took the floor to consider the question of *Taxation and the
Rights of the States.* He pointed out the dependence of the
members of the Congress upon their constituents, the provision
in the new government of a system of checks, and the instituting
of a balance in legislative authority. He considered the question of the division of powers between state and Federal governments to be a matter of convenience, since both governments
derived from the people. He discussed the leading objects of
governments in relation to revenue and the comparable ex-
penses of different services of government, being careful to
show that the state governments could not be destroyed by a
national legislature. He declared for the expediency in a Federal system of instituting a dual system of taxation and discussed the kinds of taxes probable and their relation to the welfare of the states. He endeavored to show that New York
would not suffer peculiar disadvantages from the granting of
the taxing power to the Federal government.

The organization.—Hamilton's speech on *Taxation and the
Rights of the States* has a beginning, a middle, and an end.
Each part of the speech is clearly distinguishable, and, unlike
his earlier speeches delivered in convention, there is no notice
of the break caused by adjournment. The speaker gave no conclusion on June 27, and began on June 28 without a formal
introduction.

Hamilton's introduction is one calculated to place him in the
character of a man appealing to judgment. At the same time,
while establishing his own character as a speaker of reason,
Hamilton flatters the members of his audience with the supposition that they are susceptible to arguments based on reason

rather than to those based on prejudice. The introduction is short and can be given in full:

This is one of those subjects, Mr. Chairman, on which objections very naturally arise, and assume the most plausible shape. Its address is to the passions, and its first impressions create a prejudice, before cool examination has an opportunity for exertion. It is more easy for the human mind to calculate the evils than the advantages of a measure; and vastly more natural to apprehend the danger than to see the necessity of giving powers to our rulers. Hence I may justly expect that those who hear me will place less confidence in those arguments which oppose, than in those which favor, their prepossessions.[146]

The great part of the speech—and it is the longest and most thoroughly developed of the speeches delivered at Poughkeepsie—was devoted to the body of argument, to proof and refutation. In the speech on *Taxation and the Rights of the States* Hamilton advances his own position and attacks his opponent's arguments simultaneously. He is never on the defensive; he is never apologetic; he is never at a loss for the next step. He proceeds from argument to argument and from point to point by steady progression, always with careful attention to transition. If the change in his line of attack is not clear, he announces it in so many words, as, for example: "I shall proceed now more particularly to the proposition before the Committee." [147] In Hamilton's argument, when a contention is to be refuted, the contention is, without exception, clearly stated as the very first step in refutation, as, for example, in the discussion of the forms of taxation: "Sir, it has been said that a *poll tax* is a tyrannical tax." [148] And concerning the merits of state governments,

A gentleman yesterday passed many encomiums on the character and operations of the *state governments*. The question has not been,

---

[146] Elliot, *op. cit.*, II, 347.   [147] *Ibid.*, p. 367.   [148] *Ibid.*, p. 364.

whether their laws have produced happy or unhappy effects. The character of our confederation is the subject of our controversy.[149]

Throughout the entire body of Hamilton's discourse, he seems never to be unaware of the listener's problem of reference. Uniformly, he tells his hearers what he is about and how the argument he is producing fits into his pattern. Yet, because of his skillful use of stylistic devices, particularly the rhetorical question, his speaking was not tedious. Hamilton's organization appears, in the body of his argument, to have been careful without being pedantic; and, so far as the evidence in the text can justify a conclusion, it was a form developed out of the speaker's full comprehension of his own meaning at the time of his speaking and in a complete understanding of the problem of the audience in listening to a speaker.

Nevertheless, although the careful organization of the body of his argument was Hamilton's main concern, his speech on *Taxation and the Rights of the States* held a powerful conclusion. Hamilton's very eloquence made him an object of some suspicion. Men were afraid, perhaps, of being seduced by eloquence into doing what they did not want to do. In his conclusion, therefore, after offering an explanation and apology for any strong phrases which he may have used, Hamilton adverted to an expression uttered during the course of the debate that "ingenious men may say ingenious things, and that those who are interested in raising the few upon the ruins of the many, may give to every cause an appearance of justice." [150]

In answer to the insinuations, Hamilton delivered a forceful peroration, which, for power and directness of utterance, as well as for felicity of expression, deserves to appear among the masterpieces of parliamentary speaking.[151]

Special characteristics.—Hamilton's style in his speech on *Taxation and the Rights of the States* insofar as it can be

[149] *Ibid.*, p. 365.   [150] *Ibid.*, p. 370.   [151] *Ibid.*, pp. 370, 371.

judged from the text, is direct, clear, and free from adornment. The rhetorical question is in this, as in his other speeches, a notable characteristic of his style. Often one question follows another, as in the discussion of the legislative authority:

Now, what do gentlemen mean by coming forward and declaiming against this government? Why do they say we ought to limit its power, to disable it, and to destroy its capacity of blessing the people? Has philosophy suggested, has experience taught, that such a government ought not to be trusted with every thing necessary for the good of society? [152]

And again, concerning the powers of government:

What is your state government? Does not your legislature command what money it pleases? Does not your executive execute the laws without restraint? [153]

In the speech on *Taxation and the Rights of the States*, Hamilton speaks a great deal of "the sword and the purse." [154] But the metaphor is not Hamilton's own; it is borrowed by way of refuting Melancton Smith. He refers to "the yoke of *aristocracy*"; [155] in his conclusion, he personifies "Fortune"; [156] and, in another instance, he asserts that the "human affections, like the solar heat, lose their intensity as they depart from the centre, and become languid in proportion to the expansion of the circle in which they act." [157] But he proceeds as a rule without benefit of hyperbole, simile, or metaphor. His speech is ordinarily the direct, unadorned language of sober, serious conversation. It is the language of exposition just as fully as it is the language of argument.

Hamilton's ethical proof in the speech on Taxation and the Rights of the States.—Both in his introduction and in his conclusion, Hamilton makes special effort to establish himself with his hearers. The conclusion, it has already been noted,[158] was

---

[152] Elliot, *op. cit.*, II, 348   [155] *Ibid.*, p. 354.   [157] *Ibid.*, p. 354.
[153] *Ibid.*, p. 349.   [156] *Ibid.*, p. 371.   [158] *Supra*, p. 167.
[154] *Ibid.*, p. 348, *et passim*.

chiefly refutation; but it was refutation in ethical proof. Hamilton is careful to defend his moral character and his disposition to good will toward the audience, two of the chief elements of a speaker's personal standing, from any insinuations against them. Hamilton's defense of his ethical character is a most interesting example of the use of antecedent probability in establishing ethical proof; for Hamilton does not rely on mere protestation, on assertion of innocence, or on bold proclamation of virtue. Without sacrificing his dignity or placing himself in a position of compromise, Hamilton brings logical proof to bear in an ethical question concerning his own character.

Except for his conclusion, Hamilton's effort to establish ethical proof is limited to his endeavors to keep the debate on a plane of judgment and to avoid personalities. "If anything has escaped me," he says, "which may be construed into a personal reflection, I beg the gentlemen, once for all, to be assured that I have no design to wound the feelings of any one who is opposed to me." [159]

Hamilton's emotional proof in the speech on Taxation and the Rights of the States.—In his conclusion, Hamilton's emotional proof is bound up with his ethical and logical proof, and all three modes are really directed, as he frankly states, to the end of showing "that it cannot be the wish of any reasonable man to establish a government unfriendly to the liberties of the people." [160] But the body of the speech is almost completely dependent upon logical development. The impression which Hamilton's speech made on his audience must be accounted for by his energy and animation, by the personal adaptation he made in attempting to secure a favorable disposition on the part of his hearers, rather than by the language of his argument. Hamilton himself testifies,

I have ever condemned those cold, unfeeling hearts, which no object can animate. I condemn those indifferent mortals, who either never

---

[159] Elliot, *op. cit.*, II, 370.   [160] *Ibid.*, p. 371.

form opinions, or never make them known. I confess, sir, that on no
subject has my breast been filled with stronger emotions, or more
anxious concern.[161]

*Hamilton's logical proof in the speech on Taxation and the
Rights of the States.*—In his speech on *Taxation and the Rights
of the States,* Hamilton is at his best in the refutation of opposing argument. He uses easily and skillfully the methods of
reducing to absurdity,[162] of exposing inconsistency,[163] and of
turning the tables.[164] In refutation, he sometimes accepts his
opponent's premises, and he almost invariably states them.[165]
His own care is first of all to begin with an acceptable truth.
For example, he states that there

are certain social principles in human nature, from which we may
draw the most solid conclusion with respect to the conduct of individuals and of communities. We love our families more than our
neighbors; we love our neighbors more than our countrymen in
general.[166]

And he goes on to the conclusion that "the attachment of the
individual will be first and forever secured by the state governments: they will be a mutual protection and support." [167]

But not content with one line of reasoning he develops another:

Another source of influence . . . is the various official connections
in the states. . . . The state officers will ever be important, because
they are necessary and useful. Their powers are such as are extremely
interesting among the people; such as affect their property, their
liberty, and life. What is more important than the administration of
justice and the execution of the civil and criminal laws? Can the
state governments become insignificant while they have the power of
raising money independently, and without control? If they are really

---

[161] Elliot, *op. cit.,* II, 370.   [163] *Ibid.,* p. 350.
[162] *Ibid.,* p. 349.   [164] *Ibid.,* p. 363.
[165] See, for example, Elliot, *op. cit.,* II, 354.
[166] *Ibid.,* p. 354.   [167] *Ibid.*

useful, if they are calculated to promote the essential interests of the people, they must have their confidence and support. The states can never lose their powers till the whole people of America are robbed of their liberties. These must go together; they must support each other, or meet one common fate.[168]

Hamilton rarely depends either in refutation or in constructive argument on a single approach to an argument. Almost invariably, he returns to the attack from another aspect of the question. His refutation is never half-hearted. His constructive proof is built up item by item from enthymemes presumably acceptable to his audience. Departing from his usual habit of depending on evidence within the immediate experience of the group, the speaker, in his speech on *Taxation and the Rights of the States*, introduces documents [169] designed to prove "that this state was once on the verge of destruction, for want of an energetic government." [170] Although the opposition objected to the introduction of the documents,[171] Governor Clinton himself was forced to admit "that the representations made in them were true." [172]

The effect of Hamilton's speech on Taxation and the Rights of the States.—The immediate effect of Hamilton's speech was to provoke a rejoinder from Lansing, who professed not to be impressed with it, declaring it to be diffuse and repetitious; but Lansing continued, nevertheless, to spend a great deal of time in attempting to refute it. During the course of his speech, Lansing declared that Hamilton had entertained different views at Philadelphia from those which he now advocated; and the ensuing warm personal altercation between the two gentlemen occupied the remainder of the legislative day (June 28) and a considerable portion of the next (Monday, June 30).[173]

The altercation between Lansing and Hamilton was confined to the two men. It concerned a question of fact which Yates, who had kept a record of the Philadephia Convention, settled

---

[168] *Ibid.*, p. 355.   [170] *Ibid.*   [172] *Ibid.*, p. 359.
[169] *Ibid.*, p. 358.   [171] *Ibid.*   [173] *Ibid.*, p. 376.

in Hamilton's favor.[174] Once the point was settled and the debates resumed, the body continued to discuss Hamilton's speech. While Melancton Smith did not accept the speech, he was obviously impressed by it; [175] and on July 2 Gilbert Livingston, of the Antifederalists, was still engaged in the attempt to refute Hamilton's argument concerning concurrent jurisdiction.[176] In fact, after having taken a slight excursion into personalities between Robert R. and Gilbert Livingston, the convention was still discussing the sword and the purse when, on July 2, news was received of the ratification of the Constitution by Virginia. The proposition for debate had changed again.

THE THIRD PERIOD

Governor Clinton was making a speech when Colonel Livingston arrived at the Convention Hall carrying the news of Virginia's ratification. The news "occasioned such a buz through the House, that little of his Excellency's Speech was heard." [177] A number of Federalists promptly held a meeting to congratulate one another and to fire ten cannon in honor of the ten adopting states.[178] If the news from New Hampshire had failed to convince the Antifederalists, the news from Virginia necessarily brought some change in their attitude, for the real proposition for debate, even though it was not stated, now became "Resolved: That the state of New York should join the United States of America with reservations." The Federalists adopted

---

[174] Hamilton "accused Mr. Lansing's insinuation as improper, unbecoming and uncandid. Mr. Lansing rose, and with much spirit resented the imputation. He made an appeal to Judge Yates, who had taken notes in the Federal Convention for a proof of Mr. Hamilton's expressions. This produced some disorder in the Committee, and the Chairman was obliged to call to order. A motion for adjournment put an end to the altercation." *Daily Advertiser*, July 4, 1788. Another description of the altercation is found in a letter from Christopher P. Yates to Abraham Yates, June 30, 1788. New York Public Library.

[175] Elliot, *op. cit.*, II, 378.   [177] *Daily Advertiser*, July 8, 1788.
[176] *Ibid.*, p. 387.   [178] *Ibid.*

a policy of watchful waiting, and on Thursday, July 3, the
convention made unexpected progress, chiefly owing to the
Federalists's taking no notice of any amendments offered and
refusing to engage in debate. It is said that "the silence of the
Federalists seemed to confound the opposition, who in about
two hours, having offered all the amendments they could *then*
think of, moved for an adjournment in order that they might
have time to prepare *more* against the next morning." [179]

Again, on Friday, July 4, and on Saturday, July 5, the
Antifederalists proposed many amendments of which the Federalists took little notice.[180] The convention had now got to
the second section of the third article concerning the judiciary.
An observer at the convention noted at this time that "since
the news from Virginia, notwithstanding the proposition of
amendments . . . there appears to be a disposition in the opposition, rather friendly to the Constitution." [181] On Monday,
July 7, the convention met and finished going through the Constitution by paragraphs; after the last amendment had been
proposed, Mr. Lansing submitted for the consideration of the
house an extensive declaration of rights. The convention then
adjourned, in order to give the proposers of amendments time
to organize them.[182] On the following day the convention met
and, having no business, adjourned until Wednesday, July 9,
at twelve o'clock.[183] But on Wednesday there was still no business and the convention again adjourned.[184]

On Thursday, July 10, the *Daily Advertiser* published in
New York the news that the Continental Congress had voted
to put the new Constitution into operation, Mr. Yates of New
York having cast the only vote against it. But still the convention at Poughkeepsie came to no terms. A Federalist observer
at the convention, however, was hopeful, even if mistaken.
"Our labors," he said, "are now drawing to a conclusion." He

---

[179] *Ibid.*
[180] *Ibid.*, July 9, 1788.
[181] *Ibid.*

[182] *Ibid.*, July 10, 1788.
[183] *Ibid.*
[184] *Ibid.*, July 15, 1788.

was of the opinion, perhaps correctly, that the Antifederalists had been convinced by the arguments of the Federalists, but were too proud to confess it.[185] At any rate, Lansing came forward with the final terms which the Antifederalists were willing to accept. These terms involved the acceptance of four conditional amendments, providing that there should be no standing army in time of peace without the consent of two-thirds of Congress, that no direct taxes should be levied, that the use of the New York state militia should be limited, and that the national government should have no right to interfere in elections. Lansing proposed a committee of both parties to consider the phrasing of amendments, but the committee was unable to come to any conclusion, since Jay insisted that the erasure of *conditional* was preliminary to any discussion. However, Melancton Smith and Samuel Jones were found in the committee to be somewhat moderate in their state of mind.[186]

Jay, on the morning of Friday, July 11, "brought forward the grand question, by a resolution for adopting the Constitution; he spoke forcibly, and commanded great attention." [187] The chancellor and the chief justice were strong for the resolution, but Smith, Lansing, and the governor opposed it. During the close of the week the Antifederalists had met frequently in caucus. Some of them were still for rejecting the Constitution, but others, more moderate, insisted on an adoption with conditions.[188] Probably the knowledge of this situation within the Antifederalist ranks caused Jay to introduce his motion which led, on Saturday, July 12, to an extended debate on the main proposition of ratifying the Constitution.[189] Hamilton opened the debate and "in a most argumentative and impassioned address, demonstrated that the propositions before the Committee, would be a total rejection of the Constitution." He opened with an exordium in which he described the various

---

[185] *Daily Advertiser*, July 14, 1788.   [188] *Ibid.*, July 16, 1788.
[186] *Ibid.*, July 15, 1788.   [189] *Ibid.*
[187] *Ibid.*

attempts which had been made to prejudice the minds of the convention against him personally.[190] He called on the world to point out a single instance in which he had deviated from the line of public and private duty. "The pathetic appeal fixed the silent sympathetic gaze of the spectators, and made them all his own." After his exordium, Hamilton proceeded, according to his observer, to refute the fallacious reasonings of his opposition. In true Hamiltonian fashion, he showed first, from the series of papers on which the convention was founded, that the convention had no power to make a provisional adoption of the Constitution; second, that under the new Constitution, the new government had no power to accept a provisional entrance; and third, that even if the new government had the power to accept a conditional membership in the new Union, the other states would never submit to granting conditions.[191]

"Mr. Hamilton," a reporter observed, "after recapitulating his arguments in a concise and cogent manner, entreated the Convention . . . to make a solemn pause, and weigh well what they were about to do . . . on a subject so infinitely important." The reporter, obviously a man of Federalist leanings, continued his account by noting that the

orator then closed his address, and received from every unprejudiced spectator the murmur of admiration and applause.—Very different was the effect upon his opposers.—They sickened at the splendor of his triumph.[192]

On Monday, July 14, the Antifederalists called for the question, but they were overruled by a motion, made by Hamilton and seconded by G. Livingston, that the question be postponed until the following day, when Hamilton brought forward a

[190] One of the charges Hamilton had to answer was the statement, "industriously circulated," that he was a man of such talents as to carry any cause. McKesson, "Notes of the Proceedings of the Convention." New York Historical Society.
[191] *Daily Advertiser,* July 16, 1788.
[192] *Ibid.*

plan similar to that by which Virginia had ratified, except that it contained more declarations.[193] Considerable debate took place upon Hamilton's proposal, much of it repetitious, and the decision was again postponed. On Wednesday, July 16, Judge Hobart, acting for the Federalists, brought forward a motion to adjourn the convention and report for further instructions to the constituency.[194] It was Hobart's motion which really put the Antifederalists's difficult position in its true light.[195] The Federalists were now sufficiently hopeful to be willing to go again to the people, but the Antifederalists had no inclination to leave the question unsettled or to stir up further strife. In a parliamentary sense, Hobart's motion marks off a fourth period of the convention.

THE FOURTH PERIOD

The actual, though unstated, proposition before the house during the fourth period was "Resolved: That the state of New York should join the United States of America without reservations," with the Federalists carrying the affirmative. On the morning of July 17 Hamilton made a speech, presumably to Judge Hobart's motion for adjournment.[196] Actually the speech seems to have been designed to secure support not for adjournment, but for the adoption of the Constitution. In the peroration of his stirring speech, Hamilton admitted that distinguished patriots were to be found on both sides, but he pointed out also that most of them were for the government. Hancock, he said,

[193] *Daily Advertiser*, July 17, 1788; July 22, 1788.
[194] *Ibid.*, July 21, 1788.
[195] Before Hobart's motion was offered, Abraham Yates had confessed his apprehension that the Federalists might seek an adjournment. Yates feared that the separating of the Antifederalist group would lay the members open to management by the newspapers. Yates to Abraham G. Lansing, June 29, 1788. New York Public Library.
[196] Gilbert Livingston, "Reports of the Poughkeepsie Convention." See also *Daily Advertiser*, July 21, 1788.

acquiesces in a situation which might tempt him not to support the Constitution; Adams, who first conceived the bold idea of independence, is for it; Governor Livingston, a republican, is for it; Dickinson and Franklin are for it; General Washington, disinterested patriot, in whom all parties admit confidence, is for it. At the close of the war, at the head of a discontented army, did Washington take advantage of the army or of the country? No, he proved himself a patriot; and he has come forward again, hazarding his harvest of glory, because he has seen that the work he has been engaged in is but half finished. Is it human nature, Hamilton inquired, to suppose that these good men should lose their virtue and acquiesce in a government which is dangerous to the liberties of the country?

It is impossible to know exactly what effect Hamilton's speech had upon the minds of his hearers. But it is at least interesting to learn that "he was powerful in his reasoning, and so persuasively eloquent and pathetic, that he drew tears from most of the audience." [197] But whatever the audience felt and thought, the motion to adjourn was lost, as Hamilton perhaps wished it to be. And immediately afterward the convention went again into a committee of the whole to consider a new proposal for amendment by Melancton Smith. Duane's motion that Hamilton's proposal for amendment be substituted in the convention for that of Melancton Smith was defeated.

On Friday, July 18, when the convention met, silence pervaded the house,[198] and, it being apparent that no one was ready for action, the convention adjourned for the day.[199] On

---

[197] *Daily Advertiser*, July 21, 1788.

[198] During this period, differences were growing among the Antifederalists. Lansing wrote on July 20, "Mr. Jones it is said is so much Intimidated by the Threats of the Federalists that he does not any more take an active part. Mr. Smith is—Likewise charged with some improper Steps—I cannot give Credit to what is alledged—but if it is true he has injured the cause of our Country more than any Federalist." Abraham G. Lansing to Abraham Yates, July 20, 1788. New York Public Library.

[199] *Ibid.*

Saturday, July 19, the house discussed Smith's new proposal for amendment and referred it to a committee for redrafting.[200]

When the convention met in a committee of the whole on Monday, July 21, Hamilton made a speech specifically concerning the amendment limiting the right of Congress to call out the militia.[201] He supposed that such a limitation was most impolitic, and Jay supported him. But Nathaniel Lawrence observed that the right of Congress to call out the state militia was a source of much uneasiness among the constituency. The result was that the "amendment was carried by all the Antis on one side, and all the Federalists on the other." [202] The discussion of Smith's proposals continued, Hamilton being strong in opposition to them. But his reasoning was of no avail. The amendments concerned were all carried by the entire voice of the opposition. On Tuesday, July 22, the convention, in committee of the whole, continued the consideration of the amendments proposed by Melancton Smith. Most of them were carried without any debate.[203] But on Wednesday, July 23, when the committee had finally finished the consideration of all the amendments and began to look into the proposition of adopting the Constitution with the conditions annexed, Samuel Jones came forward to move that the words *"in full confidence"* be inserted in the main motion instead of the words *"upon condition."* [204] The effect of Jones' motion was to grant the Federalist contention that the ratification should be final and absolute.

Melancton Smith rose and declared his determination to vote against a condition. Not limiting himself to acceding to the Federalist cause, Smith gave a substantial speech favoring the adoption of the amendment:

---

[200] *Daily Advertiser*, July 25, 1788. Gilbert Livingston's "Reports of the Poughkeepsie Convention" should be consulted for the period from July 16 to July 26.

[201] *Daily Advertiser*, July 25, 1788.

[202] *Ibid.*   [203] *Ibid.*   [204] *Ibid.*, July 28, 1788.

He was as thoroughly convinced then as he ever had been, that the Constitution was radically defective—amendments to it had always been the object of his pursuit, and until Virginia came in, he had reason to believe they might have been obtained previous to the operation of the Government. He was now satisfied they could not, and it was equally the dictate of reason and duty to quit his first ground, and advance so far as that they might be received into the Union. . . . On the first suggestion of the plan then under consideration, he thought it might have answered the purpose; but from the reasonings of gentlemen in opposition to it, and whose opinions alone would deservedly have vast weight in the national councils, as well as from the sentiments of persons abroad, he was now persuaded the proposition would not be received, however doubtful it might appear, considered merely as an abstract and speculative question. . . . He then placed in a striking and affecting light, the situation of the State in case we should not be received by Congress. . . . He therefore concluded that it was no more than a proper discharge of his public duty, as well as the most advisable way of obtaining the great end of his opposition, to vote against any proposition which would not be received as a ratification of the Constitution.[205]

Gilbert Livingston and Zephaniah Platt joined Smith and Jones in supporting the amendment, but Clinton said he stood there as a representative of Ulster County and he would vote for conditions.[206] Sixty members were present, besides the chairman; thirty-one voted for the amendment and twenty-nine against it. The Federalist fight had at last been won.

But on the next day, July 24, Lansing, who was still unconvinced, made a motion providing for the right to withdraw from the new government under certain conditions. Hamilton and Jay spoke against Lansing's motion, and Hamilton "read part of a letter from a gentleman of high public distinction [James Madison], containing in explicit terms . . . that the

[205] The reporter commented, "I was so well pleased with Smith's speech, that I have given you the substance of it with fidelity, and as nearly as I could in his own language." *Daily Advertiser*, July 28, 1788.
[206] *Ibid.*

reservation would amount to a conditional ratification, and would not be received by Congress."[207] Duane and Livingston supported Hamilton in expressing the hope that the convention might now conclude in harmony, and so it did. On Friday, July 25, the question on the motion as amended was brought up, with Smith speaking for the motion, and the committee of the whole voted thirty-one to twenty-eight for the Constitution. Finally, the house accepted the committee's report, and by a vote of thirty to twenty-seven ratified the Federal Constitution.[208] The thirty men who voted for the Constitution included eighteen of the nineteen Federalists (Richard Morris not voting) and twelve of the Antifederalists, as follows: John D'Witt, Gilbert Livingston, Zephaniah Platt, Melancton Smith, Jesse Woodhull, Stephen Carman, Samuel Jones, Nathaniel Lawrence, John Schenk, Jonathan N. Havens, Henry Scudder, and John Smith. Seven Antifederalists who, according to report, would have voted for the Constitution if necessary, abstained from casting their ballots. These men were Dirck Swart, Anthony Ten Eyck, Peter Vroman, Ezra Thompson, Christopher P. Yates, David Hedges, and George Clinton. On Saturday, July 26, after having considered the Constitution by paragraphs in continuous session for nearly six weeks, the delegates passed the motion to adjourn *sine die*.

The adjournment of the convention at Poughkeepsie marked the close of an epoch in American political history and gave the signal for the construction of a new social order. At the same time, it concluded, for New York and for its sister states as well, one of the most brilliant national discussions of which we have record and closed a chapter in the history of American oratory.

[207] *Daily Advertiser*, July 28, 1788.
[208] Several members were out of doors, but, according to Childs's correspondent, they were all for the Federalists. *Daily Advertiser*, July 28, 1788.

VII. HAMILTON'S WAY OF
PERSUASION

. . . HE IS *rather a convincing speaker than a blazing orator.*—
WILLIAM PIERCE.

THE RATIFICATION at Poughkeepsie was considered to be a
victory for the Federalist forces and a personal triumph
for Alexander Hamilton, who received the honor of carrying
the certificate of ratification to the Congress in New York.[1] The
"Federal Ship Hamilton" graced the parade in the victory
march of the Federalists.[2] It was Alexander Hamilton whose
name appeared in the songs of celebration.

> Behold Columbia's empire rise,
> On freedom's solid base to stand;
> Supported by propitious skies,
> And seal'd by her deliverer's hand.
>
> *Chorus*
>
> Raise, Columbia, raise thy voice,
> Union is thy noble choice.
>
> .   .   .
>
> The hero, statesman and the sage,
> Matur'd this noblest work of man;
> And HAMILTON's instructive page
> Illumes his fellow-patriot's plan.

---

[1] "Col. Hamilton who has brought with him the ratification of the
Constitution, . . . will have the honor, this day, to present it to Congress." *Albany Journal*, Aug. 4, 1788.
[2] *Daily Advertiser*, Aug. 2, 1788.

Raise, Columbia, raise thy voice,
Union is thy noble choice.[3]

The question whether the popular opinion was correct in the simplicity with which it attributed victory to the Federalists and triumph to their leader is one which will warrant reflection, for it has a bearing not only on Hamilton's oratory but also upon the very nature of persuasion. It will be wise, however, to defer an answer until the speaker, the audience, the occasion, and the speeches have been reconsidered.[4]

THE SPEAKER

The student of public speaking, like the layman, is interested in the orator as a man; and, in the case of Alexander Hamilton, in the development of those powers which enabled the obscure boy who came as a stranger to the city of New York in 1773 to become, fifteen years later, the dominant character in a significant parliamentary struggle for the establishment of a new government for the Commonwealth.

It is possible to characterize the speaker and, in some measure, to trace the development of his powers. As a speaker, Alexander Hamilton represents the orator in the classical tradition, the child of the marriage of rhetoric and politics. Oratory, Hamilton thought, was a means of communication; but it was a means of communication to the end of energizing knowledge for an audience. And the knowledge which Hamilton wished to energize related almost without exception to politics, the nation, and the state. Even though Hamilton's concept of oratory is unstated, it is to be found in the text of his speeches and the testimony of his witnesses. Oratory, written or spoken, was not in Hamilton's idea and practice a vehicle of display; it was a social force, to be used like other social forces and even in conjunction with them.

[3] *Albany Journal*, Aug. 4, 1788.   [4] *Infra.*, p. 190.

Equipped with the utilitarian concept of oratory, Hamilton also possessed other qualifications for the role he had to play in the convention at Poughkeepsie. A man of notable personal charm, which he was well disposed to use among those whom he considered to be his peers; a veteran of the Revolution with a reputation for bravery under fire; an established citizen of the Commonwealth, connected by marriage with one of its first families; a practicing attorney, with a wide acquaintance and with many friends—Hamilton was an accepted member of the aristocracy of New York. But Hamilton's most distinguished characteristic as a man, and thus as an orator, appears to every critic who approaches him to be the fertility of his mind and the rare quality of his insight into probable courses of action. The combination of exceptional intelligence and tireless energy which observers both prejudiced and unprejudiced have agreed in noting was not an unmixed blessing to the orator; for the evidences of his genius, even in 1788, before he had set the people against him by his funding measures, by his plan for paying the soldiers of the Revolution, and by his suppression of the Whisky Insurrection, made him the object of some suspicion. It was felt that "ingenious men may say ingenious things," and Hamilton, known to his fellow delegates as a brilliant man, was nevertheless suspected to a degree for that very reason in an attitude which people of honest but humble mentality, correctly or incorrectly, not infrequently display toward those of high intelligence. If Alexander Hamilton was in a measure an alien in the group at Poughkeepsie, it was rather because of his brilliance than because of any other circumstances. Often a convincing speaker, not ordinarily a "blazing orator," Hamilton could never in any circumstance achieve the character of "a plain, blunt man."

To indicate in summary the development of Hamilton's powers during the fifteen years from 1773 to 1788 is another problem and a more difficult one; for Hamilton's growth seems to have been lateral rather than vertical. His early pamphlets thus exhibit a quality of political and rhetorical sophistication hardly exceeded by his final efforts, and the evidences of his development are chiefly in breadth of view and extent of experience rather than in depth of insight. His change during the fifteen years from 1773 to 1788 thus appears as one of maturation of abilities already uncommonly mature and of the addition, in school, camp, and legislature, to those learnings which he had already acquired from real situations in home and countinghouse.

Although it is possible to characterize Hamilton as a speaker and to describe his development, it is hardly possible fully to relate his developed powers to any single effective agent. One will note, to be sure, his salutary experiences in Cruger's store, his interest in reading, and his education at King's College, particularly in rhetoric and oratory. Yet it would be indiscreet to relate Hamilton's abilities too closely to such agencies, for many youths of his time had similar experiences with dissimilar outcome. No doubt his ability as a speaker in 1788 was directly associated with his writing of letters and pamphlets, particularly *The Federalist*, with his previous experience as a parliamentary and forensic speaker, and even with his military service. But such an accounting merely defers an answer to the essential question and leaves open to conjecture the reasons for his unusual performances in polemic and forensic contest. Perhaps the most that can be said with wisdom concerning the education of.the orator is that following the experiences which he knew in school, camp, courtroom, and legislative halls, he was, when he appeared at the convention in Poughkeepsie, a remarkable man and, like his opponent, Melancton Smith, one "formed for investigations and debate."

THE AUDIENCE

But it may well be inquired whether Hamilton was more remarkable than his audience. For, although a large section of the population of New York in 1788 did not rise to the audience level, a highly significant group of men found participation in politics to be a primary concern. To these members of Hamilton's remote audience the discussion of public questions was undertaken for no light or sentimental reasons, but for the sternly practical purpose of protecting themselves in their rights, privileges, and perquisites. Politics and the discussion of public questions were commonly undertaken frankly from the point of view of self-interest, enlightened or otherwise; and the motives appealed to were as often as not soundly based on economic realism. Considered as a whole, Hamilton's remote audience was unsentimental in attitude and highly sophisticated in the discussion of public affairs. This audience of determined realists studied the constitution proposed by Hamilton and his colleagues thoroughly and discussed it pro and con, considered every line of it, and formed their judgments on the basis of their political experience and their conjectures concerning the future. For the future, they feared most of all a leviathan state which might raise their taxes,[5] set up lucrative offices of government,[6] and call their sons out of the state to fight a foreign war,[7] perhaps in Massachusetts or Pennsylvania. And in spite of every effort that Alexander Hamilton and his colleagues could put forth in the way of persuasion, the citizens decided, with George Clinton and his party, that the proposed constitution was an instrument of tyranny; and they sent to the convention at Poughkeepsie a great majority of representatives who opposed its ratification.

[5] Elliot, *The Debates in the Several State Conventions*, II, p. 338, *et passim*.

[6] "This is an extensive country, increasing in population and growing in consequence. Very many lucrative offices will be in the grant of the government, which will be objects of avarice and ambition. How easy will it be to gain over a sufficient number, in the bestowment of offices, to promote the views and the purposes of those who grant them!" Speech of Melancton Smith, June 21, 1788. Elliot, *op. cit.*, II, 249.

[7] *Daily Advertiser*, July 25, 1788.

Having been defeated by the vote of the people, Hamilton, as Federalist leader, had still to deal with the people's representatives. In the assembled convention he observed that there were nineteen members of his own group and forty-six members of his opposition. His difficult audience problem—to secure votes from his opposition without losing any from his own ranks —was somewhat simplified by the unity of the Federalists and the developing disunity of the Antifederalists. In the debates Hamilton found a skillful opponent in Melancton Smith, the floor leader of the opposition, and a subtle collaborator in John Jay.

Hamilton and Smith carried the burden of the debate throughout the convention, for most of the delegates were silent, and of those who spoke only a few spoke often or at length. The debates became to a certain degree an endurance contest, with both parties holding out for advantages by negotiation, compromise, or arrangement; and Dirck Wynkoop, the Antifederalist, had reason to complain, as he did, that "many arguments have been thrown out—that we should forget from whence we came . . . we are brought down from one point to another till we are brought to an unconditional adoption." [8] Indeed, the Federalist observer who wrote to Mr. Childs after the Constitution had finally been ratified was quite correct when he said the "Constitution has, comparatively speaking, undergone an ordeal torture, and been preserved, as by fire." [9]

Despite the variations in abilities and temperament of individuals in the group and despite the continued silence of many of the members, the audience which Hamilton addressed at Poughkeepsie was one which set a high standard of parliamentary excellence. The convention at Poughkeepsie in its audience aspects demonstrated the peculiar quality of common sense, of reason, of sportsmanship, or of whatever it is that enables men to settle their differences on the plane of persuasion rather than

[8] Gilbert Livingston, "Reports of the Poughkeepsie Convention."
[9] *Daily Advertiser,* July 28, 1788.

at the level of force. Henry Wisner, veteran legislator and consistent opponent of Federalism,[10] explaining in the same speech why he had to vote against the Constitution and how he would do all he could to make the result satisfactory to the people, was an exemplar of parliamentary government.[11] George Clinton, bitter in defeat, yet volunteering to enforce the decision of the convention and to support it before the people, was a genuine practitioner of government by persuasion.[12] Indeed one who looks closely at the Antifederalist group will observe that it is a great simplification to say that Melancton Smith was beaten and, like all simplifications, one containing an element of falsity. Concerning Smith's change of mind, James Kent, the eyewitness and constant observer, expressed a sensible, if somewhat partisan, point of view:

I always considered that the gentlemen who made this memorable and unbought sacrifice of prejudice, error, and pride on the altar of patriotism and their country's welfare, were entitled to the highest honor. It was quite an heroic effort to quit such a leader as Governor Clinton, and such men as Yates and Lansing, who had been delegates to the General Convention, even though it was to follow their own convictions.[13]

Considered as audience, Melancton Smith and the members of his group, together with the Federalists and the determined Antifederalists, constituted a body which cannot fail to interest the informed student of persuasion.

THE OCCASION

Neither the speaker nor the audience need be of greater interest to the informed person than the occasion in which they

[10] Spaulding, *New York in the Critical Period*, p. 233.
[11] *Daily Advertiser*, July 28, 1788.
[12] *Ibid.*
[13] Kent, *Memoirs*, p. 311.

participated. As the participants themselves were well aware, the occasion of their controversy was one of moment. Hamilton's first words in *The Federalist* explained to his readers that on their decision hinged "the fate of an empire in many respects the most interesting in the world." [14] And he continued by calling to attention the accepted opinion of the time:

It has been frequently remarked that it seems to have been reserved to the people of this country, by their conduct and example, to decide the important question, whether societies of men are really capable or not of establishing good government from reflection and choice, or whether they are forever destined to depend for their political constitutions on accident and force. If there be any truth in the remark, the crisis at which we are arrived may with propriety be regarded as the era in which that decision is to be made; and a wrong election of the part we shall act may, in this view, deserve to be considered as the general misfortune of mankind.[15]

The perspective of history will hardly alter Hamilton's prejudgment of the importance of his occasion; and if what he says is true, the speeches which he delivered in convention are all the more significant.

THE SPEECHES

The available evidence concerning Hamilton's speeches at Poughkeepsie can be related to the speaker's method of delivery, to the text of his utterance, and to the effectiveness of the speaker.

Hamilton's delivery was vigorous, animated, and energetic.[16] His method of dealing with his subject involved thorough analysis, complete examination, and a full revelation of the sequence of his argument to his audience. The subject matter of his speeches was based not upon a superficial knowledge of his

---

[14] *The Federalist*, No. 1. Edward Mead Earle, ed., p. 3.
[15] *Ibid.*
[16] Kent, *Memoirs*, p. 305.

materials, but upon a comprehension of his audience and upon a complete investigation of the evidence within the scope of his argument. "He never omitted to meet, examine, and discover the strength or weakness, the truth or falsehood of every proposition with which he had to contend." [17] Hamilton's purposes were clear, his preparation was easy and adequate, though often limited, in the immediate situation. The organization of his speeches was systematic, and the arrangement was consistently in terms of his hearers. Though Hamilton always attempted to dispose the audience favorably toward himself and toward the argument which he had to present, the element of thoughtfulness was so dominant in all of his speeches as to represent him primarily as a man of judgment.

In the development of his appeal to reason, Hamilton demonstrated a surpassing skill in extempore refutation. Some of the most striking instances of his argument in refutation were developed in the course of strenuous debate, in reply to arguments which his opponents had prepared in advance. In reasoned analysis, his first reliance was on the seeking and exposing of causal relation. During the course of his speeches he exemplified the use of almost every type of refutation and special argumentative method. But perhaps the most distinctive feature of Hamilton's approach to the problem of persuasion was that of his completeness. Characteristically, Hamilton's development in the argumentative situation was diffuse and versatile. He was rarely content with a single answer to an opponent or with stressing a single point in support of his own position. He left one point of attack only to return at another point. In proceeding by versatile methods, Hamilton was careful to validate his conclusions by the use of acceptable evidence, depending more often upon items of fact known to his hearers than upon appeal to authority.

Furthermore, he was careful always to present himself to the audience in the light of one who should be believed, and a

[17] *Ibid.*

significant portion of his speeches was subtly devoted to establishing ethical character. In style, Hamilton was not inclined to metaphor. His speaking was simple rather than bombastic, straightforward rather than hyperbolic, convincing rather than merely expressive.

The primary problem of the orator, however, is one of communication to effect an end, and no speaker can ever be far removed from the question of expediency. One is entitled, therefore, to ask the following question: In the dramatic occasion at Poughkeepsie, what was the probable effect of Hamilton's rhetoric?

The forces which played on Melancton Smith, Samuel Jones, and the other adherents to the Antifederalist cause were so many and so varied as to defy complete analysis. Conversation, negotiation, personal appeals, the speeches of Harison, Robert Livingston, Jay, and other Federalist leaders, the movement of events, perhaps some sense of irritation with Governor Clinton, or even countless other unknown factors may have influenced the final decision of Melancton Smith to subscribe to the Federalist cause and to lead some of his party with him. Nevertheless, some factors concerning the effectiveness of Hamilton's speeches can be suggested.

THE EFFECTIVENESS OF HAMILTON'S RHETORIC

In the first place, Hamilton's speeches had a unifying value, a quality of effectiveness easily obscured in the total persuasive situation. The debater must do more than convince his opposition; indeed his first concern is to persuade his own followers, to keep them united, and to maintain their interest and allegiance. Neglecting for the moment Hamilton's effect upon the hostile or neutral section of his audience, immediate or remote, one observes that Hamilton, as the Federalist leader, was effective with his own forces. His speeches provided common ground for the Federalists and gave them renewed confidence

in their position. Even the Antifederalists conceded his eloquence and the power of his leadership.[18]

In the second place, Hamilton's speeches had a high time
value. The function of the speaker in a controversial situation,
particularly when events are moving in his favor, is sometimes
that of delaying or preventing precipitate action. This attitude
should not be confused with the filibuster. There was nothing
resembling a filibuster at Poughkeepsie and, indeed, the Federalists were not in a position to follow such a course had they
desired to do so. But Hamilton, as generalissimo of the Federalist forces, encouraged every inclination to full discussion in
the convention. Hamilton's view of the situation was confirmed
by at least one Antifederalist, who wrote

. . . I am inclined to believe that our Friends *have* or *are* ready to
consent to debate the Constitution by Paragraphs.—If this is determined on, the Business will unavoidably be retarded to the disappoint-
ment of our Country Friends with whom it is now the Busy Season.
—This Circumstance the Federal Gentlemen will no doubt avail
themselves of, and procrastinate the Business as long as they possibly
can.[19]

In the same letter, Lansing wrote, ". . . I am apprehensive
we will eventually be injured by delay,—notwithstanding the
decided majority—the determination of Massachusetts has
shewn us what Federal Chicanery can Effect." [20]

In the third place, Hamilton's speeches, along with the plan
of the Federalists, had a defensive value. One goal of the Federalists was to secure the unconditional adoption of the Constitution; another was to prevent either an outright rejection

[18] Tillinghast to John Lamb, June 21, 1788. New York Historical
Society. De Witt Clinton to Thomas Greenleaf, June 22, 1788. Columbia
University Library. McKesson, "Notes of the Proceedings of the Con-
vention." New York Historical Society.

[19] Abraham G. Lansing to Abraham Yates, June 22, 1788. New York
Public Library.

[20] *Ibid.*

or a conditional adoption. Hamilton's speeches throughout represent defense as well as attack; they were made in an effort to prevent the clear majority against ratification from being registered as the final decision of the convention. He was thus supporting the watchful-waiting policy of the Federalists, which culminated, after the news of Virginia's ratification had reached the house, in the motion for a recess. Early in the session, Yates had anticipated the Federalist attack:

The principle object the other side have in view is to get an adjournment which I confess is the only apprehension I have For if they can obtain an adjournment the Members During that time will be Seperated and open to their management both in the Newspapers—and the state the whole time in Convulsions.[21]

When the motion for adjournment was actually proposed, Lansing analyzed the situation:

If this Measure should take place, [adjournment or recess] all the Exertions we have made and the anxiety we have experienced for the Liberty of our Country will end in nothing—much as it is against my wish to adopt the Constitution without previous amendments—I should prefer the Virginia Form to an adjournment—for we will have to go over all the Ground of the Election again without any prospect of Success—The Baneful Manor Interest will be exerted to obtain Instructions to the Delegates, and the poor deluded well meaning Yeomanry of our Country, not having it in their power to follow the dictates of their own Consciences, will be compelled to sign these instructions to keep well with their Masters.[22]

If Hamilton was not actually the leader in the movement to allow the resolving factors of time to prevent a rejection, as his expressed policy would indicate, he was certainly one of the

[21] Abraham Yates to Abraham G. Lansing, June 29, 1788. New York Public Library.

[22] Abraham G. Lansing to Abraham Yates, July 20, 1788. New York Public Library.

tacticians in charge, and to that degree was one of the authors of the parliamentary success of the Federalists.[23]

In the fourth place, Hamilton's speeches were effective in their association with events. No one knew better than Alexander Hamilton the relation between oratory and the force of circumstance. Hamilton was a field marshal of persuasion rather than a corporal, and, knowing both the value and the limitations of oratory, his tactics in persuasion were to use the ratification of New Hampshire and Virginia, with every other device possible, as a means to a favorable result. The whole scope and range of Hamilton's argumentative plan best represent his power in the organization of effective persuasion. One is reminded of the sentences inscribed in the youthful captain's Pay-Book:

As a general marches at the head of his troops, so ought wise politicians, if I dare use the expression, to march at the head of affairs; insomuch that they ought not to await *the event*, to know what measures to take; but the measures which they have taken ought to produce the *event*.[24]

Finally, Hamilton's speeches were effectively established in the line of persuasion. Melancton Smith's own statement offers testimony that Hamilton had convinced him not only of the expediency of surrendering from a position of recalcitrance, but also of the earnestness of his opposition.[25] A specific point in this connection is the ground on which Smith finally capitulated. Neither Melancton Smith nor Samuel Jones was convinced of the merits of the Constitution—nor were the Antifederalists generally.[26] Although the early speeches of

[23] Hamilton to Madison, May 19, 1788. Alexander Hamilton, *Works*, Lodge, ed., IX, 430.

[24] "Extracts from Demosthenes's Orations. Philippic I." Alexander Hamilton, *Works*, John Church Hamilton, ed., I, 6. Quoted from *supra*, p. 49.

[25] *Daily Advertiser*, July 28, 1788. See also *supra*, p. 179.

[26] On January 14, following the adjournment of the convention at Poughkeepsie, Smith wrote to Gilbert Livingston as follows: ". . . You

Hamilton may have had some effect on Smith, the ground upon which Smith finally capitulated was that which Hamilton described in his speeches of July 11 and July 17, during the third and fourth periods of the convention. The issues were, in fact, those which had been mentioned publicly, even before the convention opened, in the statement that "the grand question now is, not whether the Federal Constitution is a good one, but whether it will be for the interest of this State to belong to the Union, or to enjoy the benefits of independence?"[27] Without being convinced on the first issue, that of the merits of the Constitution, Smith was yet willing to surrender to Hamilton on the second, that of the expediency of ratifying it. At the same time, he established his intention of urging amendments to secure his position, so that the real point of his capitulation was in agreeing to ratify in advance of specific official commitments for his proposed amendments.

Therefore, even though Melancton Smith acknowledged the force of Hamilton's arguments and their agency in effecting his change of mind,[28] it is not good judgment to say uncritically and without explanation that Hamilton vanquished Smith in

---

may rest assured that a number of us retain the same sentiments respecting it [the Constitution] we ever did." Smith to Gilbert Livingston, Jan. 14, 1789. New York State Library. On Aug. 8, 1788, Abraham Yates signed a formal statement, which was witnessed by Ezra L'Hommedieu, Egbert Benson, and Alexander Hamilton. It said in part, "Being confident that the Constitution for the general government in its present form will be destructive to the liberties of the People: and as Such by every means to be avoided as one of the greatest of all Evils: and that the convention of New York in adopting it without express conditional amendments have been mistaken Both in their expectations and apprehensions." New York Public Library. Abraham Lansing described one basis for the acceptance of the accomplished fact: ". . . upon the whole I believe or *endeavour* to believe that it is best so both in a political and private light—for had the Constitution been so adopted as that Congress would not accept it—yourself and our Friends would have incurred blame & Censure if any serious commotions had ensued." Abraham G. Lansing to Abraham Yates, Aug. 3, 1788. New York Public Library.

[27] *Daily Advertiser*, June 14, 1788.
[28] *Daily Advertiser*, July 28, 1788.

debate, any more than it is wise to suppose that the speeches of
Alexander Hamilton were the only persuasive factors which
need to be considered.

Yet Hamilton's speeches were effective and would have been
so, even if they had not been associated with complete success.
For in the Aristotelian theory, absolute persuasion is not required of the orator. Complete and unqualified persuasion is a
sophistic rather than an Aristotelian ideal. What is required of
the orator in Aristotle's view is that he shall be persuasive—not
that he shall accomplish an absolute. Their being associated with
success heightens the dramatic interest in the speeches which
Hamilton delivered at Poughkeepsie; but their association with
success does not represent the only judgment, nor the final one,
in their criticism. If the tellers, on the final ballot, had found
twenty-seven members voting for the unconditional ratification
of the Constitution and thirty members voting against it, instead
of finding, as was actually the case, thirty members voting for
it and twenty-seven members voting against it, Alexander Hamilton's speeches would still have been remarkable for their sustained cogency, their organization of refutation, their vigor and
animation in delivery, their straightforward and convincing
presentation, and for their effectiveness as well.

Aristotle's favorite analogy between the speaker and the
physician [29] can be carried out in point. The physician is not
required to effect a cure; he is required only to treat the patient
with all the skill at his command. Likewise, the orator is not
required to effect complete persuasion. He is required only to
discover and to present as best he can the line of argument
adapted to his hearers. The physician and the orator should
thus be praised for the high quality of their performances,
rather than for any immediate success following their efforts;
and, likewise, they should be reprehended for the poor quality
of their performances, rather than for any immediate failure
following their efforts. The event is in the hands of the gods.

[29] Aristotle, *Rhetoric*, 1356b, 1361b.

One word more should be said about the effective quality of Hamilton's speeches. In arriving at a judgment concerning an orator, one should ask not only "Was he persuasive?" One should ask also, "With whom was he persuasive and on what subjects?" Alexander Hamilton's speeches at Poughkeepsie concerned subjects of high seriousness in the life of the state. His audience, including his chief adversary, were hard-headed and experienced men of genuine political sophistication, inured to rhetoric and not easily moved. When, therefore, Melancton Smith declared himself convinced of the merits of Hamilton's arguments for unconditional ratification and was joined by eleven of his colleagues in leaving the Antifederalists to vote for unconditional ratification of the proposed constitution, the task of persuasion accomplished was, far from being an ordinary one, rather one of the most remarkable on record.

CONCLUSION

From the Aristotelian point of view, Hamilton's speeches at Poughkeepsie deserve the highest commendation. In fact, the whole—if so large a whole can be assessed—the speaker, the audience, the occasion, and the speeches, represent a culmination of circumstances, a concurrence of events which must always remain of unusual interest to the student of American oratory. The story of the young and brilliant Hamilton delivering speeches of emotional, ethical, and logical power to an audience of high political intelligence, on an occasion of dramatic interest, suggests inevitable conclusions. The first is that the biographer of Hamilton, when he appears, must be competent to understand the man as a public speaker in the long tradition of classical rhetoric, as an orator in the schools of Aristotle and Quintilian. The second is that the history of American oratory, if it should be written, must give ample room to the speeches of Alexander Hamilton. The third is that the critics of American life and literature should seek to discover the ways in which the American genius has expressed itself in communicative language as well as in fantasy and image, in rhetoric as well as in poetic. Perhaps there is a fourth. It may be that some historian, seeking to understand American culture, not as an established historic fact with all the resultants known, but as a series of problems in courses of action, will be willing to forget what comes after and to see the people of each successive generation engaged in the process of persuading one another to do what they want done. Such a historian will be likely to rediscover persuasion as a force, like wealth or generalship; and he may even discover a rhetorical theory of history at least as plausible as certain phases of the economic interpretation which seem to govern current historical thought.

SELECTED BIBLIOGRAPHY

PRIMARY SOURCES

I. PRINTED MATERIAL

Bibliographical Aids

Of the bibliographies used, the following, in addition to the special aids available in various libraries consulted, have been most serviceable:

Beers, Henry Putney, Bibliographies in American History: Guides to Materials for Research (New York, 1938).

Burchfield, Laverne, Student's Guide to Materials in Political Science (New York, 1935).

Dutcher, George Matthew, Henry Robinson Shipman, Sidney Bradshaw Fay, Augustus Hunt Shearer, and William Henry Allison, editors, A Guide to Historical Literature (New York, 1931).

Evans, Charles, American Bibliography (Chicago, 1903+), 12 vols.

Ford, Paul Leicester, Bibliography and Reference List of the History and Literature Relating to the Adoption of the Constitution of the United States (Brooklyn, 1888).

—— Bibliotheca Hamiltoniana; A List of Books Written by or Relating to Alexander Hamilton (New York, 1886).

—— Check List of Bibliographies, Catalogues, Reference-Lists, and Lists of Authorities of American Books and Subjects. (Based on Reference list to Bibliographies, catalogues, and reference lists on America in Library Journal, XIII, Feb.-Oct., 1888).

Greene, Evarts Boutell, and Richard Brandon Morris, A Guide to the Principal Sources of Early American History (1600-1800) in the City of New York (New York, 1929).

Sabin, Joseph, *et al.*, Bibliotheca Americana . . . (New York, 1868-1936).
Winsor, Justin, Narrative and Critical History of America (Boston, 1888-1889), 7 vols.

Public Documents and State Papers

Childs, Francis, editor, The Debates and Proceedings of the Constitutional Convention of the State of New-York Assembled at Poughkeepsie on the 17th of June, 1788 . . . (New York, 1788).
Elliot, Jonathan, editor, The Debates in the Several State Conventions on the Adoption of the Federal Constitution . . . (5 vols., Philadelphia, 1891).
Farrand, Max, editor, The Records of the Federal Convention of 1787 (3 vols., New Haven, 1911).
Hamilton, Alexander, Report of the Secretary of the Treasury to the House of Representatives . . ., United States Treasury Department, January 9, 1790 (New York, 1790).
State of New York, Journal of the Convention of the State of New York Held at Poughkeepsie, in Dutchess County, the 17th of June, 1788. Poughkeepsie: Printed by Nicholas Power, a few rods East from the Court-house.

Writings of Public Men

Adams, John, Works of John Adams, Second President of the United States: with a Life of the Author, . . . etc. Charles Francis Adams, editor (10 vols., Boston, 1856-60).
Ames, Fisher, Works of Fisher Ames: with a Selection from His Speeches and Correspondence. Seth Ames, editor (2 vols., Boston, 1854).
Burr, Aaron, The Private Journal of Aaron Burr Reprinted in Full from the Original Manuscript in the Library of Mr. William K. Bixby, of St. Louis, Mo. (2 vols., Rochester, N. Y., 1903).
Clinton, George, Public Papers of George Clinton, First Governor of New York . . . (10 vols., New York and Albany, 1899-1914).

Hamilton, Alexander, A Few of Hamilton's Letters Including His
Description of the Great West Indian Hurricane of 1772.
Gertrude Atherton, editor (New York, 1903).
—— Industrial and Commercial Correspondence of Alexander Ham-
ilton, Anticipating His Report on Manufactures. Arthur Harrison
Cole, editor (Chicago, 1928).
—— Papers on Public Credit, Commerce, and Finance. Samuel Mc-
Kee, Jr., editor. Foreword by Elihu Root (New York, 1934).
—— The Works of Alexander Hamilton. . . . John C. Hamilton,
editor (7 vols., New York, 1850-51).
—— The Works of Alexander Hamilton. Henry Cabot Lodge,
editor (12 vols., New York, 1904).
Hamilton, Alexander, and Thomas Jefferson, Representative Selec-
tions with Introduction, Bibliography, and Notes. Frederick C.
Prescott, editor (New York, 1934).
Hamilton, Alexander, John Jay, and James Madison, The Federalist;
A Commentary on the Constitution. Paul Leicester Ford, editor
(New York, 1898).
—— The Federalist; A Commentary on the Constitution of the
United States. . . . John C. Hamilton, editor (Philadelphia,
1866).
—— The Federalist and Other Constitutional Papers. Erastus H.
Scott, editor (Chicago, 1894).
—— The Federalist. Edward Mead Earle, editor (Washington,
1937).
—— Selections from The Federalist, Edited, with an Introduction
by John Spencer Bassett (New York, 1921).
—— The Federalist on the New Constitution Written in 1788
(Philadelphia, 1818).
Jay, John, An Address to the People of the State of New-York on
the Subject of the Constitution (New York, 1788).
—— Correspondence and Public Papers of John Jay. H. P. John-
ston, editor (4 vols., New York, 1890).
—— The Diary of John Jay, during the Peace Negotiations of
1782 . . . , Frank Monaghan, editor (New Haven, 1934).
Jefferson, Thomas, The Writings of Thomas Jefferson, Albert
Ellery Bergh, editor (20 vols., Washington, 1907).

Kent, James, An Address Delivered before the Law Association of the City of New York (New York, 1836).

—— An Anniversary Discourse Delivered before the New York Historical Society, December 6, 1828 (New York, 1829).

—— Memoirs and Letters of James Kent. William Kent, editor (Boston, 1898).

Lansing, John, Jr., Proceedings of the Convention, in The Delegate from New York or Proceedings of the Federal Convention of 1787, from the notes of John Lansing, Jr., edited by Joseph Reese Strayer (Princeton, 1938).

Maclay, William, The Journal of William Maclay, United States Senator from Pennsylvania, 1789-1791, Edgar S. Maclay, editor (New York, 1927).

Madison, James, Writings of James Madison, Comprising His Public Papers, and His Private Correspondence. . . . Gaillard Hunt, editor (9 vols., New York, 1900-1910).

Smith, Melancton, An Address to the People of the State of New York (New York, 1787).   .

Washington, George, The Writings of George Washington. W. C. Ford, editor (14 vols., New York, 1891).

—— The Writings of George Washington, from the Original Manuscript Sources, 1745-1799. John C. Fitzpatrick, editor (26 vols.,+ Washington, 1931——).

Miscellaneous Primary Sources

Barnard, Daniel D., A Discourse on the Life, Character, and Public Services of Ambrose Spencer . . . (Albany, 1849).

Callender, James, Bibliography and Iconography of Alexander Hamilton. (Typed manuscript of an incompleted work projected by the late Mr. James Callender, New York).

Callender, James Thomsen, The American Annual Register, or Historical Memoirs . . . for the Year 1796 (Philadelphia, 1797).

Daggett, David, Esquire, An Oration Pronounced in the Brick Meeting-House, in the City of New-Haven, on the Fourth of July, A. D. 1787: It Being the Eleventh Anniversary of the Independence of the United States of America (New-Haven, 1787).

Duer, W. A., Reminiscences of an Old New-Yorker (New York, 1867).

Hamilton, James A., Reminiscences of James A. Hamilton, or Men and Events, at Home and Abroad during Three Quarters of a Century (New York, 1869).

Sedgwick, Theodore, Jr., A Memoir of the Life of William Livingston. . . . (New York, 1833).

Sullivan, William, Familiar Letters on Public Characters and Public Events (Boston, 1834).

Newspapers and Ephemera

Albany Journal.
[New York] Daily Advertiser.
New-York Journal and Weekly Register.
New York Packet.
[Philadelphia] Aurora and General Advertiser.
[Philadelphia] National Gazette.
[Poughkeepsie] Country Journal and Poughkeepsie Advertiser.
Handbills. (Broadside Collection, New York Public Library).
Order of Commencement in King's College, New-York, May 21, 1771. (Columbiana. Library, Columbia University.)

II. MANUSCRIPTS

Columbia University Library

De Witt Clinton Papers. Includes 15 volumes of letters, 8 volumes of letter books, and a volume of miscellaneous papers. The first volume (1785-1801) includes family letters and some letters bearing on the convention of 1788.

Minutes of the Board of Governors of King's College, May 7, 1755 to July 5, 1781.

Hamilton College Library

Alexander Hamilton Manuscripts. Some fragmentary unsigned notes in Hamilton's handwriting concerning the building of a navy.

Huntington Library

Alexander Hamilton Papers. Letters to or about Philip Schuyler, James McHenry, John Hancock, Egbert Benson, James Duane, George Washington, and John Lansing.

George Clinton. Account current with George Washington, esq. deceased with a Statement of Monies received as his atty. since last acct. rendered.

—— Order Book: 1778-1783. A valuable record of Clinton's executive service during the Revolution, including his activities in setting up courts martial, assessing and remitting fines, receiving petitions, and conducting affairs of state.

George Clinton Letters. Correspondence with C. Wadsworth, Horatio Gates, James Clinton, and others.

Letters. The Huntington Library contains sundry letters to or from John Jay, John Lansing, De Witt Clinton, Robert R. Livingston, James Duane, Robert Morris, Philip Schuyler, Israel Putnam, Arch McLean, and Samuel Huntington, some of which concern the Poughkeepsie convention of 1788, together with other papers which bear no direct relation to it.

Maps and Description of Certain Lands belonging to Stephen D. Beekman & Maria his wife being their share or Estate of the late George Clinton Esquire. . . .

Notice of Appointment of Alexander Hamilton and Samuel Jones to act as Counsellors and Solicitors on behalf of the State of New York. New York, June 9, 1785.

Journal of Cadwallader Colden, Esq., during the Revolutionary War, 1776-1779.

Library of Congress

Alexander Hamilton. Notes of Speech in Convention of N. York. A topical outline of material presented before the convention at Poughkeepsie. A section of his Sketch of Journal of Convention of New York.

—— Sketch of Journal Convention of N.Y. Hamilton's own account of the speeches, largely those of his opposition, in the Poughkeepsie Convention.

Alexander Hamilton Collection. The Library of Congress is the major depository for Hamiltoniana. The collection includes Hamilton's legal papers, briefs, pleas, depositions, indentures, and a great number of miscellaneous items, indexed. Among the briefs are those for People vs. Croswell and Rutgers vs. Waddington. The collection includes valuable material which has not been printed.

Correspondence of Melancton Smith, De Witt Clinton, Rufus King, and others relating to the political situation in New York in 1788.

New York Historical Society

De Witt Clinton Papers. Letters from De Witt Clinton to Charles Tillinghast concerning the Poughkeepsie convention.

John Lamb Papers. Includes correspondence with Hugh Ledlie, George Clinton, Charles Tillinghast, Richard Henry Lee, and others concerning the convention at Poughkeepsie.

John McKesson Papers. McKesson served as secretary of the Poughkeepsie convention. The papers include notes, proceedings, and records.

New York Public Library

Abraham Yates Papers. Includes useful correspondence concerning the ratification of the Constitution in New York.

Alexander Hamilton Papers. One file of letters, documents, and miscellaneous papers.

George Bancroft Transcripts. From papers of Robert R. Livingston.

George Clinton Papers. Includes personal letters.

Gilbert Livingston. Reports of the Poughkeepsie Convention.

Gilbert Livingston Papers. Mostly letters concerned with land transactions.

Johnson Livingston Redmond Collection of Livingston manuscripts. Eight files.

Olin Collection. 2 vols., about a hundred pieces, including letters of the Lynch, Livingston, and Olin families.

New York State Library

Alexander Hamilton Papers. Includes an undated letter (*ca.* 1791) to Elizabeth Schuyler Hamilton and notes in Hamilton's handwrit-

ing, without date or signature, for an argument relative to Westen-
hook Patent, 23 pages folded into 16mo Book shape.
Correspondence and documents concerning the following men:
Samuel Jones, Melancton Smith, John Sloss Hobart, Gilbert Liv-
ingston, Robert R. Livingston, George Clinton, James Clinton,
Henry Oothoudt, James Duane, John Lansing, De Witt Clinton,
and Peter Van Schaack.
George Clinton Papers. Most of this collection is of little importance
in connection with the Convention of 1788; but the drafts of
Clinton's notes for his speeches given at the Poughkeepsie Conven-
tion, though damaged, are valuable.
Legislative Papers, State of New York, 1780-1803. Five boxes.
Chiefly petitions and documents of no special relevancy to the Convention of 1788.
Melancton Smith Papers. Chiefly business correspondence papers and
letters of friendship, with a bearing on Smith's character and personality. Includes Smith's bill for services in Congress from
November 6, 1786, to November 5, 1787, with a deduction for
50 days absent and 44 Sundays.
Philip Schuyler Letters and Papers. Personal and business correspondence.
Van Rensselaer Letters. Includes items bearing on the campaign for
delegates to the Poughkeepsie convention.

SECONDARY WORKS

Biographical and Historical Works

Alexander, Edward P., A Revolutionary Conservative: James Duane
of New York (New York, 1938).
Atherton, Gertrude, The Conqueror (New York, 1916).
Bailey, Ralph Edward, An American Colossus: The Singular Career
of Alexander Hamilton (Boston, 1933).
Baldwin, Jo. G., Party Leaders: Sketches of Thomas Jefferson,
Alex'r Hamilton, Andrew Jackson, Henry Clay, John Randolph,
of Roanoke, Including Notices of Many Other Distinguished
American Statesmen (New York, 1855).

Bancroft, George, History of the United States from the Discovery of the Continent (6 vols., 1886-1891).

Beard, Charles A., The Discussion of Human Affairs: An Inquiry into the Nature of the Statements, Assertions, Allegations, Claims, Heats, Tempers, Distempers, Dogmas, and Contentions Which Appear When Human Affairs Are Discussed and into the Possibility of Putting Some Rhyme and Reason into Processes of Discussion (New York, 1936).

—— An Economic Interpretation of the Constitution of the United States (New York, 1921).

Beveridge, Albert J., The Life of John Marshall (4 vols., Boston, 1916).

Boutell, Lewis Henry, Alexander Hamilton: The Constructive Statesman (Chicago, 1890).

Bowers, Claude G., Jefferson and Hamilton: The Struggle for Democracy in America (Boston, 1925).

Cardozo, Ernest A., A History of the Philolexian Society of Columbia University from 1802-1902 (Columbiana. Library, Columbia University).

Channing, Edward, A History of the United States (6 vols., New York, 1905-25).

Cheetham, James, A Narrative of the Suppression by Col. Burr of the History of the Administration of John Adams . . . 3d edition (Baltimore, ca. 1802).

Cochran, Thomas C., New York in the Confederation (Philadelphia, 1932).

Conant, Charles A., Alexander Hamilton (Boston, 1901).

Culbertson, William S., Alexander Hamilton: An Essay (New Haven, 1916).

Curtis, George Ticknor, Constitutional History of the United States (2 vols., New York, 1889-96).

Dictionary of American Biography, Allen Johnson and Dumas Malone, editors (20 vols., New York, 1928-36).

Dunlap, William, History of the New Netherlands, Province of New York, and State of New York . . . (2 vols., New York, 1840).

Farrand, Max, The Framing of the Constitution of the United States (New Haven, 1913).

Fiske, John, The Critical Period of American History (Boston, 1888).

—— Essays: Historical and Literary (2 vols., New York, 1902).

Flick, Alexander C., editor. History of the State of New York (10 vols., New York, 1933-7).

Ford, Henry Jones, Alexander Hamilton (New York, 1925).

Fox, Dixon Ryan, The Decline of Aristocracy in the Politics of New York (New York, 1918).

Fox, Fontaine T., A Study in Alexander Hamilton (New York, 1911).

Granrud, J. E., Five Years of Alexander Hamilton's Public Life 1786-1791 (Ithaca, New York, 1894).

Graybill, James Edward, Alexander Hamilton: Nevis-Weehawken . . . (New York, 1897).

Greene, Francis Vinton, The Revolutionary War and the Military Policy of the United States (New York, 1911).

Hamilton, Allan McLane, The Intimate Life of Alexander Hamilton Based Chiefly upon Original Family Letters and Other Documents, Many of which Have Never Been Published (New York, 1910).

Hamilton, John Church, The Life of Alexander Hamilton (2 vols., New York, 1840).

—— Life of Alexander Hamilton: A History of the Republic of the United States of America as Traced in His Writing and in Those of His Contemporaries (7 vols., Boston, 1879).

Hicks, Howard, Alexander Hamilton (New York, 1928).

History of Columbia University, 1754-1904 (New York, 1904).

Hockett, Homer Cary, The Constitutional History of the United States (2 vols., New York, 1939).

Hunt, Charles Havens, Life of Edward Livingston, with an Introduction by George Bancroft (New York, 1864).

Jameson, J. Franklin, The American Historian's Raw Materials . . . (Ann Arbor, 1923).

—— The American Revolution Considered as a Social Movement (Princeton, 1926).

—— The History of Historical Writing in America (Boston, 1891).

Leake, Isaac Q., Memoir of the Life and Times of General John Lamb. . . . (Albany, 1850).

Libby, Orin Grant, The Geographical Distribution of the Vote of the Thirteen States on the Federal Constitution, 1787-8 (Madison, Wisconsin, 1896).

Lodge, Henry Cabot, Alexander Hamilton (Boston, 1882).

Lord, John, Beacon Lights of History (8 vols., New York, 1884-96).

Lossing, Benson J., The Life and Times of Philip Schuyler (2 vols., New York, 1873).

—— The Pictorial Field Book of the Revolution (New York, 1860).

Loth, David, Alexander Hamilton: Portrait of a Prodigy (New York, 1939).

McLaughlin, Andrew C., The Confederation and the Constitution, 1783-1789. In The American Nation: A History, edited by Albert Bushnell Hart (New York, 1905).

McMaster, John B., History of the People of the United States from the Revolution to the Civil War (8 vols., New York, 1883-1900).

Miner, Clarence E., The Ratification of the Federal Constitution by the State of New York (New York, 1921).

Monaghan, Frank, John Jay: Defender of Liberty . . . (New York, 1935).

Morison, Samuel Eliot, The Life and Letters of Harrison Gray Otis, Federalist, 1765-1848 (2 vols., Boston, 1913).

Morse, A. D., "Alexander Hamilton," in Political Science Quarterly, Vol. V. (1890), pp. 1-23.

Morse, John T., The Life of Alexander Hamilton (2 vols., Boston, 1876).

Mott, Frank Luther, A History of American Magazines 1741-1850 (New York, 1930).

Mullett, Charles F., Fundamental Law and the American Revolution 1760-1776 (New York, 1933).

Nevins, Allan, The American States during and after the Revolution, 1775-1789 (New York, 1924).

O'Brien, Michael J., Hercules Mulligan: Confidential Correspondent of General Washington (New York, 1937).

Oliver, Frederick Scott, Alexander Hamilton: An Essay on American Union (New York, 1920).

Parton, James, The Life and Times of Aaron Burr (2 vols., Boston, 1876).

Pound, Arthur, Native Stock: The Rise of the American Spirit Seen in Six Lives (New York, 1931).

Read, Conyers, editor, The Constitution Reconsidered. Edited for the American Historical Association (New York, 1938).

Renwick, H. B., Lives of John Jay and Alexander Hamilton (New York, 1841).

Riethmüller, Christopher James, Alexander Hamilton and His Contemporaries; or, The Rise of the American Constitution (London, 1864).

Salvemini, Gaetano, Historian and Scientist: An Essay on the Nature of History and the Social Sciences (Cambridge, Massachusetts, 1939).

Schmucker, Samuel M., The Life and Times of Alexander Hamilton (Philadelphia, 1856).

Schuyler, Robert Livingston, The Constitution of the United States: An Historical Survey of Its Formation (New York, 1923).

Seligman, E. R. A., The Economic Interpretation of History (New York, 1902).

Shea, George, The Life and Epoch of Alexander Hamilton: A Historical Study (Boston, 1881).

Smertenko, Johan J., Alexander Hamilton (New York, 1932).

Spaulding, E. Wilder, His Excellency George Clinton: Critic of the Constitution (New York, 1938).

—— New York in the Critical Period, 1783-1789 (New York, 1932).

Stephens, Frank Fletcher, The Transitional Period, 1788-1789, in the Government of the United States (Columbia, Missouri, 1909).

Stephens, Louise Irby Trenholme, The Ratification of the Federal Constitution in North Carolina (New York, 1932).

Sumner, William Graham, Alexander Hamilton (New York, 1890).

Tuckerman, Bayard, Life of General Philip Schuyler, 1733-1804 (New York, 1903).

Vandenberg, Arthur Hendrick, If Hamilton Were Here Today (New York, 1923).

Van Tyne, Claude Halstead, The Loyalists in the American Revolution (New York, 1902).

Warshow, Robert Irving, Alexander Hamilton: First American Business Man (New York, 1931).

Williams, John (*pseud.*, Anthony Pasquin), The Hamiltoniad . . . (Boston, 1804).

Wilson, Woodrow, A History of the American People (10 vols., New York, 1918).

CRITICAL AND RHETORICAL WORKS

Aristotle, The Poetics of Aristotle: Edited with Critical Notes and a Translation by S. H. Butcher (Fourth Edition, London, 1911).

—— The Rhetoric . . . , translated by Lane Cooper (New York, 1932).

—— Rhetorique d'Aristote traduite en français et accompagnee de notes perpetuelles par J. Barthelmy Saint-Hilaire (2 vols., Paris, 1870).

—— The Works of Aristotle. Translated into English under the editorship of W. D. Ross. Volume 11 (1354-1462); Rhetorica, by W. Rhys Roberts; Rhetorica ad Alexandrum, [by] E. S. Forster; De Poetica, [by] Ingram Bywater (Oxford, 1924).

Baldwin, Charles Sears, Ancient Rhetoric and Poetic Interpreted from Representative Works (New York, 1924).

—— Medieval Rhetoric and Poetic (to 1400). Interpreted from Representative Works (New York, 1928).

—— Renaissance Literary Theory and Practice: Classicism in the Rhetoric and Poetic of Italy, France, and England 1400-1600. Edited with an Introduction by Donald Lemen Clark (New York, 1939).

Blair, Hugh, Lectures on Rhetoric and Belles Lettres (Dublin, 1793).

Brunetière, Ferdinand, Essays in French Literature, translated by D. Nichol Smith (London, 1898).

Cambridge History of American Literature, The, edited by William Peterfield Trent, John Erskine, Stuart P. Sherman, and Carl Van Doren (3 vols., New York, 1917).

Campbell, George, The Philosophy of Rhetoric (New York, 1851).

Cicero, Oratory and Orators with His Letters to Quintus and Brutus, edited by J. S. Watson (London, 1884).

Clark, Donald Lemen, Rhetoric and Poetry in the Renaissance: A Study of Rhetorical Terms in English Renaissance Literary Criticism (New York, 1922).

Cope, E. M., An Introduction to Aristotle's Rhetoric With Analysis Notes and Appendices (London, 1867).

De Vilbiss, Ora Beatrice, A Rhetorical Criticism of the Early Pamphlets of Alexander Hamilton (typed manuscript, Master's thesis, University of Missouri, Columbia, 1939).

Dyer, Armel C., Hamilton's Rhetoric in The Federalist (typed manuscript, Master's thesis, University of Missouri, Columbia, 1938).

Fulton, William McKinney, The Speeches of Alexander Hamilton in the New York Convention for the Ratification of the Federal Constitution: A Critical Study in Argumentation (typed manuscript, Master's thesis, State University of Iowa, Iowa City, 1930).

Goodrich, Chauncey, Select British Eloquence (New York, 1852).

Hardwicke, Henry, History of Oratory and Orators (New York, 1896).

Jebb, R. C., The Attic Orators from Antiphon to Isaeus (2 vols., London, 1893).

Jephson, Henry, The Platform: Its Rise and Progress (2 vols., New York, 1892).

Parrington, Vernon Louis, Main Currents in American Thought (3 vols., New York, 1927).

Plato, The Dialogues of Plato Translated into English with Analyses and Introductions, edited by B. Jowett (4 vols., Oxford, 1871).

Platz, Mabel, The History of Public Speaking: A Comparative Study in World Oratory (New York, 1935).

Quintilian, Institutes of Oratory: or Education of an Orator in Twelve Books Literally Translated with Notes, edited by J. S. Watson (2 vols., London, 1888).

Reid, Loren Dudley, Charles James Fox: A Study of the Effectiveness of an Eighteenth Century Parliamentary Speaker (Iowa City, 1932).

Sears, Lorenzo, The History of Oratory from the Age of Pericles to the Present Time (Chicago, 1897).

Shaw, W. C., History of American Oratory (Indianapolis, 1928).

Smith, D. Nichol, The Functions of Criticism (Oxford, 1909).

Studies in Rhetoric and Public Speaking in Honor of James Albert Winans (New York, 1925).

Trent, William Peterfield, A History of American Literature 1607-1865 (New York, 1903).

Tyler, Moses Coit, The Literary History of the American Revolution, 1763-1783 (2 vols., New York, 1897).

Wendell, Barrett, A Literary History of America (New York, 1900).

Whately, Richard, Elements of Rhetoric . . . (New York, 1854).

Wilson, Thomas, The Arte of Rhetorique, edited by G. H. Mair (Oxford, 1909).

INDEX